The Perilous Vision of John Wyclif

LOUIS BREWER HALL

NELSON-HALL nh CHICAGO

LIBRARY OF CONGRESS CATALOGING IN PUBLICATION DATA

Hall, Louis Brewer.
  The perilous vision of John Wyclif.

  Bibliography: p.
  Includes index.
  1. Wycliffe, John, d. 1384.   2. Reformation—
Early movements.   3. England—Church history—Medieval
period.   1066-1485.   4. Catholic Church—England—
Clergy—Biography.   5. Reformation—England—Biography.
I. Title.
BX4905.H34   1983   282'.092'4 [B]   82-18890
ISBN 0-8304-1006-6

Manufactured in the United States of America

10 9 8 7 6 5 4 3 2 1

The paper in this book is pH neutral (acid-free).

In memoriam supplicem
Guillelmi T. Costello, S.J.,
sacerdotis mei, magistri mei,
etiam amici mei.

FOR ALFRED CAMDEN HALL

Now challenged by nature
The great gust of the Hall spirit
Will in letters live on still.

CONTENTS

PREFACE

OFTEN WE SEE historical figures only as statues, stolid and gray, frozen into an artificial stance and polluted by the acids of nature and the chemicals of the twentieth century.

No fourteenth-century portraits of John Wyclif have survived. In most imaginations he is colorless, shadowy, and mottled. John Wyclif lived six hundred years ago in what Francis Petrarch, the Italian poet, labeled the Middle Ages, or the medieval era, a time that existed between imperial Rome and his own Renaissance Florence. To Petrarch's misunderstandings of those Middle Ages, we have added many errors of our own.

We picture Arthurian knights pursuing the Holy Grail or rescuing maidens in distress. John Wyclif, living at the time of knights, knew that they were soldiers and policemen, brutal in both roles. We see castles and imagine their crumbling turrets and roofs of slate only a slightly darker blue than the sky. John Wyclif visited a castle in London where his friend, John of Gaunt, directed his own political machine, recruited his own army, and managed a million-dollar wool business.

We picture monasteries and fill their decayed cloisters with monks chanting *Gloria in excelsis Deo* (Glory to God in the highest). John Wyclif knew monasteries as the conglomerates (though he did not know the word) that controlled towns, farms, mines, forests, and cattle. And he also knew that the monks preserved and expanded the finest libraries of England and Europe, and if he could have looked into the future, he would have seen that their plumbing was four hundred years ahead of its time.

If these Middle Ages are to be faithfully reported from the perspective of the twentieth century, then the reporter must not view any medieval person as if he were a statue, or any institution as if it were a myth.

The reporter is first an information seeker. He cannot be satisfied with secondhand statistics, summaries, or the judgments of others. He must seek the details of everyday living—the eating, working, dressing, talking—all the activities that occupy the hours and days in all the years of a man's life.

This information has been left behind in journals, letters, and reports, official and unofficial. Abundant records are preserved in the great libraries such as the Bodleian at Oxford and the British Library in London, for which every English-speaking reporter should be thankful. I especially owe a decade of thanks for the use of the personal library and the hospitality of the late Dr. W.S. Scott, of Frensham, Surrey.

The truth about medieval life must also be sought beyond libraries. In seeking to know Wyclif, I walked the border country between Yorkshire and County Durham where Wyclif grew up and helped his father raise sheep. I escaped the congested streets of Oxford, and inside the walls of Merton College stared at the steep roof of its Treasury, the only building in Oxford that still looks the same to us as it did to Wyclif.

Any reporter of the Middle Ages finds himself in an alternate world. He quickly discovers that the rhythms of daily life at that time were very different from those of today. People at that time were not protected from heat and cold, sleet and sun, or in any way isolated from the extremes of nature. Medieval life did not move to the rhythm of switches or thermostats, nor to the explosion of gasoline squeezed by the pistons of internal combustion engines.

Discovering this different quality of life forces the reporter to perceive patterns of living unique to the Middle Ages—patterns linked to ideas inherited from the past and signaling ideas yet to come. The patterns of living must be expanded the way a filmmaker animates a flower blooming or clouds flying—illuminating new patterns that were always there but had been invisible in the protracted moments of laggard time.

The most important patterns are patterns of thought—sometimes logical, sometimes passionate—that motivate choices. There have been no physiological changes in man since the Middle Ages; but there have been great psychological changes. As daily life in the Middle Ages did not move to the flow of electricity, so choices were not made according to the concepts of Rousseau, Jung, or Erik Erikson. The medieval man made his choices according to the concepts of Plato, Augustine, and Aristotle, though, like modern men, he believed he was "making up his own mind."

The routines of daily life and the newly perceived patterns finally coalesce. When the reporter writes his story, he is only incidentally typographic; he must be biographic. The word is familiar, but we have forgotten its true meaning: "life writing." The subject of the information and of the patterns must be made flesh again. It must be reincarnated.

I hope that in the following pages, John Wyclif of the fourteenth century will be reincarnated for the twentieth. He deserves to be.

CHAPTER ONE

Early Years at Wycliffe Manor

I N 1328 A KNOWLEDGEABLE midwife would be carrying an eagle-stone with her on the three-mile journey from Richmond, Yorkshire, to Wycliffe farm where a child was soon to be born.

The eagle-stone, a stone with a pebble inside it that rattled, was a token that would insure a safe delivery, the midwife believed. It had received its name because the best authorities thought an eagle brought it to her nest to help her lay her large eggs. If Catherine of Wycliffe, the mother-to-be, held it as tightly as she could during the birth, it would bring her assistance. But, the midwife thought, if Catherine had worn it around her neck during the pregnancy, it would have been even more effective.

That day in 1328 Catherine gave birth to a boy, later baptized John. Seconds after he was born, the midwife would have washed him with soap and water, then rubbed him with oil ground from acorns. Then she would swaddle the baby by laying him on a board the length of his body and wrapping him tightly with a long, twelve-inch-wide cloth bandage, pulling his feet straight and binding them together, then binding his arms tight to his sides. The midwife continued the bandage around his neck, over his ears and across the top of his head until baby John was absolutely immobile.

Midwives who were more up-to-date left a hole in the swaddling so the baby could urinate outside the bandages. New ideas like that probably had not reached northern Yorkshire in the fourteenth century, for Wycliffe was more than two hundred miles from the more modern London,

1

erefore very isolated in the days when walking or _____ were the chief means of transportation. London-born Geoffrey Chaucer considered northern England so distant that he referred to it as "way up north," indicating the home of the devil in one of his *Canterbury Tales*.[1] There was little opportunity for new ideas to reach way up north, so baby John wet inside his swaddling. Of course, he was washed several times during the day, provided that lambing or a raid of the Scots from even farther north did not interfere.

The mothers and midwives of that time did not realize that the tight bandages compressed the baby's arterial system, slowing his circulation and heartbeat. So John Wyclif, like all fourteenth-century babies, spent the first four months of his life in a cocoon, sluggish and apathetic, too inert even to cry.

Only the first four months of John Wyclif's fifty-six years, however, could be characterized as sluggish, inactive, or dull. Later at Oxford University he would acquire an encyclopedic knowledge of fourteenth-century learning and the skills that made him England's most famous scholar and preacher.

Like Galileo two centuries later, Wyclif attempted to bring church beliefs into accord with scientific theory. Like Thomas Jefferson and James Madison four centuries later, Wyclif believed in the absolute separation of church and state powers. He preached that the hierarchy of the fourteenth-century church had forgotten the ideal of Christian poverty. He guided the first translation of the complete Bible into English. His superiors in the church hierarchy did not like what Wyclif believed and preached and would attempt to bring the force of the Inquisition against him.

---

[1] "The Friar's Tale," III, 1413, p. 130.

Only as a swaddled infant was John Wyclif's life quiescent. If he were at ease in his cocoon, it was also the only time in his life when he experienced physical comfort. Even the best fourteenth-century houses were tenebrous and dank, and the Wycliffe house was not one of the best. It was a manor, with a church, a water-powered mill, and a few cottages, all of them part of 2,239 acres. About 700 acres were arable. Most of the land consisted of grass on steep hillsides interspersed with heather and trees, mostly fir, beech, and dwarf oak.[2]

The word *manor* has an elegant sound, but in rural areas in that period, windows were small and not glazed, for only the rich could afford glass. To keep out the northern cold, Yorkshiremen forced into the window openings greased cloth stretched on a wooden frame. The cloth dimmed the interiors even more. Wycliffe manor also had no chimney. The idea of a chimney had been imported from France a century earlier, but had been incorporated only into the best and up-to-date mansions. This advance in comfort had not yet reached farm houses as far from the centers of fashion as northern Yorkshire. At Wycliffe the smoke from the fires drifted slowly out the windows, through the thatch on the roof or through cracks between the thatch and the stone walls of the house. Catherine probably did not worry about the lack of light, for it was generally believed that babies, for their health, should be kept from

---

[2]Authorities are not in total agreement that John Wyclif was born at Wycliffe. A tradition has survived that the birth took place at Hipswell, a tiny village, now vanished, on the River Tees, which separates Yorkshire from County Durham. Wyclif's surname contradicts the tradition. It is obviously derived from Wycliffe, and surnames, just beginning to be used in the fourteenth century, were usually assumed from the place of birth when not from a trade. Spelling was inconsistent in the fourteenth century, and about thirty spellings of "Wycliffe" exist in various records: Wicluf, Wykliff, Wycleph, even Vikkeluf. For the sake of convenience in this book, his name—Wyclif—will be differentiated from the place—Wycliffe.

both sunlight and moonlight, and smoke was accepted as inevitable from the cooking and heating.

One of the first sounds that John heard came from outside. It was the wailing of orphan lambs and the bellow of rams nearby. Raising sheep was the main business of Wycliffe farm. At four acres a head, the land supported a band of about three hundred sheep. Roger Wyclif, John's father, was no elegant country squire, but a hard-working sheep farmer.[3]

The forces that influence daily life in rural Yorkshire—the climate, the geography, the vegetation—have changed little in six hundred years. Like his modern counterpart, Roger ran his sheep and raised barley, wheat, and oats. From these grains Catherine made her own bread and ale. On one of the cascading streams running into the Tees was a water mill where the grain raised on the farm was ground into flour.

The return for raw wool was good in the 1330s and the first five years of the 1340s. Roger received high prices from brokers in the cities of Richmond and York, who represented the London exporters.

Roger was probably illiterate. Illiteracy in the Middle Ages did not indicate a lack of intelligence. He kept his accounts by notching sticks to record the number of ewes he had, the lambs they dropped, the wool he sheared, to whom he sold the wool, and how much he received for it. Later he would dictate the information from the notches to the priest of the manor church who wrote them down, and the permanent written records would be kept in a chest in the manor house.

---

[3]Nothing specific is known about John's father or mother, for only their names have survived in a few documents. Many Wyclifs are recorded in this area of north Yorkshire, and in isolated areas of medieval England, everyone tended to be related. The word *cousin* was a general term for descendant in Middle English, the language spoken by the Wyclifs.

Roger notched his sticks while waiting for the evening meal, sitting on a stool in the center hall, which extended two-thirds of the length of the house. Near him a girl might be stitching leather shoes. Closer to the slow flame of the fire burning on the earth floor, a tenant boy might be carving a wooden spoon out of a piece of birch. Another girl, probably a daughter of one of the tenants, might comb and card lambs' wool that Catherine would spin, not on a wheel, but on a spindle she twisted back and forth with her thumb and forefinger.

While the rest of her family was busy in this center hall, Catherine was preparing the evening meal in the kitchen, behind the wall screen that cut off the south end of the hall. She worked at the only permanent table of the house. It had to be heavy enough to withstand cleaver blows as Catherine and a helper, either her daughter or a neighbor's daughter, prepared a pig, sheep, fish, or game bird, from butchering to dicing. Beyond the table, baby John hung in his swaddling on the wall, drowsy in the smoke and clatter.

At meal time in the late afternoon the center hall was transformed into a dining room as Catherine laid planks across trestles. The planks had been taken down and stacked against the wall after the earlier meal of the day, eaten between eight and ten in the morning, depending on the season.

At supper, Catherine, Roger, and children older than seven dipped diced pieces of boiled meat into a spiced sauce with their fingers. (Forks would not reach England for another hundred and fifty years.) The excess sauce dripped on a piece of bread in front of each person, and the last thing eaten was the sauce-soaked piece of bread.

At the north end of the hall a wall formed a third room called the "parlor" after the French word *parler*. Roger used this room when he wanted to talk in private. The chest containing the written records was here, and here the Wyclifs kept the valuables they especially treasured—a few pieces of linen cloth as part of a daughter's dowry, possibly a tapestry of the life of a saint embroidered over a generation, or a silver bowl and one or two spoons.

When the sun went down and marked the end of the day, Catherine and Roger climbed the steep stairs, almost a ladder, from the parlor to the bedroom. Everyone in the family slept here, baby John in a cradle, and his brothers and sisters together in their own bed. The number of John's brothers and sisters is uncertain. If there were only a few, they slept with their parents, the girls on the mother's side, the boys on the father's. The most valuable piece of furniture was that master bed, larger than today's largest double beds, accommodating four members of the family without too much crowding.

The four months of swaddling does not seem to have harmed the babies of the fourteenth century, but their arms and legs were not any straighter than the arms and legs of their twentieth-century counterparts. Psychologists who specialize in history guess that a swaddled child may have had a sense of security and trust that a nonswaddled child lacks. Just as much rebellion and conformity, cruelty and kindness emerged from the centuries of swaddling as from the centuries since swaddling stopped.

John was breastfed for a year or two; breastfeeding was also supposed to have given a baby a sense of security. If Catherine was dry of milk, one of the tenant wives nursed John with a child of her own, but Catherine would not allow just any mother to nurse her baby. She believed baby John could take on the characteristics of the nurse from her milk, so the nurse had to be someone who was mature, with a clear complexion, a sound body, and of "approved virtue, discretion, and gravity," a Doctor Spock of the Middle Ages advised.[4]

---

[4]Jane Bruce Ross, "Middle Class Children in Urban Italy, 14th to 16th Century," in deMause, pp. 183–288. She cites diaries and memoirs of the period.

When he was finally taken from his cocoon for the last time, John was dressed in a skirt; his clothes would not differentiate him from a girl until he was seven years old. Roger and Catherine had no interest in raising John to develop his individuality or his whole personality. These are modern concepts. Individuality was not prized in the Middle Ages, because medieval society functioned as a society of uniform groups. Wycliffe manor was one group, a group that gave John his name, his food, his clothes, and the start of his education. The Wyclifs went to a manor church which was in the diocese of York, another group. Later in his life John would be a member of a group at Oxford, then a priest in the diocese of Lincoln.

None of these groups demanded individuality. On the contrary, they emphasized conformity to their standards of strict behavior. As a result Roger and Catherine raised baby John in moral virtue, for parents knew that sin could easily and quickly corrupt a child. "The fruit of a soft and tender bud might easily grow wild," the manuals warned. So to prevent any tendency toward growing wild, Roger and Catherine undoubtedly beat John and his brothers and sisters and beat them often.[5]

"Who does not beat his child does not love his child," parents believed. Their beatings were not easy. These manuals on child raising recommend that a child should be beaten with "a smooth, pliant, willow stick." He should not be kicked or hit with an open palm or with fists. Stories and histories, however, report that anything handy was used for beating—canes, rods, bundles of sticks, even shovels. A child was also urged into action with a sharpened stick in the same way sheep or cattle were prodded.

Eating was also made a part of childhood discipline. John never ate with Catherine or Roger, but with the cook and all the other children of the household. Nor did he eat

---

[5]Ibid. The theory was widely held even into the nineteenth century.

sitting down, but stood at the edge of a table eating the roughest food—coarse bread and tough meat—to accustom him to additional hardship.

If Catherine continued to follow the advice she received from the medieval Doctor Spock, once a week John was made to sleep on one of the wooden benches in the hall downstairs or on the damp straw of the dirt floor.

Infant John was never allowed to crawl. Only animals used four legs, and John was a human being with a soul. As a toddler he was made to stand, leaning on a bench or stool. To move he pushed the stool in front of him. Or he stood inside a small keg, its top and bottom removed, so John could use it to move around.

The advice on child rearing that has survived from these centuries seems unfeeling, even brutal, compared to modern ideas. However, attitudes toward pain and suffering changed dramatically beginning in the late eighteenth century. In the twentieth century, medicines and physical conveniences have been developed to protect and shield people against all but the worst that nature can inflict. Drugs, warm clothing, weatherproofed homes, and comfortable furniture are taken for granted.

Roger, Catherine, and John had none of these protections or conveniences. Pain and discomforts were to be endured, and in the course of any lifetime, suffering, horrifying to us, was taken for granted. Houses did not protect people from the weather. The shutters on the windows or the oiled cloths did not prevent the winds of Yorkshire from howling through the hall and depositing the winter snow in little drifts on the floor, as damp and as cold as the ground outside.

If baby John had a stomachache, a headache, sliced a finger with a knife, or broke an arm or a leg, Catherine had no painkiller other than a decoction of betony, the herb simmering over a fire until it was concentrated. The decoction could be mixed with ale. When John had a choking spell, Catherine held him by his feet and pounded his back or gave him a mixture of horehound and ale. She treated childhood diseases with bleeding, laxatives, or purges.

Many women gave birth to ten or twelve children, of whom only three or four lived to maturity. For every child who survived many more brothers and sisters were buried in the graveyard next to the church than lived in the house. More playmates vanished than survived.

During the fourteenth century, there was no way to protect anyone—child, adult, or ancient—from any chronic misery or affliction. An arthritic old farm laborer could not even escape his aches in alcohol. The ale could be strong, but the hunched old worker could not drink enough to kill his pain—he would throw up first. Distilled liquors were known in Italy, but in England no distillers guild would exist for a hundred years.

The best defense against a lifetime of misery was personal discipline, parents knew. The beatings and proddings eventually helped a child to develop endurance by self-discipline.

The arduous task of raising sheep was discipline in practice. As soon as he himself was the size of a newborn lamb, young John was expected to help, and the work continued throughout his days at the manor. Newborn lambs, in Yorkshire as everywhere, combined three disastrous characteristics: mobility, hunger, and ignorance. A new lamb will push itself down any animal hole it finds, squeeze under every bush, fall into every brook. To protect the lamb from itself, every man, woman, and child in Wycliffe had to be out in the fields at lambing. As a child young John could clean the newborn lamb, hold it close to his body to keep it warm, then take it to its mother to feed.

John also worked at shearing in June or July. One of the streams next to a meadow was dammed into a pool, the pool divided into pens just big enough for one sheep. Young John in mountain-cold water up to his waist scrubbed the caked dirt from the fleece, then drove the sheep out of the pool to the meadow where it would soon dry enough to shear and, with luck, remain clean. By the end of the day of washing John would be tired but would never allow the herder, his father, or any of the other children to notice. He would not realize that they all had been as tired as he was until he was much older.

From working with sheep John quickly learned to accept responsibility and recognized that adults had faith in him. The harder the drizzle, the colder the snow at lambing or while hunting for a lost sheep, the greater the challenge to fulfill that faith. So John learned that the beatings and discipline he had suffered had been given without hate. The discipline developed into self-discipline, and the self-discipline became a lifelong habit. For John Wyclif, more than for many in the fourteenth century, it proved to be a necessary habit.

There was still time for play, away from sheep, and book miniatures of the period have left us illustrations of a variety of toys and games. As John grew up he could make toys out of anything he might find around the farm. He could find a hoop that once girdled an ale barrel and chase it down the hills toward one of the streams. The sheep dogs of the fourteenth century were too small and nervous to allow themselves to be made into a knight's charger, so sticks became stallions. Someone on the farm might carve a wooden horsehead for the stick. Child-knights carried staves with flowers tied on one end, and whoever kept his flower from being knocked off won the tournament. In winter the same carpenter might make a sled out of boards with bones as runners. Two boys on sleds locked arms, and in a tug-of-war, opposing chains of boys tried to pull the sleds apart.

John played games with a ball made of sheepskin filled with straw. A book miniature shows a ballgame that does not look much different from modern baseball or cricket. A boy is hitting the ball with a stick, and others are crowding around him trying to catch the ball.

At Wycliffe all games suddenly stopped one day when John saw a column of black smoke curling toward the sky several hills away. Grain and houses were burning. A horseman galloping from that direction jerked his horse to a stop in front of the manor house. "The Scots are coming! The Scots are coming!"

Catherine, John's brothers and sisters, and the tenant children ran out of the house, and Roger, herders, and other tenants dashed in from the fields, and all of them scurried down the road to Richmond. The walls of Richmond only enclosed the market and a few of the houses, but the heavy walls and tower of the castle, high above the Swale River on a 120-foot precipice, made it easy to defend. The Scots raiders would not bother with a siege, anyway, and the farmers who had time to crowd inside the walls were safe. This time the smoke and the rider had given warning in time.

The raiders covered thirty to forty miles a day, carrying no food or baggage. They lived off the land, taking what sheep they found in the fields and "cooking them in their skins," a history of the times reported.[6] Some of the Scots hung a griddle from a saddle and cooked oatmeal cakes to eat with the boiled mutton.

They attacked in a swoop, shouting and yelling, burning houses, villages, abbeys, even larger towns, taking off wagon-loads of spoils, the wagons themselves confiscated from the farms. Isolated abbeys in Yorkshire were

6Clarkson, p. 29.

especially vulnerable, for their silver and gold candlesticks, crucifixes, chalices, and plates were valuable spoils. Bylands Abbey, Rievaulx, and Egglestone, not far from Wycliffe manor, were looted. Furness, richer than most abbeys, paid the Scots ransom.

The chronicles report the number of raiders as between four thousand and ten thousand in a group, but medieval historians used numbers for psychological effect, not for mathematical accuracy. Four hundred raiders would have been enough to produce the damage the English writers attributed to four thousand.

As soon as the farmers who had crowded into Richmond learned that the Scots had ridden away, they drifted back to their cottages. Young John and everyone at Wycliffe then helped find the dislocated sheep. They seemed to scatter over the whole North Riding of Yorkshire, but it was fortunate they did, for the raiders took only what they could easily grab.

Many times the Wyclifs could locate only half the band. What sheep the raiders did not boil drowned in the turbulent streams, tangled themselves in low yew branches, or were trampled by others. The ones they found were still jumpy and hysterical and as hard to drive back to the manor fields as they had been to find. The herder showed John how to rope two or three in a line and drag them in the right direction. After they started these moving off, the rest followed. One of the other boys held the yapping dog in the rear to keep the stragglers from bolting crazily.

In May 1318, all the countryside around Wycliffe was burned and ravaged, though Wycliffe manor itself escaped damage. During the 1330s, when John was growing up, the manor twice lost half its income from damage by the raiders.

The Wyclifs were victims of an early guerilla war, though the term was not used for this kind of military expedition until the nineteenth century. The raids did not completely stop until John was nineteen years old and living in Oxford. In 1346 the archbishop of York, William La Zouche, led an army of local knights supported by stone masons, butchers, bakers, shopkeepers, farmers, serfs, even priests, and together they defeated and captured King David II of Scotland at Neville Cross near the city of Durham.

CHAPTER TWO

John's Future Is Chosen

*J*OHN WYCLIF SURVIVED THE swaddling, beatings, proddings, sheep tending, and the raids of the Scots. He survived with a sense of security that was medieval
and with a sense of freedom and independence that was
much more modern.

Once a year, after the sheep were sheared in July, a bailiff
from the chief steward of the earl of Richmond arrived at
the farm to collect his rent from Roger, fourteen pounds
silver; Roger paid not in silver but its equivalent in wool.[1]
Wycliffe manor was part of the holdings of the earl of Richmond, a title that belonged to King Edward III when John
Wyclif was born. In 1342 the king's third son, John of
Gaunt, was born in Ghent, Belgium, and the king made
him the earl of Richmond, so the rent went into his
treasury. The annual visit by the bailiff was the only
physical tie the Wyclifs had with their feudal earl, and they
were glad of it. The more than two hundred miles that
separated them from the king's palace in Westminster,
south of London, gave Roger and John a freedom that most
feudal tenants did not have. If the Wyclifs had been tenants
of a local lord or of one of the big monasteries nearby in
Yorkshire, they might have been forced to take care of their

---

[1]It is difficult to give an accurate, modern equivalent to fourteenth-century
money. A skilled worker in the fourteenth century, a carpenter, roof thatcher,
or a miller, depending on the circumstances of his employment, could earn
fourteen pounds of silver in three months. On this basis, the Wycliffe rent is
about equal to a quarter of the annual wages of a skilled worker today in North-
eastern United States, about four or five thousand dollars.

owner's sheep during lambing while their own lambs dropped or died, or to cut their owner's grain while theirs rotted.

In their scenes of comic relief, medieval plays give a realistic picture of these problems of everyday life, though most of the little playlets were gathered into a cycle that dramatized stories from the Bible from the creation of the world to the Last Judgment. In the cycle given at Wakefield, Yorkshire, south of Richmond, the shepherds in the fields "keeping watch over their flocks by night" while unknowingly waiting for the Christmas angels to appear, complain of their harassment by feudal landlords:

> We plain shepherds who watch on the moor,
>   It's no wonder we hardly endure
> When all these rich lords watch over our door,
>   and the fields that we plough are hard as the floor.
>
>> As ye very well know,
>> From cold we're all lamed
>> Overtaxed and overstrained;
>> From a nobleman's blow
>> Of a fist are we tamed.[2]

On the contrary, when John Wyclif was disciplined, it was by his own father or mother, and as he matured, he learned that the discipline was for the good of the sheep, the good of the manor, and therefore his own good. Unlike the shepherd of the Wakefield play, he was not beaten by some arrogant lord who owned the land or by one to whom the Wyclifs owed work. The Wyclifs' feudal lord was only a name—John of Gaunt—far away in London.

John Wyclif took this freedom for granted. No one could explain it to him, just as no one could explain the furze on

---

[2]"Shepherds' Play II," from the *Towneley Plays*, pp.116–17. Language has been modernized by the author.

the hills or the streams that scrambled down to the River Tees or the heartbeat of a newborn lamb that he felt through his tunic on a cold Yorkshire night.

This was a modern freedom that would not come to everyone in England for five hundred years. With other children of the fourteenth century John shared a particular sense of security. Certainly, the Scots ran the family off the manor for a short time, and twice they lost half their band. However, when they returned to the manor, the family and neighbors worked together gathering in the sheep they had left, counting them, cursing the Scots not only for killing sheep but also for letting the rams out so no one knew which ewes were fresh and which were not. Their ill fortune was shared.

Sitting on the ground outside the sheep pen, they all drank out of a mazer of ale, John included, even when he was only a boy. A Yorkshire sheepman could catch a mazer of ale thrown to him without spilling any. If he spilled, the others made him lap it off the ground. But they all laughed together at his dirty mouth, and a boy could laugh with them, sleepy with the ale he drank. All this gave John a sense of peace that wiped out any worries the raids might have brought.

John also had a deeper sense of security. During his adolescence he had no need to worry about "finding himself" or "seeking his role in society," stages of growth that a modern child must go through.[3] A medieval adolescent saw his future in front of him. His future was determined early, governed by his family and the group to which it belonged. A shoemaker's son would be a shoemaker's apprentice, in all probability, and he was raised at the shop which was part of his home. A tiler's son learned to cut and set tile for a roof or a floor. A baker's son mixed dough and kneaded loaves from the time he was big enough to stand

---

[3]Erikson, pp. 258–60.

over the baker's table and pound his fists into the swollen leaven.

There is evidence that John Wyclif had an older brother who was being raised to become lord of the manor. However, that is all that has been learned about him; even his name has been lost. There is no way of knowing about the relationship that may have existed between John and his brother, their rivalry, their friendship, their love. This influence of one on the other must remain a vacuum in history that unfortunately cannot be filled.

The English laws of primogeniture have always been strict. John could not inherit the farm. As a second son, if he remained on the farm, he would always be little more than a tenant. John was always described as physically small, though wiry and energetic. Even by the time he was seven years old, it must have been apparent to Roger that John was not going to be of the size and strength needed for farm work.

Many Wyclifs in this area of England were priests; the priesthood must have been a family tradition for second sons. When John was born, a Wyclif was the parish priest of the manor church and was probably the one who christened him.

Roger decided early that like other Wyclifs, young John would find his role in the church. The decision was not very dramatic, for one-third of the people of England worked for the church bureaucracy in some capacity. Like the baker's son or the tiler's son, all around him John could see his future in the church as a monk, a friar, or a parish priest. Wycliffe manor was surrounded by Cistercian monasteries: Jervaulx, south of Richmond; Fountains, farther to the southwest; Rippon, not far from Fountains; and Bylands and Rievaulx, to the east.

As a boy John would have been impressed by the size of these monasteries and by their huge bands of sheep. The Cistercians were the best farmers in England of both grain and sheep. Fountains Abbey ran a thousand sheep and two thousand cattle. Supervising all this livestock was a full-time occupation for a monk. If he became a Cistercian, young John might simply transfer his expertise from one sheep farm to another.

The Cistercians brought mechanization with them when they emigrated from France about two hundred years earlier. Most of their abbeys were equipped with water wheels not only for crushing wheat and barley but also for fulling cloth, which utilized a great power wheel that raised two-hundred-pound weights and released them to crash down on the woven wool. Their abbeys were piped for water, which went into their kitchens and toilets. These factories and conveniences required planning, organization, maintenance, and record keeping by monks with the training and skills of an engineer.

The Cistercians did not operate the largest monasteries in England; the largest belonged to the Benedictines, like the monastery at Bury St. Edmunds, Suffolk. The abbot himself controlled thirteen manor farms in his own name, most of them bigger than Wycliffe. The abbey supplied priests for thirteen small parishes. The cellarer who ran the abbey farms had his own staff of forty-eight brothers and numerous laymen.

Even knights were pledged to the service of Bury St. Edmunds, and the monastery needed them for its protection. Once its tenants rebelled and looted the monastery of a hundred horses, a hundred and twenty cows, three hundred oxen, ten thousand sheep, and thirty hogs. The rebels left only enough livestock on abbey lands to allow it to continue operation.

The eighty monks at Bury St. Edmunds were a minor part of the establishment, though the farms and livestock existed to support them. Monks supervised carpenters, masons, glazers, tilers, and blacksmiths just to keep the buildings of the monastery complex in repair. Bury St.

Edmunds also controlled smaller monasteries, or daughter houses. A bright young man could find a place at St. Edmunds with whatever skill or training he had, and the chances for advancement in the hierarchy of the monastery were unlimited. If John did not become abbot of the mother house, he might still become abbot of a daughter house.

St. Albans, another Benedictine monastery in Hertfordshire, nearer London, was not as large as Bury St. Edmunds. Still it owned extensive forests where carpenters cut wood for the monastery buildings and for fuel and where the monks had exclusive rights to hunt their deer, boar, and rabbits for food. A monk who enjoyed hunting combined his career and his hobby like the monk who joined Chaucer's pilgrims in the *Canterbury Tales:*

> He was an expert hunter, and did all right;
> Greyhounds he had, as swift as birds in flight;
> For riding and for hunting of the hare
> Was his chief love, and no cost would he spare.[4]

The monasteries were also centers of intellectual life of England outside of the universities, Oxford and Cambridge. Both Bury St. Edmunds and St. Albans had fine libraries and scriptoria where monks wrote, copied, illuminated, and stored books, some of which were copied again in other monasteries. Some illuminations were reproduced as murals on walls of cathedrals throughout England. If John were trained in scholarship, the scriptoria would provide him with a stimulating and challenging career. John Wyclif never forgot his early impression of the monasteries, for later in his life he would condemn them for their size and great wealth.

---

[4]"Prologue" to the *Canterbury Tales,* I, 189-92, p. 13. Language has been modernized by the author.

Roger might have preferred John to be a friar rather than a monk. Monks were supposed to stay in their monasteries; friars were permitted to go out among people to beg for money and gifts. Roger had four orders of friars to choose from: Franciscan, Dominican, Augustinian (nicknamed Austin), and Carmelite. John knew of the Franciscan church in Richmond near the Frenchgate on the north wall of the city and often saw the Franciscans in their gray habits, a cloak with a cowl over it. They begged in Richmond and on the surrounding farms, even traveling to Wycliffe.

In addition to begging, friars performed some of the duties of a parish priest: preaching, hearing confessions, marrying, and burying the dead. Some of the most famous names John heard were those of the friars: St. Francis of Assisi and St. Dominic, who were the founders of the two basic orders; famous scholars like Albert the Great and his pupil, Thomas Aquinas, who had died two hundred years earlier; and if John had not heard of Robert Grosseteste, he would learn of him at Oxford. Roger Bacon had been Grosseteste's pupil, but Bacon was not as famous as Grosseteste in the fourteenth century, for Grosseteste had been the bishop of Lincoln.

The friars were not popular everywhere. Any priest at the Wycliffe church would be unhappy to see one of them come into his parish. The church was tiny, a little over thirty feet long, with no tower, no stained glass; it was just a square, stone structure with a thatched roof. The Wyclifs and their neighbors supported their church, not with money but with wool, mutton, and grain, and the priest had to sell some of these to buy the wine for his mass. The begging friars carried off to their own houses in Richmond and to York what little was available for the Wycliffe church.

Everyone knew the story of St. Francis and his voluntary poverty, his simplicity, and his sincerity. But by the fourteenth century, two hundred years after St. Francis, the friars were rich, and poverty was no longer one of their virtues. Even a priest was not above repeating stories of how the friars violated their oaths, not only to poverty but also to chastity. It was common for friars to seduce wives while their husbands were away. The people repeated these stories to one another on market day and in the taverns. Boccaccio in "The Decameron" and Chaucer in the *Canterbury Tales* have preserved some of these accounts. On the seventh day of "The Decameron" story three, a roving lover finds seduction is easier when he becomes a friar and persuades a wife it is only proper that she should sleep with the godfather of her child, who he is. Of course, the husband returns home unexpectedly, and the wife quickly explains that the friar is casting a spell to rid her child of worms. Upstairs, a second friar, seducing the housemaid, reports that he added his prayers to those of the godfather. The grateful husband rewards the friars with wine and candies for their doctoring.[5]

The friars knew these stories were being passed around, and within the order a small group, the Spiritual Franciscans, were trying to bring their practices into accordance with the principles that St. Francis originally prescribed. They dressed themselves in the clothes of the lowest serfs. They begged only what they needed to eat and nothing more to support abbeys or churches.

John did not have to become a monk or a friar to enter the bureaucracy of the church. The representative of the church most familiar to him was his parish priest, and the priest at Wycliffe church did not personify the glamor of the monk nor the garrulousness of the friar. Roger knew,

---

[5]The stories of the Seventh Day in "The Decameron" are to illustrate tricks women have played on their husbands. Chaucer's portrait of the friar in his "Prologue" I, 208–69, synthesizes the general attacks made on the friars in the fourteenth century. In his "Summoner's Prologue and Tale," III, 1665–2294, pp. 134–43, Chaucer has demonstrated the allegations in action.

however, that the parish priest had as good a chance for advancement in the church bureaucracy as any monk or friar. Priests sometimes became bishops, bishops became archbishops, archbishops cardinals, and cardinals popes.

Neither Roger nor John had seen a cardinal in Wycliffe, but undoubtedly both had seen the archbishop of York in the gigantic York Minster. These great churches were the largest buildings they had seen; the Wycliffe church could be hidden in the Minster and no one would know it was there.

CHAPTER THREE

A Farm Boy Masters Latin

*T*HE WAY OF THE PARISH PRIEST was the way Roger chose for John, and he began his studies when he was seven. First John had to learn a foreign language—Latin, which was the language of the church system. For the second and last time the Western world had a truly international language. Since the fall of the Roman Empire, every educated man spoke the language of the Romans: Peter Abelard, the Frenchman; Thomas Aquinas, the Italian; Moses Maimonides, the Spaniard; Albert the Great, the German; Robert Grosseteste, the Englishman; and in the years after them Nicholas Copernicus, the Pole, who read Robert Grosseteste, Galileo Galilei, the Italian, who read Copernicus; and Rene Descartes, the Frenchman, who read Galileo. Every university—Bologna, Palermo, Toledo, Paris, Oxford, and Cambridge—taught in the same language.

Even when John was seven years old, Latin was not altogether foreign to him. He had heard it from the time he had heard English. The Wyclif family probably went to mass every Sunday and on Holy Days of Obligation. John had heard the Latin of the mass so many times he knew most, if not all, of it by heart. Most people in the fourteenth century did, provided they went to church more often than to be baptized, married, and buried.

First John absorbed the Latin prayers: *Ave Maria gratia plena* (Hail, Mary, full of grace); *Pater noster qui est in coelis* (Our Father, who art in Heaven); then he absorbed the longer parts of the mass, the creed: *Credo in unum deum* (I believe in one God); the beginning of St. John's

25

gospel: *In principio erat verbum* (In the beginning was the word).

In a world without clocks or watches, the easiest method of measuring short durations of time was by reciting these memorized parts of the mass. When John was told to watch a pot in the kitchen, his mother told him to let the fish boil only as long as it took to say two *"in principios."* When John brushed down a sweaty horse, he brushed it five *"pater nosters"* on each side.

At seven years old, John was no longer considered a child but rather a little adult. He had abandoned his skirt and now wore a bright tunic about knee length, of green, blue, red, or brown, and tied about the waist with a leather thong. He wore woolen socks dyed in colors different from his tunic, and his hood, a third color, could be rolled down in the sun or pulled over his head in the rain. His shoes were leather but little heavier than modern slippers.

In his new, colorful clothing, he walked over the hill to his school, the Wycliffe manor church. His first teacher was the parish priest, now no longer a Wyclif but John of Clairvaux. For his lessons John sat on the floor around the pulpit with other boys of the area. In his lap rested a wax tablet, and he used a wooden stylus to write on the wax. Only John of Clairvaux had a book, so John's thirty-four-year journey to a doctorate of theology began as the priest dictated a rhymed Latin grammar, which the students memorized. As soon as he could recite the cases and conjugations of Latin nouns and verbs, John learned a practical, everyday vocabulary of Latin conversations with his teacher, a modern method of teaching a foreign language still in use today.

As soon as he demonstrated that he was able to easily converse in Latin, John memorized a collection of Latin proverbs. Actually, they were not the works of any single author but were attributed to a Dionysius Cato and were accumulated from the fifth through the sixteenth centuries and even used by Shakespeare's schoolmaster. Polonius' advice to Laertes in *Hamlet* was adapted from a sixteenth-century Cato.

The proverbs introduced a more complicated Latin syntax, but were not especially suitable to a seven-year-old boy raised on a north Yorkshire sheep farm. In Latin, the pupils were warned to "flee prostitutes," and were informed that "a prostitute kisses but not for love" and that "A bath helps neither a crow nor a whore." Young John had certainly met no prostitutes at Wycliffe. "Love and wine are knit in lust," John was told, but wine was too expensive for Roger's table, and the Latin did not warn against ale, which John drank, though it made him more sleepy than lustful. Cato's advice on marriage was uniformly cynical. "A woman hates what the husband likes," John learned. "Bear a wife's sharp tongue if she is frugal." And "a leaky roof, a smokey fire, and a chiding wife drive a man from his home."

Although the advice John received from the proverbs was somewhat inappropriate, his skill in Latin grew enough so that John of Clairvaux could now tell stories from the Bible and from the Latin classics. For the first time in his schooling John did not just memorize; now he composed and delivered speeches based on the stories—St. Michael's speech when he expelled Adam and Eve from the Garden of Eden, or Julius Caesar's speech when he defeated Pompey at Pharsalia. Then John debated in Latin with another pupil on whether Adam was personally responsible for disobeying God, whether St. George was greater than St. Paul; whether Aeneas should have married Dido at Carthage before he deserted her for the trip to found Rome.

With this training Latin became John Wyclif's first language, not his second. He thought in Latin, wrote in Latin, declaimed in Latin, debated in Latin, for at Wycliffe church he began the most exacting educational curriculum the Western world has known. It provided John Wyclif with the skills to put together a gigantic intellectual puzzle, a synthesis of knowledge a thousand years old. It incorporated the knowledge of the Greeks (Plato and Aristotle), Romans (Virgil and Seneca), Hebrews (Jeremiah and the Psalms), and the church (St. Paul and St. Augustine), and names, contemporary to John Wyclif, but now long forgotten: Peter Lombard, Robert Grosseteste, Richard Fitzralph, and Thomas Bradwardine.

The synthesis blended arithmetic and philosophy; physics and theology; geometry and music. It explained what we now call the solar system, what the medieval teachers called the universe. The scientists of the fourteenth century were more fortunate than those of the twentieth, for the fourteenth-century synthesis explained the ultimate source of the universe, its power, and its cosmic force. The cosmic force was called God, and God was the source of all power: physical, spiritual, even political.

John Wyclif may have been educated at the local church for seven years, or he may have received only the fundamentals there, the basics of his Latin, for example. He may have completed his early education at a grammar school, perhaps at the one taught by the Franciscans in Richmond. Whether at Wycliffe church or Richmond, his education would have been about the same, for John Wyclif was educated between the ages of seven and fourteen in the only way possible for him to continue assembling the pieces of this medieval, intellectual macrocosm. And assembling and rearranging the pieces would occupy him to the end of his life.

In 1345 he did not know the long process that was before him. However, John of Clairvaux, or any master, knew that if his pupil's education was to continue, he must move from Yorkshire two hundred miles south to Oxford University.

In the fourteenth century, Oxford had taken the place of the University of Paris as the leading university in the West. Most leaders of the church bureaucracy in England had come from Oxford. The bishops and archbishops were chosen from Oxford, and its graduates filled the most important posts in the civil government: the keeper of the privy seal, the treasurer of the Royal Household, or the chancellor of England. The leaders of the church bureaucracy usually filled the most important posts in the civil government.

If the Wyclifs had been one of the great families, John might have progressed in the church system without the help of Oxford. A few did. If the son of a small sheep farmer in northern Yorkshire wanted to advance in the system, however, he could progress only if he were a doctor of divine theology, of civil law, or of ecclesiastical law from Oxford. And John Wyclif could survive the long years to the doctorate only if he had been well prepared. The tools of John Wyclif's education at Oxford were the tools that John of Clairvaux gave him: Latin, declamations, and disputations. Only the subjects of the declamations and disputations would vary, and the logic that organized them both would be complicated yet subtle.

CHAPTER FOUR

Oxford

THE AUTUMN TERM AT OXFORD opened October 9, St. Denis Day. Ten days before, John said goodbye to his father and mother, the other members of his family, his teacher and priest, John of Clairvaux, and his friends at Wycliffe.

The trip to Oxford was the longest he had ever taken, more than two hundred miles, and it would be on foot, for he could not afford the luxury of a horse. Even if he had taken an old nag from the farm, the horse would need food, and on each of the eight or nine nights on the road, John would have had to pay for stable and feed. These expenses would have added more than a shilling (more than ten dollars) to the cost of the trip. In any case, the walk did not bother him, for he was used to walking. Travelers covered about twenty miles a day, walking faster than people do today.

When he arrived, John found Oxford larger than Richmond, although in 1345 Oxford had fewer than four thousand people, equally divided between scholars and townspeople. The Oxfordians were brightly dressed, but their fashions were more up-to-date than those on the northern borders of the country. In Oxford men's sleeves were wide and flaring, their tunics short and tight around their waists and chests. The women's dresses were tight around their bodies, showing off their breasts. Their skirts were loose, flowing like water around their hips and legs as they walked down the street.

The streets, though, were as dark and narrow as those of Richmond. Horses and carts had trouble pushing through the pedestrians, and two carts passed one another only with the greatest care and often accompanied by loud swearing. Most of the buildings were made of weathered gray timber beams that framed dirty brown plaster. A few of the larger houses had street floors of the golden sandstone from the Chilswell quarries, used by local masons for fifty years. College halls, private houses, taverns, and brothels stood side by side. The second stories of the buildings almost met, cutting off what little sunlight might have shone through. All the roofs were steeply peaked and gray tiled. Only a few were thatched.

The center of Oxford was Carfax, a square where the four main streets met. The town council complained that butchers slaughtered there in the early morning, allowed the blood to run down the gutter in the center of High and Fish streets to the east and south until it dried. The council had stopped the worst of the slaughtering, but a few dry puddles of blood could always be found in the gutters of High or Fish street.

John passed Richard Lynn's, the main bookseller of Oxford. He displayed manuscript books on stands, some open to a page decorated with a letter in blue and red, some closed, displaying tooled and jeweled leather covers. John knew these books were not for him. The price of one of them could pay for a small house, a sheepfold, or all the hogs his father raised at Wycliffe.

Oxford was filled with college halls where the students lived and studied, some along the streets, some up the narrow alleyways. A few of these names have survived the six hundred years and are part of Oxford today: Balliol, Merton, Queens, Oriel. When John arrived, the system was just beginning, and only a few of the halls were independent colleges. All of them were income-producing investments which cost a student about fifteen pence (about twelve dollars) a week for room and board. The price depended on the luxuries, glass windows, chimneys, and large rooms offered to its residents and was fixed by university assessors.

Many of these halls were owned by religious orders. The Augustinians of Oseney Abbey, just outside the western edge of the town, owned forty halls. St. Frideswyde, an abbey south of Oxford, also owned halls, though not as many as Oseney. Still it was as famous because it sponsored the annual St. Frideswyde fair every November 18, St. Frideswyde Day. St. Frideswyde, the patron saint of Oxford, was the abbey's first abbess. She was raped when the Vikings raided and destroyed the abbey in the eighth century.

Authorities generally agree that John Wyclif began his university life at Balliol Hall, for he qualified for one of the six undergraduate fellowships John Balliol offered to northern students as part of a penance for his sins (one of which may have been drunkenness). Balliol Castle was just over the River Tees from Wycliffe. William of Wycliffe was already living at Balliol when John arrived. It is not known how closely he was related to John, but undoubtedly he was from the general area of Wycliffe. John would call William his cousin, and when the new Wyclif arrived in Oxford, Cousin William met him and acted as his guide.

William took John down Horsemonger Street on the far side of the north branch of the Thames. Here were the horse markets where students who had ridden to Oxford could sell their horses, hoping to buy others at the end of the year. Balliol was located beyond the stables. Like most medieval buildings, it was built around the large, central hall used at Balliol for both eating and lectures. Not far away was the chapel, a new building, less than twenty years old, made of timber and plaster with a large glass window. Here John would attend daily mass and also hear some of his lectures, William told him.

John shared a room upstairs with three or four other new students. It was little more than a cubicle with thin partitions separating him and his roommates from another group in the next cubicle. The cubicles were connected to a study room with stools and a table. John had no bed. He slept on a pallet filled with straw, just another discomfort in this age of discomfort.

To enter the university John did not have to pass any examinations. He needed only to put his name on the roll of one of the regent-masters, the members of the teaching faculty with a master of arts degree. Usually a student enrolled with the master of his own hall, so it is assumed that John enrolled with Hugh of Corbrigge, the master of Balliol at the time.

As soon as his name was on the roll, John Wyclif became a clerk, the fourteenth-century name for a university student. Not all clerks took minor orders in the church, but John did. A barber came to the hall and shaved John's beard (if he had one) and the top of his head except for a few strands of hair, so John was tonsured. Later he joined the other entering clerks at St. Mary's, the university church on High Street. The bishop of Lincoln had come from Lincoln Cathedral, and as the clerks knelt at the altar, the bishop snipped those last strands of hair on his tonsure and asked God that John be accepted into His church. In reply, the clerks recited a dedication together.

John was now a subdeacon, part of the bureaucracy he had seen only from the outside during his first fourteen years of life. As subdeacon, he could assist Hugh or the chaplain of Balliol in saying mass, giving those responses he knew by heart. For the first time he could help distribute the host during communion. John Wyclif had started on his way—he was only a subdeacon, but the archbishop of Canterbury, John Stratford, was once a subdeacon at Oxford.

As a clerk at Oxford, John had to buy special clothes. In the Middle Ages clothes were used to identify a man's rank, group, and occupation, not to protect him against nature. Everyone wore the same clothes summer and winter. As a clerk John wore a toga, a tunic down to his waist of bright blue, green, yellow, or red, whatever color his hall had adopted. Over the toga he wore a cappa, a sleeveless robe, also bright, required for the lectures he attended, and over the cappa he wore a hood of fur, cheap fur as an undergraduate, more expensive after he received his bachelor's degree. This fur was the students' only concession to a change of climate.

These clothes were expensive, but William certainly knew where John could buy secondhand garments. Only about thirty percent of the students who began their course of studies successfully earned their bachelor of arts degree, and when the dropouts left Oxford, they sold their togas, cappas, and hoods, often at a tavern to pay their drinking bills. Here John could buy secondhand clothes cheaply, but if he wished to pay more, he could buy better quality garments from a tailor who repaired damaged clothing. If John knew a student who was not attending lectures at the same time he was, the two could share a cappa. This exchange was difficult to arrange, however, for halls catered to students in the same curriculum who all attended the same lectures.

The taverns of Oxford were marketplaces not only for secondhand clothes but also for secondhand books. The texts left here, however, changed hands so many times that the pages were often torn, some even missing, and the ink was illegible in many places, smeared by grimy fingers or washed out by spilled ale. For a secondhand copy of the authors he would soon be familiar with—Aristotle, Boethius, Averroes, Peter Lombard—or separate volumes of the books of the Bible, or a manuscript in better condition than those in the taverns, Cousin William would take John to the fair at St. Giles, just outside Oxford, where dealers in secondhand books set up their stalls.

After John had been tonsured and had purchased his clothes and books, he met the other clerks at Balliol, and together they elected a principal who was their leader. The principal served under a master and the master under two procurators, one a Franciscan, one a parish priest. The clerks made their own rules as long as they did not conflict with laws already laid down by the hall or the university. At least Balliol had the beginnings of a democracy, and for the first time in his life John had a voice, if a small one, in how he was to live.

All these preparations had to be finished by the day after St. Denis Day, October 10. On that day the term opened with the Mass of the Holy Ghost at St. Mary's. With all the members of the university gathered in one place, the new clerks looked one another over and stared at the masters, the proctors, and their superior of superiors, the chancellor of Oxford.

Wyclif could not help noticing that the university was divided into two distinct groups: secular clerks like himself, studying on their own to be parish priests; and members of one of the orders, either monks or friars. The seculars either paid their own way or received partial scholarships. The monks and friars were supported by their order. The seculars believed the orders had a much easier life—good wines, roasted mutton, and soft beds. But the rivalry was more serious than a difference in styles of living. The seculars actually controlled the university by a special license from the king, which guaranteed them freedom of discussion and expression. If the orders took control, as they had at the University of Paris, the seculars believed this freedom would be lost to them. It is doubtful that Wyclif had any idea, as he saw the two groups segregated on two sides of St. Mary's Church, that he would one day become a hero to the seculars in their struggle against the orders.

Three days after the Mass of the Holy Ghost, a second mass was celebrated for King Edward III and Queen Philippa, their children, and university benefactors, living and dead. Only then did the first day of studies begin. The elected principal of Balliol blew a loud horn at sunrise. The clerks cursed the principal, stumbled out of their cubicles, and gathered at a trough in the Balliol yard to wash. Before they ate, they heard mass and their first lecture. Lectures recessed for the first meal at about ten o'clock, began again at about noon, and continued until sunset, when they stopped for vespers and supper.[1]

John had light for studying only during the day, the time getting shorter as winter approached and lengthening again with the coming of spring. Candles, the only artificial light, were expensive and beyond John's meager budget. He might have made a taper by wrapping pieces of straw in a tight bundle, but students rarely did this. As soon as it was too dark to read, Wyclif was probably glad to go to sleep on his pallet.

John and his brother clerks were only fourteen or fifteen years old. It was the first time most of them had been free of the sharp discipline of home and school, free of the beatings and proddings. A young man who had his name listed on a lenient master's roll without adequate training soon found a tavern easier to frequent than the lecture hall, and the girls of Oxford more congenial companions than Aristotle. No wonder John could buy secondhand clothes and books from students with unpaid tavern bills.

But the discipline of the Wycliffe sheep farm and the resulting self-discipline that developed from it served John well, and John of Clairvaux had trained him well. Already

---

[1]These times cannot be fixed exactly, for during the fourteenth century the day was not organized by the clock. The position of the sun fixed the time for prayers in monasteries, and those outside the monasteries arranged their day according to the monastery bells which rang the "hours." The time between the prayers lengthened with the summer days. However, clocks were known, and town clocks existed in Dover, in Paris, and even in the monastery at St. Albans. When the abbot at St. Albans, a mathematical and a mechanical genius, was building his clock, both King Edward III and the monks at St. Albans accused the abbot of wasting money and time on an unnecessary luxury.

he had had seven years of Latin training and was thoroughly familiar with the process of this specialized, unique, and demanding schooling. He was still subject to comprehending lectures, giving declamations, and arguing disputations.

Lectures at the university took on a special form. John's new master began by dictating a question. John transcribed it but did not answer it; he was not supposed to, at least not yet. The master divided the question into subquestions, and the subquestions into further subquestions, and then again. Finally the master answered the sub-sub-question and worked back up the division as if the problem had gone down a flight of stairs and climbed up again. With this stair system the master analyzed an author's words and phrases, their meanings, and the implications of their meanings. John's study depended on memory as much as on his books, and the technique of subdividing, relating, and systematizing broke any subject into small units which John could easily memorize.

Through this stair process John ingested the rhetoric, logic, astronomy, physics, and ethics of Aristotle and the commentaries on Aristotle by Averroes and Avicenna. The Oxford curriculum had been built on Aristotle since the discovery of his works one hundred years earlier, along with their translations from Greek and Arabic into Latin.

Wyclif studied only two works with the same care as the works of Aristotle: *The Four Books of Sentences* by Peter Lombard, and the Bible. The *Sentences* was actually a Biblical commentary. Two hundred years earlier Peter had collected the ideas (sentences) of the Bible and various church authorities, especially St. Augustine, under a wide variety of subjects: the creation of the world, cosmology, ethics, Christ in Heaven, Christ on earth, the sacraments, the Second Coming, the Last Judgment, the end of the world.

Wyclif and his fellow clerks used the *Sentences* as if it were an intellectual trampoline—they jumped off it in great speculative leaps, twisting, turning, and flipping. Many a student and master wrote a commentary on the *Sentences* after he finished his studies. About three hundred of these remain in the British Library in London and over one thousand in the Vatican library in Rome. If Wyclif wrote a commentary on Peter Lombard, it has been lost. But Wyclif's writings that do survive are filled with references to Peter, and he was early convinced that Peter was correct in judging the Bible and St. Augustine as the ultimate authorities on truth, whenever it could be found.

John Wyclif did not only descend and ascend stairs of questions and devour Aristotle. He had to demonstrate skill in declamations every week before his fellows at Balliol and once a year before all the clerks in the school of liberal arts. Of course, the declamations at Oxford were more sophisticated than they had been at Wycliffe: declamations not on Adam and Eve but on physics; not on Dido and Aeneas but on ethics; not on Caesar and Pompey but on astronomy. These declamations at Oxford, as at Wycliffe, were set speeches designed to demonstrate not John's mental agility nor keenness in argument, but his understanding of form and style. Proficiency in declamation was acquired from the study of Cicero. Wyclif mastered it quickly.

Wyclif made his real reputation in the more demanding of the two university exercises—the disputation. Disputations were debates, but to call a medieval disputation a debate is like calling *Swan Lake* a dance. The disputation at Oxford was an intellectual ballet in which ideas pivoted in graceful turns and perfect extensions of logic.

The disputations were held on every level of the university. John had to dispute with a fellow clerk at Balliol, with another clerk during a contest between two of the college halls, and with his masters. But as part of his final examination for his degrees, he had to dispute with the whole university—undergraduates, graduates, and faculty. It was a special polemic called a *quodlibet* (anything you wish).

So important were the quodlibets that records of them have survived for six hundred years. The records demonstrate that when John Wyclif stood for his quodlibet he had to be prepared for everything: psychology ("What is the greater reward, to love or be loved?"); ethics ("Can justice and equity have the same result?"); semantics ("Does creating the word enable a person to recognize the object?"); and feminism ("May a wife give alms without the consent of her husband?").

Most of the topics disputed were religious, and no tenet of fourteenth-century theology was forbidden in the quodlibet. True, the masters were priests, the clerks were subdeacons and deacons, and all were subject to the discipline of church superiors. But Oxford was under a special jurisdiction of the king and enjoyed great freedom of investigation and discussion because of the king's protection. Disputants in quodlibets asked, "Did the power of the bishops come directly from Christ or by way of intermediaries?" "Will prayer alter a divine decree as seen in the stars?" "Can God create a vacuum?"[2] In the years ahead John Wyclif would ask questions in his disputations that would truly test this freedom of investigation and discussion.

Disputations took the place of laboratories at Oxford. In contrast to modern investigators, John Wyclif and his associates had to probe their ideas publicly, where all could listen. Their ideas were challenged, altered, and developed during the disputations as they are today during experimentation.

The medieval disputations, however, developed a tradition that modern laboratories lack—a prevaricator, or of-

---

[2]This question disturbed all scientific thinking for three hundred years until (by experiment, not disputation) Blaise Pascal, the French physicist and mathematician of the seventeenth century, and Robert Boyle, the English chemist, proved that God not only could but did create a vacuum.

ficial jester. The prevaricator added much to the appeal of the quodlibet. Someone from the audience would fire a question. After the disputant gave his answer, the prevaricator would pun, ridicule, and joke about it. An inept disputant suffered from the jibes and sneers, but John Wyclif held his own against the prevaricator. He was skilled in the declamation, but he learned to use the disputation with brilliance and success as few others in his time at Oxford.

In 1349 John Wyclif was prepared to stand before the university for his first quodlibet as part of the examination for his bachelor's degree, but he would not actually stand as disputant until 1353. During the intervening years, the howl of Black Death was to be heard across England.

CHAPTER FIVE

The Black Death

*I*N THE FOURTEENTH CENTURY the bubonic plague was called the pestilence, and it was always present, in every large city of England and of the Continent.

The disease started with a swelling in the groin or armpit called a bubo, which enlarged from the size of a pea to the size of an egg in a few hours. The following day gray spots would show on the victim's thighs, arms, and legs, and he would be very hot and sweaty. The medieval physician would give him a laxative, bleed him, and feed him the juice of an aloe spiced in myrrh, cinnamon, and saffron. He would rub a salve of hog fat and myrtle on the bubo or tie a live toad over it. When the bubo did not vanish, the physician would lance it. In a week the patient was usually dead.

During the rainy summer of 1348, merchants, pilgrims, friars, and knights coming across the English Channel saw a terrifying new pestilence. A man would be walking along the street on his way to a shop or church, when suddenly blood would gush from his mouth and nose. He would collapse where he was standing, and would be dead by the end of the day.

It was not the speed of death that frightened the travelers. They were used to speedy death. It was the numbers that were dying and the quick spread of the disease that frightened them. In the spring of that year both variations of the pestilence, new and old, had been in Palermo and Genoa, then a week later in Florence and Rome, then in Avignon, the city of the pope, then in Marseilles. Just across the Channel in Calais, six hundred people died in one day. They heard it said the lepers or the Jews had poisoned the wells.

England had lepers but, officially, no Jews. In 1290 Edward I had expelled sixteen thousand Jews in three months. The English felt safe from what was happening in France and Italy, not because they had no Jews but because they prided themselves on their holiness. They called England "the Pearl of the Blessed Virgin," and believed that the Blessed Virgin would certainly protect her pearl. But just to be safe, in August the bishop of Bath and Wells gave forty days' indulgence from Purgatory to anyone who prayed, gave alms, and fasted for the intention of saving England from this pestilence.

At the end of August, on the Feast of the Beheading of John the Baptist, a ship arrived at Melcombe Regis, a small port town on the south coast of England. Within a week not a person there was left alive. The few that had not died had fled, and the pestilence screamed through the southwest of England, through Dorset, through Devon, along the water routes, up the Bristol Channel, then up the Avon River to the city of Bristol, up the Severn to the city of Gloucester, up the River Lea, up the Stour, then down the Thames toward Oxford.

We have no record of what John Wyclif did during 1349. In times of great calamities, thoughts usually turn toward home, but Yorkshire offered no refuge from the pestilence. A local history reported that the pastures of Wycliffe became a waste, "overrun with briars, nettled, and noxious weeds." Sheep died where they stood, and as another chronicle stated, "Neither man, bird, nor beast would touch them."

The city of Richmond was on high ground, and Yorkshiremen, like the Wyclifs who lived nearby, thought that the city would provide a healthy retreat as it had done during the Scots' raids. And so they crowded within the city walls. There one-third of them died. The Wyclifs were among the two-thirds who survived. The city of York lost fewer by percent but more in numbers; two thousand of its ten thousand.

If John Wyclif decided to remain at Oxford, as he probably did, life was no safer there. During 1349 Oxford had three mayors: the first died on his way to London to take his oath of office, the second decided not to take the chance of going to London and was sworn in by the abbot of Oseney, and he and his successor both died in office.

The abbot of Frideswyde died. The vicars of St. Mary's, St. Ebbe's, and St. Giles died. An entire monastery of friars was wiped out, and the vacant abbey fell to the king by default. Wyclif had only a two-minute walk from Balliol to common trenches dug for victims on a plot of land near Smithgate on the north wall of the town. On one day he could have seen sixteen bodies carried there and dumped.

At first priests tried to give the rites of burial. Soon the dead were so many and the priests so few that the grave diggers, newly created deacons, were taught to mumble, *"Requiem aeternam dona eis, Domine,"* probably not knowing that the Latin meant, "Eternal rest give them, Lord." At least student subdeacons like Wyclif, who were pressed into service, knew what the Latin meant.

Most scholars and masters fled. They thought of themselves as temporary residents, and some of the college halls had arranged retreats in rural villages for emergencies such as the plague or serious riots. In Oxford the college halls were deserted, and the townspeople who stayed behind helped themselves to what they had been denied when the masters and clerks were in residence. They moved into the halls, satisfying their revenge. A townsman felt that he proved his superiority to any scholar by remaining behind and surviving. All goods were scarce so harness-makers, fishmongers, bakers, and millers at Oxford charged any price they wished.

Wyclif never ran with the crowd, but what happened at Oxford must have frightened him, and with good reason.

So frightened was he that he reported the population of the town had dropped from 60,000 to 3,000. Richard Fitzralph, a famed mathematician and chancellor of Oxford from 1332 to 1334, said the population fell from 30,000 to 6,000.

Even the mathematician's figures are completely exaggerated. A population of 30,000 would make Oxford the second largest city in England, with London at about 60,000. Of course, it was not. Even 3,000 may slightly exaggerate the size of the student body that lived in Oxford before the plague. If deaths there were proportional to the rest of England, Oxford's population dropped from 4,000 to 2,700. With the decrease of one-third, the streets would have seemed deserted to Wyclif, and he would have noticed empty houses. His statistics as well as those of the chancellor were the result of shock, not accurate counting.

Death hit haphazardly—sometimes the old pestilence, sometimes the new. A family, a street, a village, a monastery would be wiped out. Not far away, another family, another street, another village, another monastery would lose not a person. No one knew why.

John Wyclif read about the pestilence in the commentary on Aristotle by Avicenna, one of the most famous Islamic mathematicians, philosophers, and encyclopedists of the eleventh century. Avicenna wrote that during a pestilence he noticed that mice, rats, and animals living underground came to the surface in great numbers and acted as if they were drunk.

All scholars read Avicenna, but none connected his account of the erratic behavior of the rodents to a cause of the plague. The scientists of the fourteenth century divided the problem into a final cause—God's anger for the sins of mankind—and an immediate cause—the polluted air.

The final cause could be seen in the stars, the positions of which showed God's plan. Every astrologer claimed to have predicted the pestilence of 1348. John Aschenden at Merton College, Oxford, ten years before Wyclif, found God's purpose demonstrated in a conjunction of Jupiter and Saturn in Aquarius and a total eclipse of the moon in Libra, all of which occurred on March 20, 1345. He mentioned all kinds of calamities that these conjunctions indicated. His Oxford manuscript does mention the pestilence, but the difference in the colors of the ink indicates that Aschenden, or someone, later added the pestilence to the list of calamities.

Galen, whose writings survived from the second century A.D., was the generally accepted authority on polluted air. He warned against air that issued from marshes, stagnant water, and rotting plants, but especially air from unburied corpses. Undoubtedly the stench of the epidemic was overpowering. Everywhere living bodies were infected with the buboes and incontinent with excrement and urine. Their stink was as brutal as the putrefying, unburied dead. Authorities suggested a few remedies to cleanse the air. Some advocated burning odorous woods like juniper, ash, oak, or pine. They said that throwing spice on the fire added to its efficiency as a depollutant. One authority suggested burning sulphur. (Actually, the sulphur would kill the plague bacilli, and in a heavy enough concentration the fleas and possibly the rats themselves.)

Physicians warned against anything that generated heat. If you must bathe, they said, bathe in tepid water. They especially prescribed bleeding. One physician recommended bleeding up to ten pounds of blood, a desperate remedy indeed, for that is almost the complete human supply.

The pestilence and the attempt to eradicate its final cause brought a revived sense of community to London shopkeepers. Each Londoner had been responsible for keeping the street clean in front of his shop. Usually a shopkeeper merely pushed the dirt from in front of his shop down the street and in front of another shop when that owner was occupied with some other business. The shopkeepers hoped that the dirt was eventually picked up by cleaners hired by the watch, if the watch had not pocketed the money given him to hire cleaners. During the last months of the epidemic, however, shopkeepers cleaned the street in front of their shops with zeal, and the streets of London were cleaner than they had been before or would be after.

Everyone believed that the real cure would come when the people accepted the final cause of the pestilence—God's anger. They had to abandon their sinful ways. People streamed into London to demonstrate that they had given up sin and were truly repentant. More than six hundred of them, many from Flanders, met twice daily in front of St. Paul's Cathedral as well as other places around the city. Each stripped to the waist, and over his head wore a hood with a red cross embroidered on its back and front. Each repentant sinner carried a three-strand, knotted leather whip. Some even pushed horseshoe nails through the knots.

These marchers came to be known as the flagellants. They paraded slowly through the streets of London, at each measured step scourging themselves over their shoulders. Soon their backs were lacerated, and the blood ran down their torn skin and over the cloths bound around their waists. They chanted a litany, one group calling out, "From thy dreadful pestilence," and the other group completing, "Good Lord, deliver us."

Three times during the march at well-known corners, for example, at Bridge Street opposite the north gate of London Bridge, each man dropped face down on the ground, his arms stretched out, as if he were crucified. Then the flagellant in the rear walked over the raw backs, giving each man a cut with his lash until he reached the front of the line. They continued in this way until the line had returned to its original order, and then the flagellants rose and marched on through the streets.

Soon the plague lessened. The flagellants, not the physicians or the shopkeepers, received the credit, for the people of the fourteenth century believed the self-torture had been effective. Day by day the number of dying decreased. The spread of the disease in the countryside outside the towns slowed and stopped. The virulence of the plague was to return again in 1356 and 1361, but in the autumn of 1349 it seemed the flagellants had accomplished their purpose.

Now, six hundred years later, the immediate cause of the bubonic plague is analyzed differently. The disease is caused not by air pollution but by a bacillus, *Pasteurella pestis*, named for Pasteur but discovered by others using his methods of research. The bacillus is carried in various fleas on the black rat. In humans the bacilli attack the lymph glands and the walls of blood vessels, causing hemorrhages. With pneumonic plague, the new type in 1349, death came before the postules could form. In the older, bubonic form, in addition to the hemorrhages, the bacilli caused a fatty deterioration of the kidneys and heart and the cause of death was actually heart attack.

In the fall of 1353 the clerks and masters returned to Oxford, and the townspeople had to move out of the college halls. If the experience of that university was similar to the experience of the University of Paris, where more accurate records were kept, within five years the university had as many teaching masters as it had had before the plague, and it was awarding as many degrees.

Four years after the pestilence had emptied Oxford of its masters and clerks, John Wyclif faced them, now gathered together, in his first quodlibet. The pestilence was still on everyone's mind, and Wyclif was a good enough student to prepare for questions about it. The kind of questions asked and the answers Wyclif was expected to give, based on the latest scientific information, have been preserved:

Q: If polluted air, which is hot and moist, is the cause of the pestilence, why was the pestilence at its height in the close of summer and the beginning of autumn when the air is cold and dry?

A: It was the heat of the previous summer that made the summer and autumn air still susceptible to pollution.

Q: During the pestilence why did certain birds, usually accustomed to flying high, descend, while others rose to unusual heights?

A: They did that to escape the pollution wherever it was, and it was both low and high at different times.

Q: Why did prisoners die less than those who had not committed a crime, if sin was the ultimate cause of the pestilence?

A: Sin, the final cause, acted only according to general laws. The prisoners were subject to the immediate cause, the polluted air. The prisons, being enclosed, had less polluted air than outside.

These answers are evidence that Wyclif's studies had been in physics as well as philosophy and that his ideas had begun to be organized into the great medieval synthesis. He overcame the challenges of this first quodlibet and was now a bachelor of arts, no longer an undergraduate. He could assist at lectures by dictating the text for a few extra pence. However, the bachelor's degree did not take him far into the system of the university or into the hierarchy of the church. He stood only at the bottom of a rock face. Above him was another rugged escarpment, the three-year ascent to the master of arts.

At this time Wyclif moved across Oxford from Balliol to Merton College.[1] Merton was popular with scholars because it was endowed to give twelve of the most promising and needy clerks in the university who already had earned their first degree a chance to continue their studies. In addition, all Mertonians received six pence a week to pray for the souls of two friends of Walter de Merton, founder of the college, and each clerk at the college served a year as bursar, Wyclif among them.

These financial rewards were not the only reasons Oxfordians were glad to study at Merton. It was also the most prestigious house of learning in medieval England. With Wyclif at Merton were two clerks who later would become chancellors of the university—Alan Tonworth and William Berton. Wyclif would have good reason to remember them both.

While Wyclif was there, Richard Fitzralph, the mathematician who had so inflatedly reported the losses during the plague, visited Merton. His faulty statistics went unnoticed, for he had spent a lifetime in irascible controversy, especially concerning the friars. While he was at Avignon bringing his case against them to the attention of the pope, he wrote a book, *On the Poverty of Our Savior*, reminding the friars of their forgotten ideal of holy poverty. While he visited Merton, he left a copy in the college library, and it is still there today. Wyclif probably met the old warrior, and he certainly read the book carefully. Wyclif's quarrel with the friars would come later, but he would remember Fitzralph's cohesive reasoning, especially his basic argument that only a righteous man could hold true power in the church.

---

[1]Some of the buildings at Merton which Wyclif knew when he was there still stand. The exterior of the chapel remains, and in the Mob Quadrangle of Merton, the Treasury with its steep, slate roof has not changed in appearance for six hundred years.

The importance of Merton came from intellectuals like Fitzralph and other mathematicians, astronomers, and physicists who had been there, some of the greatest of the fourteenth century. Ralph Strode, a personal friend of both Wyclif and Chaucer, was at Merton. Strode was one of the universal men of the time, famous first as a great logician. His Latin texts on logic were used at the University of Padua. He also became a successful London city attorney, and he wrote an epic, now lost, which described an imaginary voyage to New Jerusalem, a work of speculative fiction published in the years between Dante's *Divine Comedy* and Thomas More's *Utopia*.

Robert Grosseteste, first chancellor of Oxford, had been at the university one hundred years before Wyclif. A Franciscan, not a Mertonian, he was a pioneer in optics, medicine, astronomy, acoustics, and Biblical scholarship. He suggested badly needed changes in the calendar four hundred years before they were finally adopted. An early student of Greek, he insisted that the Greek text be used to correct the Latin Vulgate Bible, and he could read enough Hebrew to direct a new translation of the Psalms from Hebrew to Latin.

John Aschenden, the astronomer who claimed to have predicted the plague, left a tradition of stellar calculation accurate enough for Wyclif to calculate the solar eclipse of August 17, 1384. The calculations Wyclif and all mathematicians needed at that time were more complicated than those necessary today, because in the fourteenth century the solar system was seen as Ptolemaic—the earth at the center surrounded by seven planets, which included the sun and moon. So that their mathematics could agree with their observations, error had been piled on error for the thirteen hundred years since Ptolemy had described his system. Wyclif's calendar was ten days off, and on this disorientation he computed epicycles within cycles for his prediction.

Like most medieval scientists, Aschenden, Grosseteste, and Wyclif were attracted to the investigation of optics. These scientists of the Middle Ages knew that, according to the Book of Genesis, the creation of the world began with light, and they believed that the properties of light—its power—made the rest of creation possible. All approved of St. Augustine's metaphor, "God is the light of the world." God used light by a kind of "divine illumination" to inspire human wisdom, Grosseteste thought.

In one of his sermons, Wyclif remarked that when he was young, he gathered information on optics from a wide variety of sources and that he was especially interested in studying the properties of light. Principally he read Robert Grosseteste. Wyclif was influenced by him not only in optics but also in the study of the Bible and of philosophy.

"This man is orthodox and holy," Wyclif wrote about Grosseteste, "eminently praised and imbued with excellence in worldly and divine philosophy, much more perceptive and clear than we are. Would that the modern world listened to the words of such a man."[2]

It is understandable that Wyclif, Grosseteste, and the other scientists would be attracted to the study of light. Everywhere that Wyclif had lived, in Yorkshire and at Oxford, he occupied rooms much darker than people are now accustomed to. In towns and cities, streets were without illumination of any kind after sundown. Candles provided the strongest artificial light available and were expensive. When the sun set, people stopped work and retired. No one ventured outside into the black and dangerous night. When the sun rose, confidence returned, people moved again in the streets, and work resumed.

---

[2]Wyclif, "*de Trinitate.*" Praise for Grosseteste and citations from his works abound in most of Wyclif's works: *de Civile Dominio, de Veritate Sacrae Scripturae, de Eucharistica*, the sermons, and many other works.

For John Wyclif and all the people of the fourteenth century light was a beautiful phenomenon and by no means taken for granted. Light became a clue to Wyclif's beliefs about God, the power of God, and God's creations. A scientific explanation of what to him was an intellectual image would not be known for six hundred years.

At the time in Wyclif's life when he was hunting for new ideas and ready to accept them, he was exposed at Oxford to the speculations of these scientists and theoreticians. Their ideas spurred him on to examine the nature of reality and to question its conventional explanation in the theology of his day.

These Oxfordians—Thomas Bradwardine, Richard Fitzralph, Robert Grosseteste, and Ralph Strode—are some of the forgotten explorers of thought, spring rains before the thunderstorms of Copernicus and Galileo. Copernicus and Galileo revealed a conflict between their science and their theology. The Oxfordians found no such conflict. Wyclif still hoped there was none and wished fervently that his science would support his theology.

CHAPTER SIX

Priesthood

THE TENTH OF FEBRUARY, A HOLIDAY at Oxford, honored St. Scholastica, the sister of St. Benedict and founder of the Benedictine order of nuns. The Swindelstock tavern on Carfax was open for business on February 10, 1355, and its customers were celebrating St. Scholastica Day by drinking great quantities of ale.

The drinkers sat on the benches and stools, and because Swindelstock, like all taverns, was open to the street, the drinkers could watch Oxfordians at Carfax coming up Great Bailey and going down High and Fish streets. Some of the customers at the tavern rolled dice, others played chess. Young Oxford girls sometimes served the ale and at intervals vanished upstairs with a customer to console him if he lost his money at dice or at chess (of course, she made certain he had at least a few groats left). Chess was a popular betting game in which players paid one another for the number of pieces they could capture.

Walter Springhouse, formerly rector of Hamden, Somerset, and Roger Chesterfield, both Oxford clerks, were being served not by one of the girls but by John Croydon, a friend of the tavern's owner, John Bereford, mayor of Oxford and formerly its representative in Parliament. Walter and Roger argued with John Croydon on the quality of Swindelstock ale, which the clerks of Oxford always claimed was diluted with lime and water, a practice in cheap taverns.

John Croydon denied the charge. The argument heated up, and Roger Chesterfield threw the wooden mazer he was drinking from at John Croydon. The friends of the two clerks and the friends of the townsmen quickly took sides. Soon the tavern was a frenzy of stools, mazers, and barrel staves, all of which bloodied noses and cracked heads. The tumult quickly spread into Carfax and down the four streets which met there. No one cared about the original dispute. Oxford clerks bashed Oxford townsmen where they found them, and townsmen hammered the clerks. Someone rang the bell of St. Martin's at Carfax to call reinforcements for the townsmen. Someone else ran down High Street and rang St. Mary's to call for student reinforcements.

Passions flamed until nightfall, and Oxfordians were bruised, battered, and broken, but in the first twenty-four hours no one was killed. That was rare in an Oxford riot. The next day it seemed the riot had subsided. At about eleven o'clock, however, a group of townsmen with bows and arrows fired into a group of students who had gathered in Beaumont Fields, north of the town. The students ran down Horsemonger Street and into the Austin priory for safety.

A few minutes later a master of theology was shot while trying to leave the priory. Now the fighting escalated. The bells of St. Mary's and St. Martin's clanged furiously all day to again summon reinforcements. The clerks rushed along the walls of the town and shut all the gates to prevent help for the townsmen from arriving. Their tactic succeeded until vespers. At that time the farmers and artisans outside of Oxford, their work over for the day, broke through the gates shouting "Slay, slay, havoc, havoc," introducing a new word, *havoc*, into the English language. The clerks, unconcerned with the history of the language, tried to free themselves from the convulsive paroxysm in the narrow streets. Friars from the various abbeys tried to bring peace by thrusting the crucifix between battering combatants, crying out "*Pax vobiscum! Pax vobiscum* ("Peace be with you"). They were driven back to their monasteries by the blows of both sides.

Finally the clerks retreated to their halls and barricaded themselves inside. For the second and third day after St. Scholastica's holiday they defended themselves, but eventually the townsmen crashed into some of the halls, and once inside they killed clerks, plundered valuables, and flung books into the streets. Five college halls were burned and sixty-three clerks were killed. The townsmen unceremoniously dumped the dead bodies into the Thames, north and south of the town. One chronicle reported that some of the tonsured corpses were scalped, the first record of this practice in English history, but not the last.

These were not the days for a frail, although wiry, clerk whose skill was in declamation and disputation. Neither the rampaging townsmen nor clerks would have been influenced by arguments on the nature of light, no matter how carefully reasoned. Hysteria is not influenced by logic. Fortunately Merton College was one of the few collegiate halls in the town of Oxford built entirely of stone, and its stone walls offered protection that some of the other halls lacked. The violence that consumed the town eddied about the Merton walls, swirled by, and spared the clerks inside, including John Wyclif and his fellows Alan Tonworth and William Berton.

Most clerks fled Oxford for their lives. The entire university was closed until June, and the bishop of Lincoln, John Glynwell, placed the town under an interdict for two years. He forbade any public worship except on important feast days like Christmas and Easter, an order which did not apply to university chapels.

King Edward ordered two hundred townsmen imprisoned and fined the town two hundred and fifty pounds (about seventy-five thousand dollars). In addition, the king ordered the town to pay for the damage done to the university. Finally, he gave the university a charter freeing it from any town control.

When these judgments assured the clerks and masters of the college halls that comprised Oxford University that their lives were safe again, at least for a time, they returned to their scholarship. Wyclif's career began again, and he started the long preparation for his second and more important examination, the master of arts. The process of the examination was as difficult as it was elaborate.

First, nine masters had to witness to his character and attainments. When his character had been guaranteed, he was permitted to give a lecture on, of course, Aristotle. Finally, he had to stand and dispute again. The bachelors and undergraduates he was leaving behind would be even more eager to trap him as a candidate for the master of arts than they had been when he had stood for his bachelor of arts quodlibet. Every step in his logic would be probed, every definition twisted, every authority challenged. He needed all his concentration, memory, and skill.

The day following this match he appeared at St. Mary's Church and from the university chancellor received a ring, a book, and a biretta (more a cap than a modern biretta). He had still to give his inaugural lecture, stand for another disputation, and take his oath. Only then would he be a master. The process culminated in a traditional banquet given by the new master of arts for his teachers, an expensive formality. John Wyclif had to pay for boards to be used for tables as well as for trestles beneath the boards, firewood to warm the hall, servants, wine, candles by the pound, and mutton.[1]

---

[1]Records at Merton show that for an examination feast given there a few years after Wyclif, a student had to pay for ten pots of honey, a pound of peppers, and forty braces of rabbit.

John Wyclif became a master, and he was also ordained a priest. He had usually assisted a priest each day at mass. It was as much a part of his day as attending lectures, disputing, and eating.

For the ordination, the bishop of Lincoln conducted a special service. Master John and others to be invested lined up in front of the altar. Possibly William Berton was one of them, for he had been behind the walls of Merton during the St. Scholastica riots and had taken his master's degree at the same time as Wyclif.

Now for the first time Wyclif put on the complete vestments of a priest and said his first mass, performing the mystery of the Holy Eucharist. He held the consecrated bread above his head and said, *"Hoc est enim corpus meum,"* the same words he had heard spoken by John of Clairvaux and every other priest he had served since he was a boy at Wycliffe. With those words, Wyclif believed, the ordinary piece of bread he held in his fingers changed into the physical body of Christ. A miracle occurred again when Wyclif raised the chalice of wine above his head, for the wine changed into Christ's blood. But eventually John Wyclif wondered about the mystery of the bread and the wine. He wondered what happened physically when the substance of the bread and the substance of the wine changed during the consecration, when he actually said, *"Hoc est enim corpus meum."* These substances felt the same and looked the same before and after the consecration yet they were changed. Just what did God do to the substances?

Wyclif studied the nature of created things in philosophy just as he studied the nature of light. He accepted as fact that the change at mass took place. After all, he would soon begin studying for his bachelor of theology degree and following it, his doctor of theology. This mystery of the Eucharist was a question for theology and could not be answered by philosophy alone. Later, when he had finished his studies in the school of theology, he would be better equipped intellectually to answer the questions he was now asking himself.

To perform the miracle he knew he had to be without sin. As a priest John Wyclif was supposed to refrain from sex. Plenty of priests at that time did not, as records of priests' children demonstrate. In Chaucer's *Canterbury Tales*, the Reeve tells the story of a miller near Cambridge who married the daughter of a priest and was proud of the fact.

Like most people in the fourteenth century, Wyclif had never been shielded from sex at any time in his life. On a sheep farm it has to be taken for granted that rams freshen sheep by mounting them and from the process lambs are born.

Further, a medieval house offered no privacy for human bodily functions. Usually a family slept in one room, and although this room was very dark, often without a window, it was not so dark that a normal child like John Wyclif would not soon realize what happened in his parents' bed. He and his friends, both boys and girls, undoubtedly experimented with what they learned from observing their parents.

There is no evidence whatever that after John Wyclif took his oath of celibacy, he violated it. Later in life, his powerful enemies would constantly accuse him of heresy, but never of sexual license, although they would have if they could have found the slightest evidence of it.

Unfortunately there is little autobiographical material in Wyclif's writings and absolutely nothing about his own sexual life. He did not tell of his trials in conquering sex, as St. Augustine does in his *Confessions*. Wyclif accommodated himself to the celibate life, but if he struggled to do so, he kept the details of the struggle to himself.

At the same time there is none of the neurotic anti-feminism in his writings which characterizes some of the writings of St. Jerome, for example. Quite the contrary. When Wyclif described the duties of a priest, he did not especially emphasize celibacy. He found that the Bible did not prohibit marriage among the early Christians, and believed it should therefore be permitted. He opposed sexual intercourse outside of marriage and condemned those priests who kept mistresses, but his argument was primarily economic: he observed that a priest should not dress his mistresses in expensive clothes from the tithe money given him by his parishioners, for they have more need for the money than does the priest's mistress.

Later, when he was debating with Ralph Strode, Wyclif remarked that if a person, because of the need for sex, "feels himself less disposed to living on God's side, he should refrain from the life of a churchman."[2] For Wyclif the lust to conquer was the lust for wealth, for in the Middle Ages wealth was harder to obtain than sex.

The medieval attitude toward love and marriage possibly accounts for a phenomenon much more common then than it is today—the surrogate family. After Wyclif made his choice to reject family life for himself, he developed a sense of responsibility for all those who suffered under the bureaucracy of the church, especially those hard-working priests in poor parishes. His students, poor priests, and later some associates at Oxford became his surrogate families.

Wyclif's first surrogate family, and a temporary one, was at Balliol College. After he became a master of arts and a priest, he was given the duties of the master of Balliol. He was older than many of the Oxford students and had already achieved a high enough reputation to survive the exacting process required for appointment to this position.

---

[2]"Responsiones ad argumenta Radulphi Strodi," in Wyclif, *Opera Minora*, p. 197.

He passed the scrutiny of the chancellor of the university, two college masters not in Balliol, the proctors of Balliol, the bishop of Durham, and the warden of Durham Hall. He knew the warden, John Uhtred of Boldon, a Benedictine monk and a doctor of theology, one of the most famous churchmen of the fourteenth century. Later Wyclif called him "my special master," and debated with him on the subject of the power of the pope.

John Wyclif discovered that the mastership of Balliol was no sinecure. A record survives indicating that he had to go to court to collect the rent for a property in London owned by the college. He won the case by establishing the ownership of the property, then taking physical possession of it for a time, and he discovered that it included a church, a tiny salary for a vicar, and an undisclosed number of pigeons for his table.

Wyclif did not remain master of Balliol long, however. He was assigned his first position outside Oxford, that of parish priest for the church in Fillingham, Lincolnshire, and Balliol required that he resign as master when he found another source of income.

CHAPTER SEVEN

First Parish

WYCLIF'S LIFE AT FILLINGHAM was not one of lectures, declamations, and disputations. At Fillingham no one had heard of Aristotle, Peter Lombard, or Robert Grosseteste, though Grosseteste had been their bishop one hundred years earlier. They spoke no Latin at Fillingham. And Fillingham was not in a soft, green valley; it consisted of swamps, and the fenland, a waste of gorse and bracken, bristly shrub, and wild fern. Fifty poor families living on a tributary of the Trent River made up the village. Some of the higher ground supported sheep, and at least the new parish priest of Fillingham knew the routine of lambing, weaning, and shearing. The woodlands of Fillingham had fir and some hardwoods—oak, birch, beech, and ash—which the parishioners cut to supplement their income from wool. The wool and the wood were floated on the Trent River nine miles to Gainsborough. Lincoln, a much larger city, was only ten miles away, but getting there over soggy roads was not as easy as using the river to float that lumber to market.

Here at his first parish, Wyclif broke with religious tradition. In the fourteenth century the sermon was not considered an important part of the mass. Contrary to this tradition, Wyclif wrote in his book *On the Duties of a Priest* that preaching should be one of the most important concerns of a parish priest. "Next to leading a righteous life," he wrote, "among all the duties of a priest, preaching is most honored. Preaching the gospel exceeds prayer and giving the sacraments to an infinite degree."

He understood preaching as teaching. As a master of arts he had been trained to be a teacher, and he had become one of the best teachers in the greatest university. Even this early in his career, he was driven to teach truth as he perceived it in St. Augustine, Peter Lombard, Robert Grosseteste, and the Holy Bible. And so the master of arts who, at Oxford, could use a Latin syllogism as either a battle axe or a delicate scalpel, at Fillingham explained Divine Providence so that Lincolnshire farmers could understand the concept. "Knowledge of God's law," he wrote, "should be taught in the language which is easiest to understand, because what is being taught is the word of God."

Wyclif quickly adapted to the change from scholar to country priest. He had his regular duties: christenings, burials, visiting the sick, and saying mass. The parish priest had to perform many other duties. He was the second most important person in the village, second only to the lord who owned the land and to whom the free tenants paid rent and for whom the bonded tenants did service. Because of his education, it was the parish priest who frequently kept records, as John of Clairvaux may have kept Roger Wyclif's records. When the rents were collected, the priest noted who paid and how much. The priest knew what tasks tenants and serfs had to perform for the lord as fiefs, for this information, hidden in old charters, was passed by word of mouth from generation to generation. He transcribed wills and deeds and administered oaths.

In addition, the priest was his own tax collector. He collected the tithes, the church taxes which were legally binding. Tithes were the only taxes the poor paid. There were no income taxes in fourteenth-century England, and the poll tax was still twenty years away.

From poor farmers Wyclif did not collect these tithes in money, of course, but in mutton, pork, maybe a chicken or a rabbit, some grain, wool, even wool cloth. The priest kept his own records of tithes, and a peasant could not challenge what the priest said, for the church court always supported the priest, not the peasant.

Sometimes if a priest were not given the tithes he demanded—perhaps more than were due him—he excommunicated the parishioner. Once excommunicated, a man could not have his children christened. He could not have a burial mass nor be buried in consecrated ground. The man could not take an oath, so he could not testify if he thought he had a grievance, even against the priest who excommunicated him. With power like this available to him, it was easy for an unscrupulous priest to fill his tithe barn, then sell what he did not need for his own use at the market. In this way, he could make enough money to pay a curate and live away from the parish in one of the big cities.

In a long Latin poem, *Vox Clamantis* ("The Voice of One Crying in the Wilderness"), John Gower, Chaucer's friend, told of a priest who received permission to go back to school, but who instead went to London and lived with his mistress. Gower wrote of another priest who had a double lock on his poor box, and a mistress who had both keys.

Wyclif inveighed against this kind of priest throughout his lifetime. He wrote that a priest had no right to extort tithes by excommunication or by any other kind of force. He wrote in *The Duties of a Priest*: "I do not see why all the clergy, following the rule set by the disciples, should not be content with just food and clothing. Even if a priest comes by his tithes justly, the tithes should be shared with the poor. For himself the priest should be moderate, then distribute what remains to the poor and needy." Wyclif did allow "some part for the upkeep of the church building, for the repair and maintenance of the parish house."

Wyclif advocated a simple method to reform a bad priest, a way in which parishioners could make their wishes felt strongly and quickly: no tithes without virtue. "If a priest notoriously neglects his duties, his parishioners should, rather ought, to keep their offerings and tithes from him," Wyclif suggested.[1]

In 1361 Wyclif's duties at Fillingham suddenly multiplied. The pestilence exploded, its most virulent eruption since 1348, and the priest of an isolated village was the only person with enough learning to act as physician.

Wyclif had seen the pestilence at Oxford. He knew the thankless task of giving aloe and myrrh to a man dying of bubonic plague. The air of Fillingham, swampy and fetid, was just what authorities on the disease warned against. Burning the fir and ash that grew abundantly in that area would purify the bad air, Wyclif knew, and undoubtedly he suggested this. But the priest's chief occupation was the melancholy one—burial. Little time was left for cures.

And the year following the plague was known for its fierce winds. An unknown minstrel sang:

> In a thousand three hundred and sixty-two
> St. Maurus wind over England blew.[2]

Fortunately, also in 1362, the pestilence lost its virulence. It was Wyclif's last year at Fillingham. He was given a license by the bishop of Lincoln to return to Oxford and continue with his studies of Aristotle and Peter Lombard. Out of his pay at Fillingham he had to provide a curate to take his place, so there would be little left to support himself.

---

[1]The concept came to Wyclif almost directly from Richard Fitzralph. It permeates Wyclif's thinking and appears frequently in *de Dominio Divino* and *de Officio Pastorali*.

[2]The winds began on St. Maurus Day, January 15. The saint's name was then given to all the high winds of that year. The scholars thought, mistakenly, that the name was derived from the Latin *amarus*, meaning "bitter," and so was doubly appropriate for the winds.

And he could no longer stay at Balliol. Balliol was for poor undergraduates. Wyclif was poor, but he was now a graduate master of arts, and was beginning his studies toward the bachelor of theology. This would take him six more years, then two years more for the doctorate. He still had a long way to go.

To survive these years he found a room at Queen's Hall off High Street in the east end of Oxford. The rooms cost two pounds for the term, and the university tried to help him with the cost. The chancellor sent a petition to Pope Urban V at Avignon asking the pope to make "their Master Wyclif" a canon at York so he might have an additional income. Instead the bureaucracy came through with an appointment at Aust in Westbury-on-Tyne, now in the city of Bristol. From this appointment Wyclif was to receive six pounds, thirteen shillings, four pence a year, but he was supposed to pay a curate five pounds a year and also pay to keep the chancel of the church in repair. Wyclif did neither and eventually lost the appointment. As a master, he gave lectures to the younger clerks, but the pay for this was slight.

Wycliffe manor in Yorkshire could not help support him. His father had died. His older brother, the one whose name is not known, had also died. John now was lord of Wycliffe manor.

He does not mention his family in his writings, but that does not mean they were not in his thoughts. The relationship of a mature man with his parents is different from what it was when he was a child, and when a parent dies, many times he leaves behind him the ache of love that should have been told. It would help to know of these changes in Wyclif's life, but unfortunately he left no writings concerning them. Only formal records remain, stating that John appointed William Wyclif in the place of John of Clairvaux as vicar. It is not known if this was the same William who was at Balliol with John.

John of Clairvaux, however, was still near Wycliffe and
not forgotten. His former pupil laid his prestige on the line
and signed a guarantee for his former master's good conduct. No more details than the record itself are known.
John of Clairvaux was old now and had retired, and the
bond Wyclif signed may have been no more than a way to
keep the old priest from fishing for salmon out of season.

If John Wyclif returned to the manor, he returned only
momentarily to accomplish his business. He left someone
else, it is not known who, to run the sheep. Wyclif's goal
was his doctorate, and his life at Oxford was arduous and
austere.

CHAPTER EIGHT

The Reverend Doctor
Becomes a Prophet

L AMBETH PALACE ACROSS THE THAMES from Westminster
was the castle of the archbishop of Canterbury, Simon
Islip. He had risen in the bureaucracy by going to Oxford, the same route Wyclif had taken. Simon was born in
the tiny village of Islip, north of Oxford, had been at Merton, and had finally received his doctorate in canon and
civil law.

After his degree he had risen through the bureaucracy to
become keeper of the privy seal for Edward III, dispensing
money for the king, later acting as his ambassador. Despite
his position he had not been affected by his rank or trap-
pings. Even as archbishop of Canterbury, Islip lived simply
and frugally.

Now he wanted to appoint a new warden to Canterbury
College at Oxford, founded to train priests since their ranks
had been thinned by the plagues of 1348 and 1361. The college was to house four monks from Canterbury Cathedral
who would be in charge of eight needy and deserving
secular clerks.

Throughout the university the orders and seculars still
glowered at one another in rancor; it was the same situation that Wyclif had found twenty years earlier when he
had attended his first mass in St. Mary's. Now the monks
and friars had petitioned for a shortened curriculum, un-
willing to endure the long and tedious grind that Wyclif and
the other secular clerks were enduring. So to their argument with the orders about luxurious living, the clerks
now added ignorance. The seculars saw any change as the

toward the friars and monks taking control of the
y.

ᴸⁱᵛⁱⁿᵍ under the same roof at Canterbury College, the
four monks and the eight clerks made the college a miniature battlefield of the university, and the civil war was taking precedence over scholarship. To stop the war, Archbishop Islip removed the monks and put secular clerks in
their places. The warden of the college, he felt, should be a
promising reverend master, one studying for his bachelor of
theology. He found such a person, unpretentious like
himself—Reverend Master John Wyclif.

However, even the archbishop of Canterbury had to
channel this motion through the bureaucracy. Wyclif's appointment had to be approved by the Benedictine monks of
Canterbury, who had lost control of the college, and then
the appointment had to be approved by the king himself.

John Wyclif was warden of Canterbury College for not
quite six months. Living was more comfortable as warden
of Canterbury than it had been as a renter at Queen's,
though he had to run the college and at the same time study
the *Sentences* of Peter Lombard and the Bible. But Wyclif's
permanent appointment vanished somewhere in the bureaucracy. Simon Islip had died. The new archbishop of
Canterbury was Simon Langham, a Benedictine monk,
formerly the abbot of Westminster. He had returned
Canterbury College to the control of his monks and had
decided to fire John Wyclif as warden and restore a Benedictine to the position.

Three monks left their monastery in Canterbury, Kent,
and after the walk from Canterbury to London and from
London to Oxford, they presented Archbishop Langham's
order to the deposed warden of Canterbury College. When
he received the order, Warden Wyclif refused to obey it. He
and his fellow seculars remained in the hall.

The monks walked this refusal back to Canterbury. The
archbishop of Canterbury withdrew the income from the

college and confiscated books that Islip had willed to the college library. John Wyclif decided to test what he thought he knew about the church bureaucracy, absorbed in his twenty-two years at Oxford. He sent an appeal to the pope in the hands of one of the secular clerks of Canterbury College.

Any bureaucracy moves like a ponderous hippopotamus, sluggish in the warm waters of complacency. The bureaucracy at Avignon moved even more ponderously than today's bureaucracies, because every document had to be handwritten and transmitted on foot or by horseback.

After a time, Wyclif's appeal reached Avignon and was examined by specialists in canon law as they passed it from one office to another. One of these specialists was Adam Easton, a Benedictine from Norwich and a doctor of theology from Oxford, a good scholar who could read both Greek and Hebrew. When he received the appeal from the warden of Canterbury College, he rejected it, and after he had added an official seal of disapproval to the petition, he passed it on to the next specialist.

Finally the appeal reached the pope with the opinions of the specialists now attached. A parish priest, one still studying to be a doctor of theology, had little chance of winning a case against the archbishop of Canterbury. The case of the secular clerks at Canterbury College was refused, and three years after the monks first walked from Canterbury to London to Oxford, they walked again. This time their walk was successful. John Wyclif, the former warden of Canterbury College, had to move back into his room at Queen's College, but now he was a hero to the secular clerks of Oxford.

But he was a poor hero. The appeal to the pope had cost money, to pay the clerks who copied the documents and to support the messengers who carried them to Avignon and back again. Wyclif needed cash, and he juggled a few accounts to get some.

Through a church broker Wyclif traded his income as rector of Fillingham for that of Ludgershall, Buckinghamshire. Ludgershall was an even poorer parish than Fillingham, but from the broker who arranged the trade, Wyclif received in cash the difference for what he would have earned at Fillingham.

With the twenty pounds Wyclif received for this exchange he paid his bills and the cost of his room for a year at Queens. Wyclif now cut himself off from university politics and submerged himself in the creation, the cosmology, and Christian doctrines as he found them in the works of Peter Lombard. And he studied God the Father, God the Son, and God the Holy Ghost as revealed in Holy Scripture.

By 1372 John Wyclif had been at Oxford twenty-eight years. His final degree was at hand. He had only to stand for his final disputation; it would determine his qualifications as a doctor in divine theology.

His opponent was John Kenningham, the master of the Carmelite monastery at Ipswich, near Oxford. John Kenningham was glad to oppose the secular priest who five years earlier had tried to keep Canterbury College for the secular clerks and away from the monks and friars. Wyclif was the champion for the seculars, and John Kenningham was the champion for the monks.

John Kenningham, however, faced more than a candidate for a degree, more than a champion for the secular priests, more than a trained churchman ready to take his place in the bureaucracy. John Kenningham faced a prophet.

The twenty-eight years at Oxford had changed the farm boy from Yorkshire. He had walked down Horsemonger Street for the first time when he was fourteen or fifteen years old. When he was nineteen he had survived the plague epidemic of 1348. He had survived it again at Fillingham in 1361. Now John Wyclif was forty-three, and soon to be a doctor of theology.

What Wyclif had seen around him gave the appearance of reality—substantial, solid, and permanent—but he knew it was only an appearance, the lie of reality. He searched for something absolutely true, an ultimate reality that was permanent and knowable.

For twenty-eight years Wyclif had been studying logic, optics, mathematics, philosophy, and theology. He had read of Robert Grosseteste's experiments in light and realized that they led to truth, and that this truth radiated from God. The mathematical system of Thomas Bradwardine led to truth, and this truth progressed from God. The *Sentences* of Peter Lombard led to truth, and this truth was in the mind of God.

The optics, the mathematics, the philosophy, and the theology were not isolated one from the other, but were different methods of understanding the universe. Logic unified what Wyclif had observed, and that unity led to the ultimate reality Wyclif was searching for—God.

Now he had finally put together the pieces of the puzzle. The synthesis that began with John of Clairvaux in Wycliffe manor church was now complete. What remained for Wyclif was to discover how the link was made between God and the state of flux he saw all around him. He did not have the atom theory to fall back on. The manuscripts of the Greek philosophers who developed that theory in the fifth century B.C. had been lost.

Of course, Wyclif could know nothing of the subatomic world, the microworld of electrons and protons, the particles inside the proton, the quark and the color-force of the quark, the gluon. These concepts help scientists in the twentieth century to understand the chain that connects the source of all matter with what is seen on earth.

Wyclif had no cyclotron, no accelerator to help him find protons, quarks, and gluons. Wyclif's only tool was his logic. Grosseteste, Bradwardine, and Lombard had taken

Wyclif to God as the Ultimate Reality. God was the source of matter and the cosmic force that brought change into the world, and Wyclif wanted to construct a strong chain of creation between God and man.

Like scientists before him, Wyclif reasoned that God operated outside the limits of time. Consequently the concepts of "beginning," "past," and "future" had no meaning when referring to God. God was beyond time, in a fifth dimension, to use a twentieth-century concept.

Wyclif believed that the chain of creation, a chain of light, went back to God's mind. Creation was the appearance of God's ideas on earth, made possible by light. Everything he saw around him once existed as an idea in God's mind, and this idea was timeless. It was only the appearance of that idea in the world that gave it the four dimensions of length, width, thickness, and time.

Wyclif explained this hypothesis in his first major work, On Logic, and decided to test it with the Bible. He maintained that like everything else the Bible was the appearance on earth of God's ideas. The words of the Bible made up one universal utterance.

In the Middle Ages reading was not silent. A manuscript book was written to be read aloud. The texts Wyclif had studied had been read aloud to him by John of Clairvaux and by his Oxford masters. As a master himself he read aloud to his students. The book, On Logic, and all his books, had originally been lectures or sermons.

The Bible was not made up of silent words on a dead page; it was made up of sounds. Wyclif correctly described sound as traveling in waves. In the chain of creation he heard the words of the Bible as sound waves from the voice of God to the ear and mind of man.

Wyclif understood that words were symbols just as mathematical numbers were symbols. All symbols change. People in the fourteenth century who had to keep records, like Geoffrey Chaucer, had started to use Arabic numbers.

Their symbol changed from *VII* to *7*, but the concept of *seven* was permanent and remained the same.

Wyclif believed that in the same way, the words of the Bible were true. He felt that they were symbols of a truth that was timeless and even more demonstrable than proof by mathematics. And it was the truth of the whole that gave truth to the parts. These were the arguments he had to defend in his final disputation with John Kenningham.

A record of this disputation still exists. Opponents in a university disputation were traditionally polite to one another, but Kenningham was superciliously polite to Wyclif. He recorded the debate after Wyclif had received the doctorate and wrote:

> How difficult it is for me to find arguments against such a doctor. For my arguments would be nothing more than small sticks to beat upon a nest which is outside our temporal globe, or like children who throw stones at the Pleiades. As we might compare the starry heavens to the web of a spider, so does my reasoning differ from the opinion of my master. Truly, the impressive words of such a doctor, imposing in learning and eloquence, almost confound me, for I know neither Aristotle nor the great Augustine could speak this way though both of them have endured many opponents.[1]

Kenningham was not so confounded that he was not able to challenge Wyclif. The Carmelite denied Wyclif's arguments, and he tried to destroy the chain that Wyclif had constructed between God's ideas and the forms of those ideas on earth. Kenningham used specific verses from the Bible which were obviously not literally true, attempting to turn upside down Wyclif's argument that the truth of the whole gave truth to the parts. Kenningham used parts to

---

[1] *Fasciculi Zizaniorum*, p. 67.

destroy the whole, ignoring Wyclif's concept that the words of the Bible were changing symbols of timeless ideas.

Actually, no one won this disputation. Wyclif was awarded his doctorate of theology, and the two debaters disagreed over a lifetime. In the church of St. Mary's, Wyclif sat on the left of the chancellor of Oxford for the graduation ceremony. He wore special boots that reached to the middle of his legs to distinguish him, about to become a doctor, from the masters in front of him, who wore low slippers.

When that day ended he was Reverend Doctor John Wyclif. His title of reverend indicated that he was still a parish priest, and his name was entered as the priest of Lutterworth, Leicestershire, a tiny church not far from Oxford. However, a curate would perform most of the duties there. Principally Wyclif was a regent-master of Oxford.

The road was open to John Wyclif, son of a sheep farmer in the north, to become a bishop, possibly an archbishop— who knows, perhaps the second English pope. After teaching at Oxford for a short while, it was expected that he would find a place somewhere in the bureaucracy and from that place make the system function smoothly. And if the bureaucracy functioned even more smoothly from his corner of the system, his name would be mentioned. The right people—an archbishop, a cardinal, the pope himself— would give their nod, or raise their eyebrows.

"Ah yes," they would say, "the Reverend Doctor John Wyclif." The name would be remembered and repeated when there was an opening for a bishop, an archbishop, or a cardinal in some more important place.

The Reverend Doctor John Wyclif wanted none of that.

Twenty-seven years before, the farm boy from Yorkshire had brought that modern sense of freedom with him to Balliol College, Oxford. And he had brought self-discipline too. The sense of freedom and the self-discipline had

grown, developed, and tempered, and with the Bibl
Lombard, St. Augustine, Robert Grosseteste, and the
tations, a completely new person had emerged. That person had no wish to find a place in the system to make it
function smoothly. That person instead had decided to
fight the system.

When John Wyclif debated John Kenningham, he had
already acquired some of the dangerous characteristics of a
prophet. A reputation for predicting the future is not the
most dangerous characteristic of a prophet, only a by-
product. Seeing a vision is the most dangerous characteristic. Wyclif had seen a vision, which came from logic, and
this vision gave him an impetus to make the truth of his vision known. This impetus becomes a sense of destiny in a
prophet and separates him from ordinary men. This is what
makes him dangerous.

Isaiah, Jeremiah, Ezekiel, Amos, Hosea—all the great
prophets—saw a vision. John Wyclif's vision simply came
from his logic, but the logic dazzled him as Yahweh and the
seraphim dazzled Isaiah, the wheel did Ezekiel, and the
plumbline did Amos. The vision that flashed from Wyclif's
logic was like the vision of Hosea, who wanted to return to
the old relationship of Yahweh and his people. Wyclif's vision was like the vision of Jeremiah, who wanted to return
to the traditions of a better Israel.

John Wyclif wanted the church to return to an age of
innocence, purity, and simplicity. He wanted to return to
the primitive church which he found described in the Bible
and extolled in St. Augustine and in Peter Lombard's
Sentences. He saw the church at its beginnings when it was
poor, when its priests were fishermen and not bureaucrats.

This vision of a lost age of innocence and purity is one of
the most fundamental and recurring of man's dreams. It is
the dream of the Garden of Eden, the dream of Lao Tzu.
Jeremiah preached it after the Babylonians had destroyed
Israel. St. Francis preached it while Assisi fought Perugia,

while France was torn in a civil war between the orthodox establishment of the north and the revolutionary Albingen-sians of the south. And in the uncertainties of the 1370s, John Wyclif brought the same vision to the English people.

All around him Wyclif saw abbots, bishops, and arch-bishops living in palaces. And he saw the tenant farmers and serfs who supported them and the poor priests who ministered to these people, all of them destitute. Today most of the English monasteries of the fourteenth century are picturesque ruins, gray and still, cats sleeping in the empty shells of window frames. But from the time he was helping to raise his father's sheep, Wyclif knew the monasteries as shining, colorful, and prosperous, and he remembered when the monks bought wool from his father.

He also knew that the monks of St. Albans were waited on by teams of servants. He knew that Bury St. Edmunds was a small town, its income derived from farms so vast that no man could ride across them in a single day. Tenant farmers and serfs plowed the fields, sowed the grain, cut the wheat, and tended the sheep that supported the monks in the monastery. The tenant farmers could not call the sheep their own. It was not "my lamb" a boy warmed in the rain, but the abbey's lamb. In the fourteenth century tenant farmers and serfs were called *villeins*, the ancestor of the modern word *villain*, a word that still expresses contempt.

John Wyclif saw the church bureaucracy as huge and corpulent. The bureaucracy had had fourteen hundred years to bloat, and like all bureaucracies, its first function was to perpetuate itself. In this effort it functioned well. The bureaucracy gathered money to supply itself so it could gather more money.

In 1309 the popes had moved the bureaucracy from Rome to Avignon in southern France. The move changed the loca-tion but not the system. The inertia of the bureaucracy kept it functioning as it always had.

The bishops, archbishops, cardinals, and consistories at the top of the system held their power because they made the bureaucracy function. They enforced their power in their own courts and with their own prisons. If these instruments were not effective, they used the king's court and the king's prisons, for the bishops and the archbishops were also the king's officers, often acting as his chancellor or his treasurer.

Like Hosea, Wyclif found "no faith, no tenderness, no knowledge of God in the country."[2] Like Jeremiah, he asked, "Where is the Lord?" Like Isaiah, he cried out against evildoers. Like Joel, he called for priests to put on sackcloth and ashes. Wyclif had read in Richard Fitzralph's book, *On the Poverty of Our Savior,* that only the righteous man can truly hold power, that there is no power without virtue.

The bureaucracy had no virtue. And so they should hold no power, he reasoned. The church should be as it was in the beginning—innocent, simple, and pure.

Wyclif had earlier suggested that tithes should be withheld from the priest who neglected his parish duties. Now he advocated withholding tithes from all the members of the bureaucracy: friars, monks, bishops, archbishops, even popes.

If his method had been widely followed, it would have undoubtedly revolutionized the fourteenth-century church. Tithes, however, were legitimate taxes. Wyclif was advocating the nonpayment of taxes, and, as might be expected, the church bureaucracy did not regard his suggestion at all sympathetically.

---

[2]Hosea IV, 1, paraphrased from Wyclif, *de Apostasia,* an attack directed primarily against friars.

CHAPTER NINE

The Prophet as Envoy

A T OXFORD THE YOUNG CLERKS now studying for their degrees listened excitedly as Master Wyclif revealed his vision of innocence, purity, and simplicity. Sitting on a high stool in the dining room (refectory) of the Austin priory north of the town, Wyclif personified this vision of simplicity.

Many prophets wore clothing that set them apart. Both Elijah and Amos did, and so Wyclif did, too. He wore a long, russet gown tied with a cord around his thin waist. His feet were bare. This was the usual dress of the peasant and the serf and had been earlier adapted by the Spiritual Franciscans.

In private life the prophet is humble and childlike. Jeremiah, like Wyclif, was raised in a small village. Amos, like Wyclif, was raised on a farm and was a shepherd. Hosea and Ezekiel were quiet and peaceful men. But in public life the prophet is not calm or temperate. His language is angry because he is driven by his vision. He always demands too much of those who listen to him and is impatient, because his listeners reject his vision.

Wyclif, small as a birch twig, still thundered. He saw no psychological grays, but only blacks and whites. To him, and to most persons in the Middle Ages, as a man lived, so he was. A man was either virtuous or sinful, and if he committed one of the seven deadly sins, he was sinful. The priests, bishops, abbots, and archbishops were committing the sins of pride, gluttony, and avarice and therefore remained sinful.

But who could sweep away the corruption that they had accumulated over the centuries between the church's happy state of original innocence and the present glittering squalor,

Wyclif asked. Who could redistribute the wealth of the monasteries and the rest of the bureaucracy to the farmers and peasants where it had originated, and thus restore holy poverty to the church? Restoring the age of simplicity needed more than withholding tithes.

Only the civil government had the right and the power to redistribute church wealth, Wyclif believed. He based the right on the separation of church and state—the church ruled over the goods of the spirit; the state ruled over the earthly goods of its subjects. Consequently the king had power even over the earthly goods of the church. On the other hand the church should advise the king and the civil government on matters of the spirit.

In the twentieth century, the civil government typifies a bureaucracy, huge and lethargic, but in the fourteenth century the idea of a central state was new. The strength of France would not be centered at Paris for a hundred years, the strength of Spain at Madrid for a hundred and twenty. England was unique in Europe with a central government, and the government was not yet altogether impersonal. The king still ruled in person and his brother, John of Gaunt, the duke of Lancaster, ruled his holdings in person. Wyclif saw nothing to fear in either rule.

The students listening to these revolutionary ideas found them exhilarating, and some of the notes they made still exist today. Thomas Netter, a Benedictine from Walden Abbey, Essex, said: "When I was young I gave careful ears to his logic. I was completely dumb-founded by his powerful statements, by the authorities he mentioned and by the vehemence of his reasoning."[1]

Wyclif published his ideas in two books, *On Civil Power* and *On Spiritual Power*, as far as "publishing" was possible in the decades before William Caxton brought the printing

---

[1]Wyclif, *Summa de Ente*, p. 24.

press from Bruges to England. A manuscript had to be duplicated by hand, of course, but enterprising book sellers had quickened the process by introducing an assembly line. After Wyclif wrote out his lecture, his copy was taken to London and divided into small sections, sometimes of just two or three pages. These sections were copied over and over again by the same scribe. Later the sections were assembled into the whole. Other entrepreneurs employed a reader who dictated a manuscript to several scribes at once.

From these book factories Wyclif's manuscripts were distributed to the larger cities of England—London, York, and Coventry—and in Westminster, the seat of the government, the lords of the state liked what they read in Wyclif's two books. They were not interested in Wyclif's desire to bring back an age of simplicity in the church, but they were very interested in his careful arguments that the civil government had power over church government, because the church now had a French pope.

A few years earlier, Pierre Roger de Beaufort had been crowned Gregory XI at Avignon. He had the nerve to demand papal taxes from England that had accrued for a generation, unpaid since Edward II's reign. When he presented his bill for these back taxes, the king's council persuaded him to negotiate, and in July 1374, the Reverend Doctor John Wyclif was one of seven commissioners who landed at the busy docks of Bruges as a negotiator for the civil government of England. The lords of the state hoped Wyclif could put his ideas of state over church into practice.

The commissioners of the king of England were all learned men led by John Gilbert, a Dominican friar. He had already led a previous commission on the same subject, and in good bureaucratic fashion, the commission had decided that the issue needed a second commission. John Gilbert had been studying at Oxford during those few years Wyclif had been warden of Canterbury College. Gilbert thought

Oxford was prejudiced against monks and friars. He transferred to Paris but never went beyond a bachelor in theology. He had a reputation as a preacher, however, and four months before this trip he had been appointed bishop of Bangor, Wales. He was to have an active career in church and state politics, and eight years after this trip he would be one of the judges who condemned the revolutionary ideas of John Wyclif.

As a regent-master of Oxford, Wyclif was second in rank to Gilbert. Wyclif had taken the place of his friend, John Uhtred of Boldon, the warden of Durham who helped approve Wyclif as master of Balliol. The king's council thought Uhtred leaned too much toward the pope's side to represent the king's point of view, so he had not been appointed a second time. Robert Bealknap was on the commission, a justice of assize, the county civil and criminal court. When he returned from Bruges, he would be made chief justice of the Court of Common Pleas and would escape, but just barely, being killed by the rebels at the beginning of the Peasants' Revolt.

The envoys of the pope were already in Bruges, but it is not certain where the conference between the two groups took place. They had a wealth of buildings to choose from and possibly chose St. Sauveur, rebuilt after a fire fifteen years earlier. It was a luxurious trip for Wyclif. Representatives of the government traveled in style. Wyclif was provided with a carriage and given travel expenses of forty-two shillings and living expenses of twenty shillings a day, almost as much as he paid for a month's rent at Queens. The pope's envoys were Spanish and were supplied with eighteen gold florins a day that the commissioners knew had been raised by a special tax on the English clergy.

The king's commissioners were churchmen and lawyers. With them was Wyclif, the prophet. But a prophet does not make a good diplomat. He has strong ideas and he expresses them strongly. After the mission was over, Wyclif wrote his ideas on the pope's tax in a book, and if he

expressed them with the same force at Bruges as
the book, it is no wonder that he failed in his first
at being a diplomat.

Wyclif called his book *The Decision* (in Latin, *Determinatio*). He presented his views in the fiction of seven lords speaking in the king's council. These lords agreed that the pope should not receive tribute, the reasons all logically argued. Many of the arguments were based on the separation of church and state. Wyclif thus repeated his contention that the state had the right, as a last resort, to deprive the church of its wealth and power. In doing this, the state was actually doing the church a favor: the less the church was concerned with wealth and power, the more she could fulfill her religious mission, Wyclif pointed out.

One of his arguments was an involved logical exercise worthy of the finest quodlibet. The pope's tax, Wyclif pointed out, had started in the time of King John, of Magna Carta fame. At that time, the pope had claimed that he was John's feudal overlord and had given the Kingdom of England back to John to rule. Wyclif observed that the present pope, if still feudal overlord of Edward III, could demand England back again, since his taxes had not been paid.

Wyclif made it sound as if he was supporting the pope's demands; agreeing with your opponent was a standard debating technique. But Wyclif had a catch waiting, also a standard debating technique. He introduced his argument that power does not exist without virtue. If the pope falls into deadly sin, he loses his lordship and cannot claim to possess England. And popes in the two hundred years between King John and King Edward had committed most of the seven deadly sins. Since all power comes from Christ, He is overlord of all, and therefore England is held directly from Christ. There is no need to pay any tax to the pope at all.

When the king's council members read *The Decision*, they agreed that Wyclif had made a strong case against paying the pope any tax, and they immediately ordered him to remain forever silent on the subject of the pope's taxes. Wyclif was puzzled; a prophet does not understand the subtleties of politics. What Wyclif did not know was that the king actually received a kick-back from the papal taxes. The council did not want the tax stopped, only slightly shaved. So Wyclif, still puzzled, returned to Oxford, his studies, and his lectures.

If John of Gaunt had not been acquainted with Wyclif's ideas on state and church before, he now read them with a great deal of interest. On September 20, 1376, he sent a messenger through the iron gates of his Savoy Palace that stood in the midst of an elegant park on the Thames River between London and Westminster. The messenger carried a summons from the ranking member of the king's council: "John, by the grace of God, King of Castile and Leon, Duke of Lancaster, Duke of Burgundy, Earl of Lincoln and Leicester, Lord of Beaufort and Nogent, of Bergerac, et cetera, et cetera, to the most esteemed Reverend Doctor, John Wyclif."

The summons officially had nothing to do with the feudal relationship that John of Gaunt, when earl of Richmond, had had with Wycliffe manor. Gaunt's father had given that title away and the lands that went with it. John of Gaunt, the only man alive in England to have ever called himself king other than Edward III, wanted the help of John Wyclif. He wanted the voice of the prophet in a complicated and dangerous political situation.

CHAPTER TEN

Preaching for John of Gaunt

JOHN OF GAUNT HAD SPENT his first thirty-six years in the shadow of his older brother, Edward, the illustrious Black Prince, and prince of Wales. They had fought together in France at Rheims and in Spain at Nájera. The Black Prince married Joan for love. Balladeers called her the Fair Maid of Kent, for she was considered the most beautiful woman in England. Surely they would be England's handsomest king and queen.

On his return from Spain, the Black Prince became ill and grew weaker and weaker. His symptoms indicated amoebic dysentery, but doctors of the time could not know that. They diagnosed his condition as an excess of blood and promptly drained great quantities of it. Other symptoms soon developed: a general swelling of the limbs, dizziness, and periodic unconsciousness. The prince conducted his last campaign in Aquitaine from a litter, curtained in embroidered silk, hand-carried or slung swaying between two horses.

Edward, the prince of Wales, died on June 7, 1376. His body encased in the famous black armor lay in state in Westminster Hall, and from all over England his subjects made pilgrimages to their prince, in whose death they saw their dreams stilled. It was now John of Gaunt's duty to preserve the power of the kingship for his nephew, Richard, eight years old and next in line for the throne.

John of Gaunt understood, as did John Wyclif, that all power came from God, including political power. God granted power to the king, the king granted it to his lords, and they to those under them. Power descended from above. King Edward III was sixty-four years old, however, and he was paying more attention to his mistress, the last of many, than to affairs of state. She was Alice Perrers, attractive, brilliant, and greedy. Already the king had given her three estates, jewels, and other gifts, all of which she flaunted. The power descending from above was weak at its source, and the new power, ascending from below, would collide with the old. John of Gaunt thought that the Oxford prophet, John Wyclif, held beliefs that might be useful to him in the collision.

The new power was rising from a parliament now known as the Good Parliament of 1376. The nobles of England, including archbishops, bishops, and abbots, had assembled at Westminster Hall. With them were 134 knights with burgesses and citizens, the knights selected by the county sheriffs, the burgesses and citizens elected in various ways. For the first time in their history these knights, burgesses, and citizens, not yet called a House of Commons, elected someone to speak for them to the lords. He was Sir Peter de la Mare, steward to the earl of March, marshall of England, and next to the boy, Richard, in line to the throne of England.

Sir Peter carried a petition to John of Gaunt, who presided over the lords of England, a petition which also broke tradition. For the first time these "commons" demanded the banishment of a king's mistress and the removal of two of the king's officers. The first, Richard Lyons, had cost the king twenty thousand pounds in taxes (about $4 million), then loaned the king the same amount, making a profit of ten thousand pounds on the deal. The second, William, fourth baron Latimer, knight of the garter, and king's chamberlain, had surrendered to the French forts, which he believed were indefensible. The petition called Richard Lyons larcenous and Lord Latimer traitorous.

John of Gaunt angrily refused the petition and would not present it to the king. But he was opposed by nine powerful lords who supported Sir Peter de la Mare, including the earl of March, William Wykeham, bishop of Winchester and former chancellor of England; Sir Henry Percy; and especially William Courtenay, a dynamic young bishop of London.

In his russet gown and bare feet, John Wyclif walked down the Oxford Road to the magnificent Savoy Palace, south of London. He was walking into the clash between John of Gaunt and the bishop of London. The Savoy was the administrative center of John of Gaunt's vast estates. Dozens of clerks toiled at long tables, bent over documents, composing and copying the duke's records and orders. Messengers were coming and going from the Lancastrian lands spread across England. The clerks and messengers were bright in scarlet, green, and blue, their tunics edged in fur and drawn up in belts of gold. Some wore a gipon, a special tunic decorated with the arms of the house of Lancaster, fleurs-de-lys, and three lions passant (that is, in a walking position, front paw raised). The arms showed that the wearers owed their feudal allegiance to John of Gaunt as duke of Lancaster.

In the midst of the activity stood Wyclif, small and drab. He might have been mistaken for a peasant from one of the ducal estates except that his hands and face were too pale. In John of Gaunt, John Wyclif had a friend devoted to him for the rest of his life. Their relationship was complicated. Each respected and honored the other. The duke respected Wyclif for his learning and piety, and he always recognized a feudal obligation for the doctor's welfare, because he was a duke and the king's son. Wyclif respected the duke because of his rank and position, a respect accepted as natural in the Middle Ages. But John of Gaunt was thirty-four years old, twelve years younger than Wyclif, and Wyclif seemed to have experienced a fatherliness toward John of Gaunt, the same feeling a dedicated teacher experiences toward an outstanding student.

John of Gaunt was no theologian and was not interested in finding his way through the labyrinth of Oxfordian logic. He respected Wyclif but could not follow the reasoning that led Wyclif to his vision of simplicity. He knew only that Wyclif maintained that the civil government might lawfully deprive unworthy churchmen of their possessions, and two of the champions of the parliamentary petition were powerful churchmen. So John of Gaunt released John Wyclif in London, and from September 1376 through February 1377, Wyclif preached in the diocese of William Courtenay that the church should distribute its wealth to the poor.

During these five months, Wyclif learned to know well the cramped, crowded, noisy, exuberant, colorful, brutal, smelly city. Like the streets of Oxford, the streets of London were made narrower by market booths and even more congested with sixty thousand Londoners jostling from sunrise to sunset. In early morning London housewives rushed to the common conduit at Cheap near St. Paul's with every kind of jug, bottle, crock, bucket, or pot to carry home the day's water. Crowding in to wait their turn, they gossiped and refused to move, so everyone not collecting water had to squeeze through Paternoster and Dean's Lane leading to the conduit. Professional waterbearers were allowed to fill their barrels early and went on their rounds just as milkmen do today.

As he pushed through the streets, Wyclif, like everyone else, had to watch out for loose pigs scrambling from garbage pile to garbage pile unmindful of the human clot. The pigs of St. Anthony's hospital had small bells around their necks and ran free legally. If a private owner let his animal roam the streets, he was taking a big chance—if he did not keep an eye on his beast, it would vanish as if by magic and become someone else's pork.

Nearly every London street had its own church, and Wyclif could expound his vision of an age of innocence and his plan for a redistribution of church wealth in over a hundred churches. Two in which he could not preach were St. Paul's, which was Bishop Courtenay's own cathedral, and St. Mary le Bow, between St. Paul's and the Tower of London, which belonged to the archbishop of Canterbury, Simon Sudbury.

Many of the churches had rectors who were Oxford men and knew Wyclif either personally or by his rapidly spreading reputation. St. Andrew's, on Holborn near Holborn Bridge over the Fleet River, had an Oxford rector. Here travellers crossed the ditch coming into the city walls. Not far from St. Andrew's were the Cow Lane and Smithfield markets, crowded with sheep, hogs, and cattle driven in from the country each day for the butchers of London. Wyclif's voice had to top the bellowing, bawling, and baying outside this church. Butchering was forbidden within the city, at least in theory, but it was tolerated in this area, provided the butchers cut up the entrails into small hunks, carted them through Newgate, and dumped them into the Fleet just on the other side of the wall.

St. Mary Coneycope was near the poultry markets where birds of all sorts—swans, geese, ducks, chickens, curlews, thrushes, larks, herons, partridges, and pheasants—raised another kind of din which Wyclif had to cope with. Like the butchers, the poulterers were not supposed to kill their birds in the city or pluck them there, but like the butchers, they killed in the early morning. The wind blew clouds of feathers that drifted into piles against St. Mary's and even into the open shops. The shouts of irate shopkeepers and their wives at this blizzard of feathers added to the commotion.

Across the city St. Mary Vintry was the home parish of the Chaucer family, but when Wyclif preached there, Geoffrey Chaucer was not there. In 1376 and 1377 Chaucer was in Flanders with Sir Thomas Percy on a secret mission for the king, possibly trying to arrange a marriage for young Prince Richard, one that would never work out.

Balliol College owned property in St. Lawrence Jewry, a quieter section of the city that Wyclif knew from his days as Master of Balliol. St. Lawrence Church was one of the most influential in London, for it supported two of the largest fraternities, clubs made up of members from the merchants' guilds who were among the most powerful men in London and well worth influencing. Many of the guildsmen became lord mayors of London, for example William Walworth, mayor during the Peasants' Revolt in 1381, and John Philipot, who lent money to the king and equipped his own navy. Wyclif did manage to influence John of Northampton, a member of the drapers' guild and another future lord mayor, then sheriff of London. As lord mayor, John would try to bring food prices down by fighting the powerful food guilds composed of fishmongers, grocers, and vintners who operated the monopolies in their various areas.

Wyclif probably preached at St. Botolph's near Aldesgate where he could renew his friendship with Ralph Strode, and at St. Magnus, near the end of London Bridge, and St. Mary Axe, which believing worshippers thought housed the very axe with which the Huns hacked St. Ursula to death along with 10,999 other virgins. The bells of St. Giles, just outside the northern gate, Cripplegate, signalled the beginning and end of the business day and of the night watch.

Wyclif preached not only on Sunday but also during the week. The most popular mass was one that was said after sunrise and before ten, when the Londoners had not yet eaten their first meal, and had come into the streets to buy food, open shops, and generally start the day moving. It was the time of noise and flurry. It was no time for hour-long sermons. Wyclif's had to be short and to the point or he would lose his congregation to their business and breakfast.

Moving from one church to another, Wyclif made a success of his London preaching. Even the unfriendly chroniclers admit that. The historian of St. Albans Abbey, Francis Walsingham, wrote:

He was not only eloquent but a deceiver. He accomplis
what he did by argument not by knowledge of God, and
the way he put words together and belched them forth. He
scurried from church to church and poured his false and
crazy notions into the ears of men. Certain lords of the
kingdom embraced his nonsense, and not only lords but
also the simple citizens of London.[1]

Wyclif took his vision of innocence and holy poverty out
of the lecture halls of Oxford and into the streets, to ordinary people. His preaching had to be simple. He stressed
the Bible and his interpretation of the Bible. In his russet
robe and bare feet, he personified the poverty he preached.

"A cup of cold water given with kindness and warm love
is a greater gift than all the lands and kingdoms of the
church," he told the Londoners in one of his sermons. "If
there is a rule most necessary to virtue, it is one which
demands the church forsake worldly riches for the riches of
God and Christ as the apostles did," he said in another.[2]

Here in London, Wyclif repeated his demand that the
church return to the age of purity, demonstrate its social
responsibility, and give back its wealth to the poor of London. And if the church would not help the poor, the civil
government had the right to force it to do so. Only in this
way would the church ever embrace holy poverty.

Wyclif repeated what he had said in his book, *On the
Duties of a Priest.* If a priest or a bishop was a notorious sinner, his parishioners should refuse him tithes. This simple,
forceful plan, had it been tested, would have been as effective in London as in Fillingham in reforming the clergy.

Wyclif did not accuse Bishop William Courtenay in St.
Paul's of being a notorious sinner. No one did; everyone

---

[1]Walsingham, *Chronicon Angliae*, p. 116.

[2]*Sermones.* II, 118; III, 39.

knew he was no sinner. But St. Paul's was the fourth largest church in the Christian world, and it was wealthy. Wyclif made its wealth sound sinful.

William Courtenay did not like what he heard coming from a parish priest of the diocese of Lincoln, especially since the priest was a regent-master of Oxford and a doctor of theology, and the Londoners were listening to him as an authority. William Courtenay did not like the fact that John of Gaunt had called this reverend doctor to London as the duke counterattacked the new power of commons and the lords who supported it.

CHAPTER ELEVEN

Wyclif Faces Courtenay

A FTER THE GOOD PARLIAMENT had adjourned, John of Gaunt had made certain that the next Parliament was made up of knights less interested in exercising the new power. After all, the sheriffs were appointed by the king, so he instructed the sheriffs to be more careful in appointing knights to represent the shires.

The sheriffs diligently followed their orders, and the new commons followed the suggestions of John of Gaunt. They petitioned to restore Lord Latimer as the king's chamberlain, and Richard Lyons and Alice Perrers to their former positions of honor.

As the second step in the counterattack, John of Gaunt disciplined the lords who had championed the Good Parliament. The earl of March, marshall of England, was ordered to inspect English garrisons at Calais and Bordeaux across the channel. Rather than leave England, the earl resigned and John of Gaunt appointed Sir Henry Percy as marshall of England. Four months later at Richard II's coronation, Sir Henry would be made earl of Northumberland.

When the Londoners heard of his appointment as marshall of England, they knew Sir Henry Percy had changed sides, from supporting the Good Parliament to supporting John of Gaunt. They resented it, and their anger against him and John of Gaunt mounted. Percy's reputation for disloyalty survived until Shakespeare's time, for in the play *Henry IV Part I*, Sir Henry deserted his own son, Hotspur, at the battle of Shrewsbury.

Another champion of the Good Parliament, William Wykeham, bishop of Winchester, was tried for his handling of finances as chancellor and found guilty. His lands were taken away, and he was exiled twenty miles from London.

Alice Perrers suggested that Sir Peter de la Mare, the former speaker who had carried that first petition to the lords, be hanged, and drawn and quartered as a traitor. John of Gaunt thought that was a little too drastic but had Sir Peter imprisoned.

To raise money for the depleted treasury, the counterattacking Parliament levied a new kind of tax. They called it a "tallage of groats," but history calls it a poll tax. From the property of every lay person above the age of fourteen, the king's officer would take a groat, or four pence worth of goods (about three dollars). The clergy, if they had an income from property, had to pay twelve pence. All other churchmen except friars and beggars had to pay the groat.

The counterattack against the Good Parliament came to a halt with William Courtenay. The bishop of London did not bend easily. His family was as aristocratic as John of Gaunt's, for the bishop was the great-grandson of Edward I, and the Courtenay family could trace its origins back to the year 1000.

His ancestors had been generals and leaders, and William had inherited their talents. At twenty-two he had been elected chancellor of Oxford where he received a doctorate in law. He was considered too young by the bishop of Lincoln, who refused to confirm him. At William's personal request the pope intervened, and William became chancellor of Oxford. At twenty-eight he was appointed bishop of London, and again he needed the intervention of the pope to be confirmed. In six years he would be archbishop of Canterbury.

William's effigy in Canterbury Cathedral still lies next to the tomb of the Black Prince. It shows him cleanshaven with the trace of a kindly smile, but his smiling marble effigy gives no indication of his great force of will.

This force was apparent in the fourteenth century. The Courtenays had been warriors. William acted like a general without an army. He never questioned anything he believed and held to the rightness of all his decisions. Like John of Gaunt, he believed he was a channel through which power radiated from God and descended to the people. But the people of London, his parishioners, did not resent him—they knew he was their champion.

On the twelfth of February, after Wyclif had been preaching in London for five months, a church summoner ordered John Wyclif, priest of Lutterworth of the diocese of Lincoln, to appear the next week before the bishop of London and the archbishop of Canterbury at St. Paul's Cathedral. A priest, even one with a doctorate from Oxford, had no muscle against the bishop of London, especially the forceful William Courtenay, nor against the archbishop of Canterbury, even the quiet Simon Sudbury.

As soon as he received this summons, Wyclif told the duke of Lancaster about it. One of the chronicles of the time reported the duke as saying, "Compared to Wyclif the bishops were practically illiterate." Nevertheless, the duke took the precaution of asking four friars, all of them doctors, to help Wyclif with his defense. Thin and wasted, Wyclif did not have the look of one who could stand up against the strength of William Courtenay. It would take more than skill in disputations to prevail against this bishop, and John of Gaunt knew it.

On the day that Wyclif was to appear at St. Paul's, the people of London learned that the new Parliament, the one controlled by John of Gaunt, had petitioned the king to transfer the government of the city to the crown, as represented by the marshall of England. The new marshall, Sir Henry Percy, could then make arrests in London as he could elsewhere in the country.

The citizens of London had been independent of outside rule since the time of William the Conqueror, and all the cities of England looked to London as a symbol of freedom. The Londoners were enraged at this threat, and their rage was directed toward John of Gaunt.

John of Gaunt decided he had better accompany John Wyclif to St. Paul's, and the news of his decision spread quickly throughout the city. On February 19, the Londoners crowded into their cathedral and onto its grounds long before the arrival of the duke, Wyclif, the friars, or their judges, the archbishop, and the bishop. The Londoners knew they could count on their bishop to defend their rights, and they were more interested in seeing their rights defended than John Wyclif censured.

St. Paul's dominated London with its 450-foot spire. The cathedral was actually a complex of buildings of glittering white stone, its decorations painted in bright colors. To the northeast of the cathedral in the yard stood St. Paul's Cross, a stone cross high on a platform, suitable for important sermons, proclamations, and excommunications. The bishop's palace and garden were to the west, and to the east was the Church of St. Gregory's. Near it was an octagonal chapter house.

The gigantic nave inside the cathedral was 585 feet long and 100 feet wide. Twelve scribes sat by the west entrance of the nave ready to prepare documents for merchants, guildsmen, or city officials. Under the huge vaults or in one of the bays, important contracts were traditionally signed and sworn to. Chaucer tells us that sergeants-of-the-law, not ordinary lawyers but barristers from whom common-law judges were chosen, had the right to see their clients in the nave.

On ordinary days St. Paul's was busy. By the afternoon of February 19 the entrances to the cathedral were mobbed, and a tightly packed throng filled the whole nave through the choir and all the way to the Chapel of the Blessed Virgin at the far east end. This chapel was a vault chamber almost as impressive as the nave itself. Here Bishop Courtenay and Archbishop Sudbury and their staffs waited for John Wyclif.

Finally Wyclif arrived and with him the duke, the four friars, and the new marshall of England, Sir Henry Percy.

An angry mob is a terrifying beast to arouse. Henry Percy had changed sides in his lifetime, but no one had accused him of being a coward. With his new authority, the strength of his body, and the power of his voice, he forced a path through the enraged and threatening Londoners, around the screen of the choir, through the choir, to the bishop and the archbishop.

The confrontation which the Londoners had waited for took place. William Courtenay spoke for the church. The duke of Lancaster spoke for the reverend doctor. The conversation has been preserved, possibly with some accuracy.[1]

When Henry Percy, Gaunt, Wyclif, and the friars arrived in the chapel, Bishop Courtenay said, "Lord Percy, if I had known what show of force you would have kept in the church, I would have stopped you out from coming thither."

"He may keep such show of force here though you say so," John of Gaunt replied without ceremony.

"Wyclif, sit down," Percy now said to the frail doctor, "for you have many things to answer to, and you need to repose yourself on a soft seat." Undoubtedly their shoving battle through the crowd had been punishing for Henry Percy, a well-built soldier. Wyclif, tiny and slight, must have seemed vulnerable to him.

"It is unreasonable that one cited before church judgment should sit during his answer," Courtenay explained. "He must and shall stand."

"The Lord Percy's motion is but reasonable," John of Gaunt put in. "As for you, my Lord Bishop, who are grown so proud and arrogant, I will bring down the pride, not of you alone but of all the prelates in England."

---

[1]Walsingham, *Chronicon Angliae*, pp. 118–21; Walsingham, *Historia Anglicana*, I, 256.

"Do your worst, sir," Courtenay answered simply.

"Thou bearest thyself so brag about thy parents, who shall not be able to help thee. They shall have enough to help themselves." The duke of Lancaster had shifted his form of address from *you*, the pronoun of respect, to *thou*, the pronoun of familiarity, a technique of insult popular in the fourteenth century, now lost to modern English.

"My confidence is not in my parents nor in any man else," Courtenay said, "but only in God, in Whom I trust, by Whose assistance I will be bold to speak."

The chronicles do not agree as to how the duke replied. Some say that he answered so that the bishop of London could hear him. Others say that he was addressing only Sir Henry Percy.

"Rather than I will take these words at his hands," John of Gaunt remarked. "I would pluck the bishop by the hair out of the church." Regardless of whom he was addressing, members of the crowd pressed close to him heard the remark. They howled, and the howl spread from the Chapel of the Blessed Virgin back through the long nave of the church. They would not allow their bishop to be insulted, let alone dragged from the church, by the man who was taking their freedom away. Bishop Courtenay tried to quiet them. Regardless of the provocation, he said, they were still in the presence of God, but during the tumult and confusion the duke, John Wyclif, Percy, and the friars managed to escape from St. Paul's.

On the day following the uproar, members of the powerful London guilds met in the great chamber of the Guildhall to debate how they could protect their liberty from John of Gaunt. They were not worried about Wyclif. The little prophet who had preached there was no power without virtue and was no threat to the independence of the city of London. John of Gaunt, though, had escaped them at St. Paul's, and there was nothing they could do about him.

Then they learned that Sir Henry Percy, already acting as marshall of England though his petition for office had not yet been signed by the king, had arrested a citizen of London, John Prentig, for criticizing the duke of Lancaster. They were told Prentig was being held in Percy's own house.

When they heard this news they exploded. Prentig's arrest was illegal. Now they could act. They were in the right and Percy was in the wrong. The debating guildsmen turned into a mob. They burst from the Guildhall and marched west on Catte Street, their angry numbers increasing as they moved. The Londoners they met were challenged. "Are you for us or against us?" The mob knew no middle ground.

Marching down Fleet Street toward the Strand and the Savoy Palace, they met a priest who asked them what they were doing. A man told the priest they were going to release Sir Peter de la Mare, unjustly imprisoned by the duke of Lancaster. Was the priest for them or against them?

"Peter de la Mare is nothing but a traitor who should have been hanged long ago," the priest replied. He was severely beaten and died a few days later.

The news of the mob reached William Courtenay at his supper. His reaction was typical of the man as well as of the operation of government, both civil and church, in the fourteenth century. He did not call the police. There were none. He did not call in a member of his staff or an assistant to act for him. He immediately left his supper and acted in person.

He rushed out of St. Paul's and caught up with the mob on the Strand nearly down to the Savoy. He stopped their momentum and brought them to a halt. It was not Courtenay's office alone that stopped them. It was his dominating presence and what he said. He said that each man's conduct would have been bad at any time, but now, during Lent, it was especially sinful.

With his words Courtenay had to reach each person in the mob as an individual. His appeal had to break the feeling of anonymity that bonded them together and gave them protection, courage, and power. The bishop's appeal to sin was much stronger in the fourteenth century than it would be today. A man then thought of himself not as a personality whose uniqueness must be recognized, but as a moral person, whose worth, whether he was sinful or virtuous, was apparent in his actions.

The bishop's appeal to each individual's sense of sin broke through their anonymity. Then he promised them that he would personally see that Peter de la Mare was released. Each man there knew he could depend on Bishop Courtenay's word. He would satisfy their goal. They could stop their violence without surrendering their courage. The mob had lost its impetus. Bishop Courtenay had probably saved the Savoy from destruction, at least for a while, and had probably saved the life of the man who, the day before, had opposed and insulted him in public.

The duke of Lancaster also learned of the riot while he was eating. He and Sir Henry Percy were dining at the home of the steward of the king, Sir John Ypres. The chronicle that remains is even explicit about their meal. It says the duke, Sir Henry, and Sir John were eating oysters at the time. The three left their oysters, dashed two streets to the Thames, and fled in a boat to the home of Joan of Kent, now the widow of the Black Prince. She later tried to smooth the quarrel between her brother-in-law, the duke, and the officials of the city, but she was not totally successful.

This was John Wyclif's first open conflict with his superiors, and he hurried back to the peace of Oxford where he could enjoy a clash of syllogisms with greater freedom. What he had preached in London about church wealth and its social responsibility had not gone unnoticed, however. Adam Easton, the Benedictine monk at the Vatican, was now a cardinal working on a new translation of the Bible from Hebrew and Greek into Latin. Ten years earlier, he had refused the appeal of John Wyclif to retain his position as warden of Canterbury College.

Adam Easton did not like someone suggesting that monks lose their income. If he could convince the bureaucrats at the Vatican that Wyclif was a heretic, Wyclif would be forbidden to attack the monks on any grounds. He would lose his mastership at Oxford and would end his life in a church prison. No heretic had been burned in England yet, but Adam Easton might have the first in John Wyclif.

Easton wrote the Benedictines at Oxford and asked them to obtain for him "the sayings of Master John Wyclif against our order," together with two copies of all of his written works.

When he sent the request to his fellow monks, the Vatican was still at Avignon. But Gregory XI had been cajoled, urged, prodded, pestered, and finally induced to leave Avignon and return to Rome by Catherine di Benincasa, an energetic and insistent nun now remembered as St. Catherine of Sienna. St. Catherine and Gregory, his consistory (the cardinals who met regularly to advise the pope), and the rest of the bureaucracy secretly boarded a ship for Genoa. By the time the pope and his court had reached Rome, Easton had received and examined the works of John Wyclif which he had requested to see. He found them glutted with heresies. Easton submitted fifty heresies to the pope's consistory. The consistory turned the matter over to the members of the Inquisition, who selected eighteen for special condemnation. When the condemnation reached England, John Wyclif could be imprisoned and "put to the question," that is, tortured. The Inquisition would now be reintroduced into England after sixty years.

During the pope's sixty-nine-year stay at Avignon, the fifth-century basilica of St. Mary Major had fallen into disrepair. Now its restoration was almost complete, and to celebrate this event on May 22, 1377, Pope Gregory chose this church from which to forward copies of the condemnation to the following: Edward III; the chancellor of Oxford,

Alan Tonworth; the archbishop of Canterbury, Simon Sudbury; William Courtenay; and Joan of Kent.

Their orders were explicit. The pope told them that if they found John Wyclif, rector of the church at Lutterworth in the diocese of Lincoln, maintaining and preaching false doctrine:

> You shall have said John seized and jailed on our authority, seek to extort a confession from him, which you will transmit to us by trusted messenger under seal, secretly and unknown to anyone, and you will keep said John under careful guard in chains until you receive further instructions concerning him. Those who object, you will restrain through ecclesiastical censure, disregarding appeal, and call in for this purpose, the assistance of the civil arm if necessary.[2]

To obtain the necessary assistance of the civil authorities, they were to inform Edward the king, Joan of Kent, princess of Wales, and widow of the Black Prince, and other lords of England that Wyclif's ideas, "when carefully scrutinized, threaten the destruction of the state." If he advocated withholding tithes from church government, he might also advocate withholding taxes from civil government, the inquisitors suggested. They wanted to call the attention of the state to this fact, for nowhere could the Inquisition proceed without civil cooperation. The letters that went to Edward and Joan acquainted them personally with the threat that John Wyclif presented to the state.

Without telling the king or Joan, Pope Gregory warned Sudbury and Courtenay that if John Wyclif had any suspicion of his imminent capture and imprisonment, and

---

[2]Walsingham, *Chronicon Angliae*, pp. 178–80; Walsingham, *Historia Anglicana*, I, 350–52.

"Heaven forbid may be able to make his escape, or with the aid of a hiding place defeat our command," they should display an edict at Oxford and in all public places where it would come to Wyclif's attention that he present himself within three months in Rome.

In still another of his letters, the pope told Alan Tonworth, chancellor of Oxford, that he "should have been a fighter and champion of the true faith, but through idleness and sloth permitted cockle to grow among the pure grain" of Oxford. The pope ordered the chancellor to seize Wyclif at the first opportunity and turn him over to the archbishop of Canterbury or to the bishop of London for the imprisonment.

What Pope Gregory and the inquisitors did not know was that Alan Tonworth had been at Merton College at the same time as John Wyclif. They were old friends.

CHAPTER TWELVE

Wyclif's Second Trial

*T*HE ORDERS FROM THE POPE in Avignon or Rome generally took about two months to be delivered to London and Oxford. Fortunately for John Wyclif, the
orders for his arrest were not received for seven months. It
is not known why.

In June 1377, Edward III died. The first Parliament of
Richard II, king at age eleven, met October 13 in the
Painted Chamber of Westminster Palace. For the second
time the king's council asked Wyclif if, in his opinion, the
king could rightfully hold back "treasure of the kingdom,
that it be not carried away to foreign nations, the pope demanding same." Wyclif left Oxford for Westminster to
deliver his reply in person. He had heard nothing about the
condemnation of his ideas, nothing about the order for his
arrest.

The painted chamber Wyclif visited was one of the most
famous rooms of England. It was large, eighty by twenty-
six feet. Its murals showed a map of the world with war
scenes of the Bible located on it: the stories of Joab, Abner,
David, Abimelech, and Jonathan, and the exploits of Judas
Maccabees, were all explained in French. In the recesses of
seven Gothic windows were statues of angels and the seven
cardinal virtues. The favorite motto of the Plantagenets
was inscribed in French on one of the walls: He who does
not give what he has, does not obtain what he wants.

William Courtenay opened the session of Parliament
with a prayer and Simon Sudbury with a sermon on the text
"Behold your king comes," inspired by the coronation of

the new king. He used the opportunity to remind the members that power came from above and that those below, by their very nature, loved and obeyed the king.

The poll tax which the last Parliament, the Parliament controlled by John of Gaunt, had levied had not collected as much as the treasury estimated, but large loans arranged with London merchants such as John Philipot and from the city itself kept the government solvent if in debt.

John Wyclif distributed in writing his opinion that the king could rightfully withhold papal taxes, and a copy was given to Sir Peter de la Mare, released from jail as Bishop Courtenay promised and again speaker for the knights, burgesses, and citizens.

On November 28, the day Parliament adjourned, Thomas Brinton, bishop of Rochester, met Wyclif, ready to return to Oxford, in the Painted Chamber. The bishop was very excited. In a loud voice so that everyone in that part of the room could hear, he announced to Wyclif that his opinions had been condemned by the pope and that he was going to be arrested.

It was the first Wyclif had heard of either piece of news. Apparently the orders had still not arrived from Rome. Brinton had heard the report from a notary in the papal court. Like Adam Easton, Brinton was a Benedictine and one of the most noted preachers of his day. He had delivered the sermon at the coronation of Richard II. The channel of communication within the Order of St. Benedict apparently moved faster than official channels.

If the archbishop of Canterbury and the bishop of London had received the orders for Wyclif's arrest, they held them back until December 18, an unlikely supposition. It was only then that they ordered the chancellor of Oxford, with the assistance of learned and orthodox doctors of the university, to ascertain if Wyclif taught the heretical doctrines listed by the Inquisition. Further, Chancellor Tonworth was to order Wyclif to appear before the papal commissioners at St. Paul's in London within thirty days.

Wyclif learned what specific doctrines the Inquisition had condemned when Alan Tonworth received them from the archbishop and showed them to him. The Inquisition had taken most of the ideas from Wyclif's book *On Civil Power.* It especially condemned Wyclif's thesis that there was no power without virtue and the political ideas he developed from it, particularly that the state could decide when a church or churchman was delinquent in his duties and could deprive him of the income that came from any lands he owned. The Inquisition also objected to Wyclif's argument that no man was excommunicated who had not first cut himself off from God by his own sins.

Wyclif answered these charges with the vehemence typical of a prophet. He knew that the Benedictines, known as the black monks because of their black robes, were led by Adam Easton and were responsible for these threats to his freedom. He said that "a black dog and his whelps" misrepresented his ideas, that children had carried fables about him to Rome.

But Wyclif also knew that insulting his accusers did not answer their charges, so he drew up a carefully reasoned defense using the authority of the Bible and of the church fathers. He tempered his stand on the state confiscation of church income properties by saying it could proceed only with the authorization of the church. He concluded his defense with the formula that "if what he said was shown contrary to faith, he would submit himself humbly to the correction of Mother Church."[1]

Wyclif's defense satisfied his fellow Mertonian Alan Tonworth, who said that Wyclif's ideas were valid,

---

[1]Fasciculi Zizaniorum, p. 179.

"though they sounded bad to the ear." Wyclif acidly replied that to condemn truth because it sounds bad to the ear would make everything in the Bible subject to condemnation.

But Pope Gregory had ordered Wyclif imprisoned, and he threatened to put Oxford under his direct control if the masters of the university did not follow his order. Alan Tonworth felt obliged to call a Congregation of all masters in the Church of St. Mary the Virgin to decide on some course of action that would keep the university free of papal control.

The monks and friars on one side of the church and the secular priests and clerks on the other debated boisterously. The monks and the friars would be happy to see Oxford's fast-rising secular priest imprisoned, especially one who had the ear of the duke of Lancaster and who advocated that their income properties be taken away.

Wyclif's fellow seculars stood by him. Some of them had known him for more than twenty years. Oxford, they said, had a great tradition of freedom of expression, even in theology. The university was capable of judging heresy and orthodoxy without the pope's threats.

They saved their strongest argument for last. They reminded the Congregation that it was against English law to imprison an Englishman on the request of the pope alone. The king also had to give his permission, and King Richard had not done this.

The vice-chancellor of the university, a monk, suggested a compromise. If Wyclif would agree, he could stay in Black Hall, one of the college halls, for the sake of appearance only. The hall had a monk at its head and was owned by Oseney. Wyclif agreed, and the monks were satisfied.

But Adam Houghton, bishop of St. David's in Wales, was now chancellor of England, and he was not satisfied. For even this token imprisonment without the king's permission he put the vice-chancellor in jail. He removed Alan Tonworth as chancellor of the university and replaced him with John Gilbert, the Dominican who had led the mission to Bruges three years earlier.

Still the summons to appear at St. Paul's in January hung over John Wyclif. Simon Sudbury preached a sermon there based on the text from St. John 16: 19: "In a short time you will no longer see me, and then a short time later, you will see me again." Wyclif thought the sermon referred allegorically to his imprisonment in Black Hall and his coming appearance at St. Paul's.

Certainly, Wyclif misinterpreted Sudbury's intentions. The archbishop of Canterbury was a quiet and peaceful man. While he would try to follow the orders of his superior, Pope Gregory, his sermon referred only to the Ascension of Christ, not to the imprisonment of John Wyclif.

But William Courtenay was neither quiet nor peaceful. He was forceful and capable of strictly enforcing the pope's order. This time, if Wyclif appeared at St. Paul's, he knew he could not have John of Gaunt there to defend him.

Wyclif did not have to appear at St. Paul's that January. Instead, in March he went to Lambeth Palace, the large castle where Sudbury lived and ruled. It was across the Thames and outside the city of London, outside the diocese of William Courtenay.

John Wyclif was tried in the chapel on the second floor. The archbishop was there, of course, along with the other great bishops of England including William Courtenay, all robed and mitred. With them were certain members of the Inquisition representing the pope. The court declared that "by no entreaties, by no threats, by no bribes would they be drawn from the pursuit of strict justice in this case." They had not forgotten what happened the year before between the duke of Lancaster and the bishop of London.

It was not long before they were drawn from their pursuit of strict justice. John of Gaunt did not appear, but Sir Lewis Clifford did. Clifford was distantly related to the duke through marriage. He had been a hard-fighting soldier at Calais in 1352 and at Nájera in 1367. He had been made a knight of the garter just the previous year.

Clifford appeared at the trial as an emissary of Joan of Kent, who had received one of the pope's letters. He told the bishops that the civil arm of the law would not support them. The church could try John Wyclif and pass judgment on him, but it could do no more than that. The Inquisition depended on the local civil government to question its witnesses when it thought the questioning necessitated torture and to carry out its sentences when the sentences called for imprisonment or execution. In his letters to King Edward, Joan of Kent, and the various lords of England, the pope had tried to persuade them to support the church against Wyclif. But this time the government would not be persuaded. Sir Lewis Clifford told the bishops and In-quisitors there would be no torture, imprisonment, or ex-ecution of heretics in England.

The trial took place outside the city, but still the Lon-doners invaded it. At St. Paul's they had ignored John Wyclif. Now they were on his side. The group was led by John of Northampton, the sheriff who had been impressed by Wyclif's preaching in London.

Clamoring and applauding, they made a shambles of what little was left of the trial. Finally the bishops were able to pass a sentence. They prohibited Wyclif from discussing the propositions condemned by the Inquisition at Oxford or in his sermons because of "the scandal thereby given the laity."

Throughout history, pomp, power, and threats of the establishment never turned a prophet from his destiny of making his vision known to the world. At Lambeth Palace Wyclif saw more pomp and threats than power because of his unexpected support by Sir Lewis Clifford. He ignored the sentence.

A few days after the trial at Lambeth Palace, Gregory XI died in Rome. Like all news, the word of the election of a new pope would have a delayed arrival in England, and John Wyclif did not learn about it for some time. When he did, he was involved in the messy business of the ransom of Alfonso, son of the count of Denia, who had been captured in Spain at the battle of Nájera eleven years earlier.

CHAPTER THIRTEEN

A War, a Pope, and a Debate

*T*HE BATTLE OF NÁJERA had been fought on April 2, 1367, when the Benedictine monks had marched from Canterbury to relieve Wyclif of his wardenship at Canterbury College, Oxford. Nájera, a village not far from Pamplona in northern Spain, is approximately one thousand miles from Oxford, and while the English and Castilian knights were battling one another, Wyclif could have no way of knowing he was going to be involved with the battle's most famous prisoner of war.

At Nájera, young John of Gaunt, twenty-seven years old, earl of Richmond but not yet duke of Lancaster, fought for the first time beside his older brother, the Black Prince. Together they were assisting Pedro the Cruel, king of Navarre, to regain the throne of Castile against Henry of Castile. The English knights chased the Castilians down a hill toward a tiny bridge over the Nájerilla River, roaring with the spring run-off from the Pyrenees further north.

The mass of Spanish knights tried to cram and squeeze their way across the bridge, but most of them, pushed from the rear, exploded into the churning water. The water bowled their horses over, and the knights, heavy as stones, drowned in their armor. Fortunately, Alfonso de Ribagorza, marquis of Villera, duke of Guardia, count of Denia, commander of the routed right Castilian wing, did not make it to the bridge but was captured by two English squires, Robert Hauley and John Shakyl. The count was of royal blood, and according to the complicated rules of chivalry, only the Black Prince was entitled to hold him captive. The prince, in turn, would compensate the two squires.

The whole affair was graciously handled. The count of Denis was allowed to go on parole, giving his two sons, Pedro and Alfonso, as hostages—Pedro to the keeping of the count of Foix, Alfonso to the keeping of the two squires with the permission of Prince Edward.

Then the business of the ransom—the really serious business of medieval warfare—became complicated. The defeated Henry of Castile advanced sixty thousand florins toward the ranson if Alfonso and Pedro would marry his two illegitimate daughters. Alfonso refused, so Henry demanded thirty thousand of his florins back. Negotiations continued for eleven years, during which Hauley and Shakyl held Alfonso but received no ransom for him.

Eventually, both the Black Prince and his father died. The count of Denia opened negotiations again with the new king, Richard. He sent two representatives from Spain with sixty thousand additional florins. William, Lord Latimer, the promoter who had been in trouble with the Good Parliament, still had a nose for money. He and Sir Ralph Ferrers put a claim on Alfonso in Marshall's Court, the court that administered the law of ransoms.

The court ordered Hauley and Shakyl to produce Alfonso, but the two squires, not trusting Lord Latimer, refused. Nor did they produce Alfonso when they received an order to do so from Parliament. Because of these refusals Hauley and Shakyl were put in the Tower of London on the grounds of contumacy, perverse and obstinate, refusal to authority, and for making their home a prison without authority.

They were in the Tower for nine months. In August 1378 they knocked their jailer over the head, escaped, and fled up river to sanctuary in Westminster Abbey Church. A few days later, on August 11, Sir Ralph Ferrers and the keeper of the Tower, Sir Alan Buxhill, along with forty soldiers, followed the two escapees into the church. They enticed John Shakyl into the belfry, which was not included in sanctuary, and he surrendered there.

Inside the church, Robert Hauley stood listening to the priest reading the gospel of the day, "If the goodman of the house had known at what hour the thief would come." At that moment Ferrers and Buxhill came up the nave of the church and grabbed Hauley. He wrestled free. The soldiers chased him around the altar into the choir behind. Here they caught him and hacked him to death at the shrine of Edward the Confessor, known as St. Edward at that time. They also killed one of the sacristans trying to stop the sacrilege. The soldiers left the body of the sacristan but dragged Hauley's body through the church, "splattering everything with his blood and brains," as the chronicles put it.[1]

The Middle Ages were especially subject to rumor. Everyone spent his daylight hours outdoors—in the streets, the markets, the fields, the courtyards, and the church-yards. It was an oral society. Wherever people met, stories true and untrue passed from one to the other. Even if a story began as true, the nature of speech and imagination soon exaggerated and distorted it. The story became false, if not in fact at least in emphasis. This law of rumor seems to have applied everywhere: in the king's palace at West-minster, in the abbey nearby, in the duke's palace at Savoy, on the streets of London—especially on the streets of London.

For three days following Hauley's death in the church of Westminster Abbey, the Londoners indulged in every sort of rumor. Most of the rumors concerned their favorite vil-lain, John of Gaunt: that the duke offered Hauley and Shakyl a reward for the prince (he did not); that the duke wanted Alfonso to marry the king's half-sister, Matilda (he did not). Actually the duke of Lancaster was crossing the

---

[1]Walsingham, *Chronicon Angliae*, pp. 207–8; Walsingham, *Historia Anglicana* I, 377–79.

channel on August 11, returning from an unsuccessful attempt to capture the coastal fort of St. Malo.

Finally, Archbishop Sudbury excommunicated all those
involved for the violation of sanctuary, but he did not spe-
cifically name the offenders. William Courtenay took it on
himself to name them. At St. Paul's Cross after he read the
solemn words of excommunication, he named Sir Ralph
Ferrers and Sir Alan Buxhill. He also named those who
were excluded from excommunication—Richard II, Joan of
Kent, and John, duke of Lancaster. At the name of John,
duke of Lancaster, the crowd in St. Paul's churchyard began
to shout. Three times a week—Sunday, Wednesday, and
Friday—Courtenay repeated the ceremony before an enthusiastic, noisy crowd.

When John of Gaunt learned what was happening, he
reacted. He threw himself into the tangle and told
Courtenay to stop repeating the curse of excommunication. One ceremony had been enough. But the bishop knew
that John of Gaunt had no authority to stop the ceremony,
and he continued three times a week. The duke compromised and told him to omit the names of those who were
excluded from excommunication. The bishop continued to
read as before, and as before the Londoners yelled when
they heard the duke of Lancaster's name. The few who had
thought that perhaps John of Gaunt was not involved in the
murder and violation of sanctuary were now convinced
that he was.

Young King Richard called a meeting of the council at
Windsor Castle and summoned the bishop of London to appear, but he did not show up. John remarked to his nephew,
''If the King so directs, I will hurry to London and drag that
obstinate Bishop to the Council in spite of those London
scoundrels.''

Richard did not so direct, but the remark was repeated in
the streets and taverns of the city. Again the law of rumor
operated, and the Londoners were now convinced that John

was plotting the destruction of the church and that he had stolen money from Parliament and equipment from the army.

The king summoned a new Parliament for October 20, but the abbot of Westminster, Nicholas Litlington, refused to sanctify the abbey church so it could be used to say mass and refused to allow commons to use the chapter house. The king's council threatened to confiscate the income-producing properties that supported the abbey.

The king did not carry out this threat, but Parliament had to move out of the town of Westminster to the Abbey of St. Peter in Gloucester. By this time John of Gaunt was so enmeshed in the Hauley and Shakyl affair, he had to defend his actions as well as challenge the government's indefensible violation of sanctuary. He needed all the logical skill he could muster, so once more he called on John Wyclif from Oxford.

Wyclif could not refuse in spite of his position as a churchman. He had escaped the chains, prison, and torture of the Inquisition when Joan of Kent sent Sir Lewis Clifford to intercede for him. Both of them were relatives of John of Gaunt, and what they did certainly had his approval if not direction.

Two years had passed. As Wyclif lectured at Oxford and stood for his annual quodlibet, his ideas had been developing and changing. Although he was still prohibited by the archbishop to discuss his theories on civil and church powers, he ignored the prohibition. He would again need a powerful friend to protect him.

John Wyclif and several other doctors of theology and of law hurried to the Savoy to confer with the duke of Lancaster. They prepared a defense for him and the government and were about to leave for Gloucester Abbey when the news from Rome finally reached them. A new pope, an Italian, had been elected—Bartolomeo Prignano had been crowned Urban VI.

Everyone praised him. He had been the archbishop of Bari and was connected with no particular party, Italian or French. He was especially praised for the purity of his life, his simplicity, his austerity, and his learning. In a letter to Richard II, Urban promised the king new freedom in the choice of English bishops. Richard and the court were so overjoyed at this that they authorized Arnold Garnier, the papal tax collector, four thousand pounds of back taxes.

Wyclif was caught up in the enthusiasm. He wrote a letter to the new pope calling him "our Urban." In the matter of Wyclif's ideas that had been condemned, he agreed to obey whatever the new pope ordered. Wyclif was especially optimistic because, in his daily life, Urban had practiced the holy poverty and self-denial that Wyclif called for in all churchmen.

In a few days the knights, burgesses, citizens, lords, and bishops joined John of Gaunt and John Wyclif at St. Peter's Abbey. Suddenly an exhausted messenger arrived from Fondi, south of Rome. He brought startling news. A second pope had been elected, Roberto, Cardinal of Genoa. Roberto of Genoa had been compared to Herod and Nero. As cardinal, he had hired Sir John Hawkwood, an English mercenary, to massacre the inhabitants of the city of Cesena. They had butchered about four thousand "old men, boys, and infants at the breast,"[2] and had stuffed their bodies into the wells of the city to pollute the water. By then even Hawkwood and his soldiers were revolted. Hawkwood's employer, now elected pope, took the name of Clement, the seventh of that name.

Members of Parliament traveled north to Gloucester Abbey where they displaced the monks, brothers, and ser-

---

[2]Pastor, Ludwig, *History of the Popes*, ed. F. I. Antrobus (St. Louis, Mo., 1891), I, 126; "Sir John Hawkwood," in *Dictionary of National Biography*, IX, 238–39.

vants who had to camp in the apple orchards or move to nearby Tewkesbury Abbey. The Parliament gave little attention to the double papal election, concerning itself only with English affairs.

As soon as Parliament opened, the archbishop of Canterbury formally protested the violation of sanctuary at Westminster. Adam Houghton was still chancellor of England, but as bishop of St. David's, he felt he could not represent a king who was attacking the privileges of the church, so he resigned.

Wyclif, Sir Thomas Percy, Hauley, Shakyl's commander at Nájera, and others debated for the crown. It is not known if Wyclif spoke, but he included his arguments in a work called *On the Church:*

> It was the intention of my lord, the Duke of Lancaster, to preserve the privileges of the Abbey. I heard him say that he would have allowed even insult to the King but not damage to the Kingdom. The actions of Hauley and Shakyl involved a case of treason; a worse crime does not exist.[3]

Later in the work, Wyclif explained the government's position further: "We detest the killing of persons, not only at Westminster but outside, anywhere in the kingdom. The killing occurred without the order or wish of the King."

Wyclif and the other doctors hoped to clear the king and John of Gaunt of any blame. They made their strongest defense on an issue that had nothing to do with the murder of Robert Hauley. They attacked the use of sanctuary by wealthy people to avoid paying debts, a popular issue. The churches which had been set aside for sanctuary were filled with this kind of fugitive. In spite of this defense of John of

---

[3]Wyclif, *de Ecclesia*, p. 150.

Gaunt and his nephew, little more than debate took place. Parliament slightly altered the rule of sanctuary for debtors, and time calmed the feelings of the abbot and of the archbishop as well as those of King Richard.

Alfonso, the hostage prince, was almost forgotten. John Shakyl kept him hidden until five years later, when in December 1383, he received twenty thousand gold francs. Law suits between Shakyl and his heirs and the Hauley heirs continued in the courts for three generations.

In November the members of Parliament left Gloucester Abbey, and the monks of St. Peter's returned from their cold bivouac in the apple orchard to their dormitories, cloister, and servants. John of Gaunt returned to Savoy, and John Wyclif to Queen's College at Oxford.

This defense of the duke at Gloucester was the last time Wyclif was directly involved in politics. In the four years since he had been an envoy for the government at Bruges, his ideas, although he did not intend them to be, had become an instrument of power. When ideas are allied to power, they are too easily compromised into dogma.

Power, however, was never a temptation for John Wyclif, the prophet. Now he cried out even more strongly, opposing church wealth and favoring a return to the age of simplicity. And his ideas were even more strongly challenged by both his orthodox friends and enemies. Ralph Strode challenged Wyclif to debate the thesis that church wealth should be given back to the poor on the basis that the wealth was necessary to perform deeds of charity. Wyclif answered that the wealth preserved the church which still failed in his deeds of charity. Their differences proved to be theoretical, not personal.

But John Wells waited to attack him personally. Wyclif had referred to his black habit, calling him "a black dog with a face yellow as gall." Wells was also known as "The Hammer of Heretics." He was from Ramsey Abbey near Cambridge and was tired of Wyclif's attacks on the monasteries, and he remembered that the Inquisition had found many heresies among Wyclif's ideas.

Once a year Wyclif still had to stand for his quodlibet disputation at Oxford. Although no authentic record of a quodlibet in which Wyclif took part has survived, the usual organization of the quodlibet has been preserved. In addition, many of Wyclif's works have survived in a form that suggests they were answers to implied or actual questions, the kind of questions that were asked at the annual quodlibet. The form of these works, then, makes a reconstruction of a quodlibet possible.

On the day of the quodlibet, the schools of Oxford were closed. The clerks and masters hurried through the narrow streets through Smithgate and over the north branch of the Thames to the Austin refectory, the largest gathering hall of the university. To find a place in the refectory they had to be there before prime, when the disputation began.

At prime the bell of St. Frideswyde rang on the south side of town and the bell of St. Osency's on the north. Inside Austin's, a ringer with a hand-bell led the participants into the hall in reverse order of rank. Once Wyclif was settled in front of the hall, someone in the audience might suggest a problem for Wyclif to examine and solve. The questioner would be aware that he might embarrass Wyclif about his stand on the two popes, for example. Originally Wyclif had joined others in praising Urban, hoping he would advocate Wyclif's ideals of simplicity, austerity, and poverty within the church. But this hope had quickly turned to disappointment.

St. Catherine of Sienna understood Urban's character better than Wyclif. When Urban was elected, she wrote to him, "Do what you have to do in moderation. For the sake of our crucified Lord, keep the hasty movements of your nature in check."

Urban had not kept his nature in check. He had declared war on the followers of the French pope, Clement. A group of Clement's followers held the Castle of St. Angelo, the great fortress on the Tiber in Rome. But they were completely isolated from the rest of the Clementists and had to surrender to Urban's soldiers. Urban ordered all the captives lined up and their hands chopped off with an axe.

Joanna, the beautiful queen of Naples, supported Clement. Urban ordered her strangled and in her place crowned her brother Charles, who, understandably, supported him. He tortured to death any cardinals who opposed him. Adam Easton was later arrested when he joined other cardinals opposing Urban, but he was luckier than many—he survived.

So Europe divided into two rancorous camps. England went with Urban. The followers of Clement in England were excommunicated. Scotland went with Clement. At Oxford, English clerks battled Scottish clerks in the streets. English holdings in France, Calais, and Bordeaux supported Urban. The rest of France followed Clement, who reestablished the court at Avignon. The German principalities and the Italian city states were divided. In Spain, Castile, Aragon, and Navarre supported Clement; Leon supported Urban.

If there was ever an example of authority without virtue, Wyclif saw it in both Urban and Clement. He said they were like ''dogs snarling over a bone'' and ''crows sitting on a carrion.'' He called the papacy ''a poisonous weed,'' ''a limb of Lucifer.''

When asked about the two popes at a quodlibet, Wyclif would have to admit he had changed his mind about ''our Urban.'' He asked himself a question: Is the pope ''a god on earth?'' He answered, ''Truly a mixed god. A simple idiot who might be damned in Hell; ... a more horrible idol than a painted log'' to whom it is ''blasphemous idolatry to pay veneration.''

Ironically, Wyclif added that he welcomed the split of the church. It made one truth obvious: the pope was not the

shepherd of the church, but its betrayer. Wyclif then emphasized the differences between Christ and the pope:
Christ was poor, the pope was rich; Christ refused power,
the pope sought it; Christ chose twelve simple men as
apostles, the pope chose many crafty, worldly men as cardinals; Christ had nowhere to lay his head, the pope lived
in a palace built with the money of the poor.[4]

This is the language of the prophet. It was the vitriolic
answer the clerks came to hear, and they regularly made
notes on Wyclif's arguments and logic. The notebook of
Adam Stocton, a clerk who came from Cambridge, still survives. In it Stocton listed twelve signs that the pope was the
antichrist, and he wrote beneath them, "One of the theses
of the venerable doctor, John Wyclif." When Wyclif
published these answers in *On the Power of the Pope*, he
reinforced his vituperation with logic and Bible citation.

Everyone at Oxford knew that Wyclif had been a friend of
the friars. He lectured in the very room where the quodlibet
was held, in the Augustinian priory. He had personal
friends among the friars, such as William Woodford, with
whom he exchanged notebooks, and John Uhtred of
Bolden, with whom he debated. He had pupils like Thomas
Netter, and he was still dressed like a Spiritual Franciscan.

But Wyclif had been recently attacking the friars for
abandoning their vow of poverty and ignoring their social
responsibility to the poor. It was a fight between old
friends, and fights between old friends always seem to
arouse a special, if morbid, interest. So someone at a
quodlibet might ask him if the friars really fulfilled Christ's
own example of holy poverty and simple living.

In addition to those earthy tales that Boccaccio and
Chaucer told about friars, writers of the period often
described friars as self-indulgent and rich. William

---

[4]Three citations from Wyclif, *Polemic Works in Latin*, I, 350–51; II, 680, 691.

Langland in his *Vision of Piers the Plowman* described a field full of ordinary people, including friars:

> I found friars there, all the orders four,
> Preaching to the people, for profit to their bellies,
> Glossing the gospel in any way seemed good.
> They covet handsome capes, and don't care how they preach.
> Many of these master friars dress fancy as they wish,
> For with them it's money and merchandize marching together.[5]

Wyclif expressed his opinion of the friars as colorfully as Langland, Boccaccio, and Chaucer: "The friars are gluttons," he said, "whose belly is the special kitchen of the devil. They love their throats and their stomachs. To indulge themselves they build kitchens grander than those of kings."

Wyclif described them as tortoises wandering over all the earth. At all hours they penetrate even the private chambers of lords and ladies, he claimed. "Like wolves or horned owls, they have animal eyes and sneak around looking everywhere for prey," he added.

In the fourteenth-century friars, he saw the betrayal of St. Francis. "They have too much wealth," he said, "wasteful houses, clothes, great feasts, jewels, treasures." They were interested only in their great monasteries, he maintained. And their monasteries covered much of the land, all supported by their begging, which left the real poor helpless and needy.[6]

Those at a quodlibet who heard his replies and knew him only by reputation would have expected a biting, satiric

---

[5]William Langland, *The Vision of Piers the Plowman*, B-text, ed. A.V.C. Schmidt (London, 1978), "Prologue," 58–63, p. 3.

[6]Wyclif, *de Apostacia*, p. 42; Wyclif, *Sermones*, I, 43.

attack on the friars. But those who were closer to Wyclif knew his break with the orders was distressing both to him and his friends in the orders. He had loyal followers within the orders who understood that he expected them to live up to the ideals which they had set for themselves.

Wyclif's attacks on the friars appeared in his *Apostasy.* He used the word *apostasy* to describe those friars who did not live according to the vision of holy poverty and who had abandoned the ideals of their founders. Those in the orders who were influenced by what he preached and wrote were suffering for their beliefs.

"I have faith in the good friends who have confidently stood by me in God's cause," he wrote, "for they are nothing like the apostates of whom I have spoken." Later in the same work he called those who followed him "my very dear sons," who "faithfully observe those things which are pure in the religion of Christ, which the devil has entangled with traditions he himself discovered."[7]

In all of his writings, Wyclif always understated his own personal feelings. That he made even these remarks shows how deeply he suffered for what his followers in the orders had to endure, and how his break with the friars cut him off from these friends. But he never left a written record expressing his own anguish over the torments his "very dear sons" suffered from believing in his vision.

At a quodlibet, if a personal enemy, such as John Wells, wanted to lead Wyclif into heresy, he would ask him to explain the mystery of the bread and wine at mass. His question might be, "What is the relationship between the substance of bread and wine and its appearance after the consecration?"

Wyclif had been studying this problem both as a student and as a master at Oxford. He believed the bread and the wine changed into the actual body and blood of Christ as he

---

[7]Wyclif, *de Apostacia*, p. 42.

performed the sacrament of the Eucharist every day. But he wanted to explain the change within that chain of creation which he had learned existed between the idea in God's mind and the physical appearance of God's idea on earth.

The authorities he had studied had always asked the same question: Why? "Why did the bread and wine change?" The authorities had an answer for that question. They believed that it changed because at the Last Supper in Jerusalem, Christ called the bread "my body," and the wine "my blood."

But Wyclif was not asking "Why?" He was asking "How?" How did the bread and wine change? This was a new question. And until men start asking new questions, the world does not find new answers. Wyclif wanted a new answer. He wanted to apply everything he had learned in physics, philosophy, and theology to explain the mystery.

Wyclif started by studying the bread itself. He wrote:

> Among all bodily senses the most sure are touch and taste. We know no corporate thing more certainly than the hardness and softness of holy bread. When it is new baked, it breaks one way and varies in sound from old baked bread. Even old bread when it is moist does not break like new bread. But philosophers say hardness and softness, brittleness and toughness cannot suggest either the true quality or the true quantity. If many consecrated hosts were mingled together with unconsecrated pieces of bread, a blasphemy, neither a human being nor an animal could tell which was which from the appearance.[8]

If the substance began as a timeless idea in the mind of God, did God in His mind destroy the substance? But in this question Wyclif found a dilemma, because destruction

---

[8]Wyclif, *The English Works*, III, 405.

implies time and space. And if the substance changed within time and space, why couldn't he see or feel it?

William Woodford followed Wyclif in his struggles to understand this dilemma. Woodford said that when he and Wyclif were studying together, Wyclif adapted an idea of Thomas Bradwardine's and tried to describe the substance of the bread and the wine as a mathematical body and the change as a kind of mathematical progression like multiplication.

But ten years had passed since the time they had studied together. Woodford said that after Wyclif received his doctorate, he believed that the same substance remained before and after the consecration. It was the sacrament of the Eucharist itself which was the body of Christ. Later still, Wyclif would find other answers. He kept searching for some answer that would fit the change that occurred within this chain between God and the world, as Wyclif understood it.

At a quodlibet in 1378, Wyclif was not ready to say that the substance did not change. That statement would be heresy. Wyclif answered with the formula that he believed as the church taught him to believe, and his enemies, including John Wells, would not catch him in heresy. Wyclif, however, had already started to investigate just what it was that the church had taught about the Eucharist since its beginnings. Perhaps he could find some doctrine somewhere in the history of the church that would help him in his scientific explanation. John Wells, the Hammer of Heretics, would have to wait to hammer him.

CHAPTER FOURTEEN

The Fame of Wyclif Spreads

AME WAS NOT THE instant phenomenon in the fourteenth century that it is in the twentieth. The sluggishness of communication made that impossible. Minstrels spread fame. On market day in a town square, minstrels entertained the shoppers with songs about King Arthur, Sir Gawain, Richard the Lion-Hearted, the Black Prince, and the Fair Maid of Kent. These ballads told stories of beautiful women, knights, and conquering heroes. No minstrel sang about an Oxford master who used logic instead of a sword and insult instead of a lance.

Still, John Wyclif's reputation spread. Londoners, such as John of Northampton, remembered his preaching; others heard his preaching at Lutterworth, and his word spread from there north to Leicester, not far away. His students remembered him and when they returned to their homes in Herefordshire, Shropshire, or Yorkshire, they repeated what he had taught them.

Some of those who heard about him secondhand became interested and wanted to hear what he said firsthand, and so they visited Oxford. They could not join the clerks at lectures, for the lectures were in Latin. But if Wyclif was pointed out to them on Carfax, on the High, or on Horsemonger Street, they stopped him and talked with him.

When the prophet speaks in public he is an actor. Wyclif's appearance had great drama. He was stark and thin, and must have looked like a pinched sparrow. Then more like a peregrine falcon than sparrow, Wyclif attacked the wealth of the monks, the friars, and the two popes. And when he told his listeners about his vision, it must have

131

seemed as if he stepped right out of the Bible, reminding them of Hosea or one of the disciples from the age of simplicity.

But the clerks at Oxford who knew Wyclif personally and the people who came to Oxford to seek him out had to be moved by more than the drama of his preaching if they were to be transformed from listeners into followers and associates. When a person talked to Wyclif on the street or in his room at Queen's, their relationship became intimate. The newcomer would be moved by the quiet side of the prophet's nature, by his moral earnestness and his careful reasoning. When that person first heard him preach, he might have been moved by the excitement of Wyclif's vision and the force of his attacks. Now he would be moved by the joy of a new, personal discovery.

Wyclif inspired enthusiastic followers early. Nicholas Hereford, a clerk working for his doctorate in theology, was one of these. The two met when Hereford was the bursar at Queen's just before John of Gaunt called Wyclif to London to preach. As bursar Hereford collected Wyclif's rent.

Hereford probably came to the university from the west country, as his surname implies, from Hereford, a town on the Wye River between England and Wales. He spoke in an accent different from Wyclif's Yorkshire Middle English, as Wyclif's dialect was undoubtedly modified by his long stay in Oxford. There is evidence Hereford may have been an Austin friar at the abbey of St. Mary de Pré in Leicester.

When Wyclif returned from the Gloucester parliament, Hereford had very nearly finished his studies and was ready for that last stretch toward his final degree. The chronicles describe him as "the most violent of Wyclif's followers." He accepted any challenge head on, rushing into it recklessly and naively.

John Aston was another of these early followers and was also an Oxford clerk. He had been a fellow at Merton after Wyclif left and was famous for his mathematics and astronomy. Computing the various positions of the planets over the span of history, he had figured that seventy-five hundred years would pass between Noah's flood and the end of the world by the fire of the Apocalypse, predicted in the Book of Revelation. He had to defend his calculations in a disputation against John Aschenden, the astronomer at Merton who claimed that he had predicted the plague of 1348 in a conjunction of Jupiter and Saturn in Aquarius and other signs.

John Aston was a scientist, but Wyclif's call to poverty altered his life. Aston left his science and, like Wyclif, walked throughout England in a long russet gown and bare feet. For food and shelter he depended on invitations to the hovels of serfs and tenant farmers. Here he talked not about astronomy or mathematics but about the vision of purity and simplicity of the early church.

Philip Repingdon was twenty years younger than Wyclif. He was born in Repton, Derbyshire, in 1350, and he was sometimes called Philip Repton. He came to Oxford, it is certain, from St. Mary de Pré at Leicester. Although Wyclif included the Augustinians in his attacks on the friars, Repingdon learned to know Wyclif's quiet side and realized that Wyclif's attacks were not directed against him personally but were the impersonal expansion of reason and logic.

Repingdon was one of the most brilliant men attracted to Wyclif. Like Hereford, he was working for his doctorate in theology, and Wyclif's ideas attracted him. He was not a fighter. He and Nicholas Hereford were friends, possibly from days together at St. Mary de Pré. As an early disciple of Wyclif, Repingdon, like Hereford, had enthusiasm and fire. In his later years, though, he lacked the zeal and stubbornness to remain on the side of revolution.

Wyclif had a group of sympathetic followers in Exeter College on Somnor Street, which ran inside the north wall of the town. Robert Rigg was living at Exeter when Wyclif was at Balliol, not far away. Like Wyclif, he was at Merton and took his turn as bursar there when Wyclif was on his mission to Bruges. Rigg would soon be elected chancellor of Oxford. He was pleasant and accommodating, but like a good administrator, he tried always to make the best of whatever situation he found himself without antagonizing those around him. As a result, his ideas and principles suffered from this accommodation.

Another follower from Exeter College was Laurence Steven, or Bedeman, as he was sometimes called. "Bedeman" was only a nickname that came from his association with Wyclif, for the name means "one who prays."

William Thorpe's parents spent a great deal of money training him to be a priest. At first he was not anxious to be one, so in addition to money, his parents tried persuasion, then force. Finally, as he testified at his trial for heresy thirty years later: "I went to those priests whom I heard to be of the best name and of the most holy living and best learned and most wise of Heavenly wisdom, and so I communed with them."

This search for the best priest led him to Oxford and to John Wyclif. Here he joined Hereford and Repingdon and the other clerks who were forming into a special group around Wyclif. About the group, Thorpe said, "A great many communed oft with him, and they loved his learning so much they writ it, and busily enforced themselves to rule themselves afterward."[1]

These special disciples within the university were Wyclif's closest and last surrogate family. This family also included many outside of Oxford, some of them completely unlearned. The family embraced one, William Smith, who was illiterate.

---

[1]John Foxe, *The Actes and Monuments*, ed. George Townsend (London, 1845), III, 826, 961; Prof. Hudson in *English Wycliffite Writings*, p. 30, edited the same passage from more authoritative manuscripts than those used by Foxe.

Smith received his name from his trade, blacksmithing. One of the chronicles said that he was so ugly and deformed he could not persuade any woman to become his wife. Regardless of his appearance, William Smith was an extraordinary blacksmith. He heard Wyclif and wanted to learn more about the vision. He taught himself to read and write, "in a short time," the chronicle admits. He began wearing the same kind of russet gown and went barefooted like Wyclif and John Aston. He established a way station for pilgrims in a broken-down, deserted chapel outside the city of Leicester near a leper hospital, and he became locally famous as William the Hermit. He was soon joined by two others, William Swinderby and Richard Waytestathe. Together they rebuilt the chapel as St. Francis had rebuilt St. Damian's at Assisi two hundred years earlier. In addition to using the chapel as a hostel, they established a school there for anyone who would listen while they described Wyclif's vision.

Parish priests, especially those of poor parishes, sought out John Wyclif. Many of these priests had parishes poorer than Fillingham. The poorest churches were made of wattles and thatch. A priest had to know something about weaving reeds and covering them with clay if he was to keep the walls of his church in repair. To keep the roof from leaking he would have to trade a chicken or some wool cloth to a thatcher who had the skill necessary to repair it.

A priest did not have to be from a rural area to know poverty. He might come from the Cornhill ward of London, the slums around Tun prison and the center for the thieves' market. William Langland, in the poem *The Vision of William Concerning Piers the Plowman*, described his life in the London slums. He lived by begging, and while not an ordained priest, once in a while he sang prayers:

I live in London and in the outlands too;
The tools I labor with and win my livelihood

Are "Our father which art in Heaven" that I sing from the
    handbook,
Or the seven psalms for the dead I know from the psalter
I sing for the souls of such that help me;
They offer me some food when they find that I hunger.
They welcome me at meals about once a month,
Now with this person, now with that, thus I beg.
Without bag or bottle I hardly fill.[2]

For a priest in a poor parish, whether in the city of London or in the country, Wyclif's sermons had a special attraction. From disputing at Oxford and explicating theology, Wyclif had developed his ideas from subtle, logical patterns into a united concept. Like Chartres Cathedral, his doctrine was formed out of myriad details, its unity best perceived at a distance.

Wyclif's sermons, however, were not like disputations and explications. They were simple and direct, as uncomplicated as a plowman's cottage. Each had a single message—short, unadorned, and easy to understand. And when that message emphasized Christian poverty, it had dramatic relevance to the parish in which a wheat cake the size of a man's fist fed wife and children for a day or even more. Priests who heard these sermons wanted to study them as models or even to read them as substitutes for their own, so at Oxford, Wyclif's surrogate family began collecting them. They translated the Latin sermons into English and arranged the sermons according to the church calendar. The church had traditionally assigned a selection from one of the gospels and one of the epistles to read at mass every day of the year, not only for Sundays but also for feast days and saints' days.

---

[2]William Langland, *The Vision of William Concerning Piers the Plowman*, C-Text, ed. Derek Pearsall (Berkeley, 1978), Passus V, 44-52, pp. 99-100.

Thirty manuscripts of completed sets of Wyclif's sermons still exist today, sets that include sermons for Sundays and for 27 feast days—294 sermons in all. They are beautiful manuscripts written on vellum (sheep skin) and not on paper, which was cheaper. Some of them have initial letters artfully decorated in red and blue. They had been produced with loving care.

His followers made digests of his sayings, observations, and ideas under various headings arranged in alphabetical order. They edited commentaries on fundamental prayers such as the Lord's Prayer, the Hail Mary, and on fundamental beliefs such as the Ten Commandments, the seven acts of mercy, and the seven deadly sins. They incorporated these into a book of instructions for priests, originally in Latin, but later translated into English as well. This book, *The Lay Folks Catechism*, is still in print today.

This effort of translating, editing, copying, and decorating required people working as an organization. It was not a matter of making a single copy for a student or a library. Many copies of all the works have survived, and many others were destroyed. To accomplish this job of copying and decorating, Wyclif's friends used professional scribes and probably one of London's factory systems for reproducing manuscripts.

Through the sermons, commentaries, digests, and books, Wyclif's ideas spread throughout England, especially into the western counties—Shropshire, Gloucester, Hereford—and the midland counties—Northampton and Oxford. Priests and laymen, such as those at the chapel of St. John the Baptist in Leicester, were preaching his vision of poverty and simplicity. Many of Wyclif's followers imitated his dress, and during the 1370s and early 1380s a new word appeared in the English language to describe them. The word was *lollard.* We are not sure where the word started. Probably it was a Dutch word, *lollaerd,* meaning someone who mutters, a word related to *lull*, as in "a mother lulls her child to sleep."

Obviously the word was not used as a compliment. The people who used it were not moved by Wyclif or his followers. By the time Chaucer used the word twenty years later, it had become a general insult for any tramp or beggar who was overly righteous. On the Canterbury pilgrimage, Chaucer's parson objects to the mildest swearing, and their guide, Harry Bailly, the host of the Tabard Inn, says to him, "Oh, Johnny, I smell a lollard in the wind."

CHAPTER FIFTEEN

The Bible Is Translated

*T*HE GREAT IDEAS IN HISTORY are easy to identify in retrospect. Looking back, we read about the discovery of one of them and think, "That's so obvious. Why didn't they think of that before?"

John Wyclif and his followers at Oxford gave the world one of these great ideas. They decided to translate the Bible into English, not just part of it, but the whole Bible, from Genesis to the Book of Revelation. Looking back, it was an obvious step for Wyclif to take. To the prophet the word itself is very important, for he receives his word directly from God.

"The word of Yahweh was addressed to me," Jeremiah wrote, and he added, "Then Yahweh put out his hand and touched my mouth and said to me, 'There, I am putting my words into your mouth.'" Isaiah received the word in a vision when one of the seraphim touched his lips with a burning coal.

Wyclif found his vision in the words of the Bible. The Bible was God's voice on earth for Wyclif—His true, universal utterance. The words were as vivid to Wyclif as the hand of Yahweh had been to Jeremiah or the live coal to Isaiah. In fact, John Wyclif heard God's voice addressed to him in sound, for during the Middle Ages a manuscript book was read aloud, not silently.

In addition, part of Wyclif's decision to translate the Bible came from his Englishman's pride in his own language. Since William the Conqueror, almost four hundred years earlier, England had been ruled by French-speaking kings. The rulers and upper classes had developed their own dialect of French—Anglo-Norman. The records of the court were in this dialect and the courts of justice were conducted in it. The literature was Anglo-Norman and Latin. When English schoolboys translated Latin, they translated it into French.

But the rulers could never impose their language on the people they ruled. An Englishman talked to his neighbor in English and to his God in English. He did not realize it, but he spoke the most flexible and adaptive language in Europe. English was a linguistic sponge. Whenever a Frenchman brought a new way of doing something to England, and had a French word for it, an Englishman took both the method and the French word describing it and went on speaking English.

The French finally succumbed. In Wyclif's lifetime a statute was issued requiring English to be used in the courts. Schoolboys began translating their Latin into English.

By the end of the fourteenth century, after one hundred years of struggle against Latin and Anglo-Norman, the literature of England was in English. Geoffrey Chaucer gathered stories for his *Canterbury Tales*, stories to be told by Englishmen into English. For his *Vision of Piers, the Plowman*, William Langland used the rhythms of English verse that had survived from the time of *Beowulf* seven hundred years earlier. The stories of King Arthur and his knights, Sir Gawain, Sir Lancelot, and Sir Kay, were being retold in English epics.

As part of its literature, England needed a Bible in English. Parts of the Bible had already been translated into English. At the beginning of the eighth century, Venerable Bede had translated the gospel of St. John, but his translation did not survive. Psalms and gospels survived from the end of the ninth century in which monks had written English above the lines of Latin. Aelfric's translations of some of the Old Testament survived from the beginning of the eleventh century. But the language of these early translations was Old English, the language of the Angles, Saxons, and Frisians who had invaded England in the fifth century. Old English was a German dialect incomprehensible to their linguistic descendents in the fourteenth.

Richard Rolle, the mystic hermit of Hampole, Yorkshire, and a contemporary of Wyclif's, translated the Psalms into English. Another translation of the Psalms, more idiomatic than Richard Rolle's and in the Midland dialect, was available. Nuns, who were not expected to know Latin, used devotional books in English. But a translation of the complete Bible had never been attempted.

Wyclif knew that Edward III had a complete Bible in French. Richard II had inherited this volume. Richard was born in France but came to England when he was four years old and so he became the first king for whom English was his native language.

"Since the rulers of England have the Bible in French," Wyclif observed, "it is not unreasonable that priests have it in English."[1]

The Bible that English priests used was in Latin, as it had been for a thousand years. In the fourth century, St. Jerome had translated the Bible from its basic languages—Hebrew, Aramaic, and Greek—into Latin, so that missionaries could tell the stories of Adam, Noah, Abraham, and Jesus to those who were familiar with the names of Thor, Odin, Loki, and Mithras.

But in the fourteenth century, not all priests could read even Jerome's Latin. Some may have attended a cathedral school or choir school, but most priests never went to any university. They learned to be priests by serving mass as boys, then advancing to subdeacon and deacon following the apprentice system of the guilds. Along the way they

---

[1]"*de Officio Pastorali,*" in *The English Works,* p. 227.

memorized the Latin of the mass. The priest they served under should have taught them the meaning of what they were saying, but some did not bother.

Before he ordained a new priest, the bishop examined the candidate on his Latin. He took some phrase from the mass and asked the meaning of the words and possibly an explanation of the Latin grammar. The bishop then asked the candidate to read some Latin aloud.

Especially in the years after the plagues, which had slaughtered so many priests, the bishop was often unpleasantly surprised. It was not uncommon that the priest already giving mass could not explain the meaning of the Latin he recited, or even read a passage that he had not memorized. Of course, the bishop had to know Latin in order to examine the priest. In a few instances, though, he was not well educated himself. Early in the century, the bishop of Durham could neither understand nor speak Latin. The education of Henry Despenser, the fighting bishop of Norwich, was deficient in everything except warfare.

The farmers who heard Wyclif at Fillingham and at Lutterworth knew no Latin, nor did the shopkeepers, grocers, and skinners of London. But they all knew English. Some of them could read and write it. As the schools started to use English, more and more ambitious young men went to school long enough to read and write their native language, especially in London. John of Gaunt conducted his business in French, but his nephew Richard and his son, Henry, earl of Derby, later Henry IV, used English.

Great ideas that seem simple when they are discovered have a way of becoming complex when they are carried out. Wyclif and the translators at Oxford needed Bibles to translate. That seems easy enough, but to fulfill the need was more complicated in the fourteenth century than it would be today.

St. Mary's, Wyclif's parish church at Lutterworth, certainly did not have a Bible. None of the priests who came to

Oxford for Wyclif's help had Bibles in their churches. A small church had a missal containing the prayers of the mass and the gospel and epistle for the day. Some larger churches had choir books that were set open on racks, large enough so all the choir could read the words and music of the chant from a distance. If a church had an illuminated missal, gospel book, or psalter, the book would be one of the church treasures and was locked in a chest or chained so it would not be stolen.

A complete Bible could be found only in the libraries of the largest abbeys, monasteries, and college halls. Merton College had two. The Queen's College Bible consisted of two large volumes of more than nine hundred pages and nine equally huge volumes of additional commentary. In other libraries near Oxford, the books of the Bible were bound into separate volumes.

Energetic Nicholas Hereford, never one to refuse a challenge, immediately took charge of the first translation. It is not certain what Latin Bible he used. It might have been the one at Queen's, since Wyclif was living there.

Hereford decided to make a word-for-word translation, giving each Latin word an English equivalent, even keeping the Latin order of the words in the translation. Nicholas Hereford and the four others working with him knew this method was not a translation into idiomatic English, but they found a precedent for their method—Richard Rolle had translated the Psalms in this way.

Hereford figured he still could produce something valuable that a priest could use. The priest would have a translation of the Latin words right in front of him; all he would have to do was to rearrange the words into good English, which he knew, of course, and he would have an English version of the Bible to use for mass or other services.

In the manuscript of this first translation, five different handwritings and two dialects can be distinguished, three of the translators from Kent and two from the Midlands. One of the latter was probably Hereford himself. Hereford was not able to finish his translation. He had been working about five years when in 1382 he had to flee England. Someone working on the translation wrote a note saying that Hereford stopped at verse twenty of the third chapter of Baruch, a prophetic book between the Lamentations of Jeremiah and Ezekiel in the Latin Bible.

John Purvey, probably a curate at Lutterworth assisting Wyclif, took over the direction of the translation. One of the chroniclers at St. Mary de Pré, Leicester, called him a "simple chaplain." No record has survived of his education, but he was a great deal more than a simple chaplain. He was ordained a priest in 1377, the year that started with Wyclif facing William Courtenay at St. Paul's and ended with Alan Tonworth receiving orders to imprison him at Oxford. John Purvey's manner must have fooled the chronicler. Purvey dressed and looked like an ordinary middle-class Englishman. Thomas Netter, the Franciscan and one of Wyclif's students at Oxford, said Purvey was the "librarian of the Lollards," an invincible disciple of Wyclif, and a strong administrator. When Netter wrote these things, he was no longer in sympathy with Wyclif's ideas.

It seems to have been Purvey who translated most of Wyclif's Latin sermons and other works into English. Netter said that Purvey took Wyclif's writings "into his mind very copiously. Even to the end of Wyclif's life, he was an inseparable companion."[2]

Before Nicholas Hereford had to leave and John Purvey took over his translation, Purvey discovered something for himself that had been known for at least two centuries— the Latin texts varied widely from one Bible to another. The pages of the larger Bibles, like the one at Queen's Col-

---

[2]*Fasciculi Zizaniorum*, pp. 383–401; Henry Knighton, *Chronica de Eventibus Angliae*, II, 178–9.

lege, for example, were divided into three columns, but only the center column was the text of the Bible. In the columns to the left and right, in the margins, and even between the lines were the glosses, explanations of difficult words, interpretations of the meaning, and etymologies. Over time, many of these glosses had been transferred into the text itself. Tags and phrases from the liturgy of the mass had found their way into the text. Variants from St. Jerome's Latin had been substituted, especially within the Psalms, for more than one translation, even by Jerome himself, was current during the Middle Ages. Those correcting the text, some of whom had little knowledge of what they were doing, only added to the damage. In the thousand years between Jerome and Wyclif, many other unintentional errors accumulated as a result of the copying itself.

The whole business of copying by hand was tedious and difficult. When they copied the Bible, the monks and friars were unusually careful, because, after all, this was the word of God. The most experienced scribe, perhaps the head of the scriptorium, was assigned to the Bible. Most scriptoria were noisy places, however. As they copied, the monks read aloud, mumbling the words they were copying. Two or three scribes and a few other droning readers raised a continual buzz in a monastery library. Copyists learned how to concentrate, but when they were tired, they heard words other than those in front of them. The names of most of these scribes have long been forgotten. A few of them, however, complained in the margins of their manuscripts, and their complaints have lasted through the centuries. Copying St. Jerome's commentary on the book of Daniel, a Bavarian monk, referring to himself in the third person, commented, "He was still with cold while he wrote. When he could not write by the light of the sun, he finished his work by the light of the night." A Swiss monk copying at St. Gall, wrote, "Those who do not know how to write think it is easy. Only my fingers hold the pen, but my whole body gets tired."[3]

A good many manuscripts end with the scribe thanking God that his task is finished, and asking the reader to pray for his health. Unfortunately blindness was a common reward for a monk who spent his life in the scriptorium.

While John Purvey was comparing the texts of the Bibles, he found not only variants but also translations that were entirely different from St. Jerome's. In the first half of the thirteenth century, Robert Grosseteste and a group of translators were studying and translating Greek commentators' works on the creation and the Psalms. Grosseteste knew enough Greek and classical Hebrew to recognize that both versions of St. Jerome's Psalms varied from the original Hebrew. To correct the errors he found, he made an interlinear translation, writing the Latin above the Hebrew. Unfortunately this work has not survived. At his urging, one of his group more proficient in Hebrew than he made a new translation. Other scholars, most of them Franciscan as well, also followed suit.

Purvey did not know Hebrew, Greek, or the Aramaic[4] in Daniel and Ezra, and he could not refer to the original languages. After he finished his translation, Purvey wrote a prologue recalling how he went about the task of resolving the differences he found among the various Latin texts. By the time he wrote the prologue, though, all of his books, including his Latin Bibles, had been taken away from him, and he was depending on his memory to recall his work.

He said that he and "diverse fellows and helpers," as he called them, gathered many old Bibles, it is estimated

---

[3]Cited by G.G. Coulton, *Medieval Panorama* (New York, 1955), p. 579.

[4]The common language of Semitic peoples between the Babylonian captivity in 587 B.C. and the rise of Islam in the seventh century A.D.

eleven, as well as glosses and commentaries. Purvey relied especially on one commentator, Nicholas of Lyre, whom Purvey said he discovered only late in his work.

Nicholas was born in Lyre, a small town in Normandy. He was a Franciscan, a doctor of theology from Paris who eventually became the Franciscan provincial of Burgundy. He was the finest Hebrew scholar of the fourteenth century who was not a rabbi. He understood some Mishnaic Hebrew, for his glosses were the only ones that used the Talmud and other rabbinical commentaries. Nicholas's scholarship was so superior that twelve hundred manuscripts of his commentaries exist in various libraries today.

The task of correlating the Bibles was colossal as Purvey and his fellows went about their work "to make one Latin Bible somewhat true." The great volumes of the Bible were open on stands in front of them. Some Bibles from one hundred years before were written in a tiny script and were small enough to be held in a person's hand. Illuminations show round bookshelves that revolved on a center shaft. When a reader went from one book to another, he had only to revolve his shelf. If Purvey and his helpers were well equipped, they might have had one of these.

As chief editor, Purvey decided on a basic text to start with, and he or an assistant read from it line by line while the helpers followed in their various other Bibles. When a helper found a disagreement, he called out, and the group stopped to discuss which version they would use for their own translation. A scribe then recorded their decision. It was a tedious process.

Of course, they were handicapped by not knowing Hebrew or Greek. However, a good many Bibles, especially those in the universities, had lists of corrections in the back that earlier scholars had discovered and recorded. Purvey made good use of these as well as the commentaries. He wrote:

> Where the Hebrew, by witness of Jerome, or Lyre, and other
> expositors, disagrees from our Latin Bibles, I have set in the
> margin by manner of a gloss, what the Hebrew has and how
> it is understood in a certain place; and I did this most in the
> Psalter, that of all our books disagrees most from the
> Hebrew.[5]

A manuscript still exists with these marginal notes, though
many differences from the Hebrew remain in the text.

Purvey's group consulted commentators other than Jerome and Nicholas of Lyre. He said they gathered "other
doctors and common glosses." He was probably referring
to the *Glossa Ordinaria*, certainly the most common gloss.
It is known that they consulted St. Augustine, Venerable
Bede, and others usually included in the "Common
Gloss."

"Other doctors" refers to a wider group than is usually
meant by the four principal doctors or teachers of the
church—Saints Ambrose, Augustine, Jerome, and Gregory—for more commentators than these were consulted,
among them Peter Comestor, whose surname means
"eater," given him because he is said to have devoured the
Scriptures, and, of course, Robert Grosseteste, who
brought his scientific techniques to Biblical scholarship.
There is evidence also that they consulted *The Golden
Chain* of St. Thomas Aquinas. There were other commentators, hard-working scholars known today only to equally
hard-working scholars: Hugh, Richard, Andrew of St. Vic-
tor (an Augustinian abbey in Paris), as well as Herman of
Cologne, who brought a knowledge of Hebrew with him
when he left Judaism for Christianity.

Many of these older scholars repeated the word or the
phrase Purvey and his group were discussing. These cita-

---

[5][Wyclif Associates], *The Holy Bible*, "Prologue," chap. 15. St. Jerome translated the Psalms twice, once from a Greek text, referred to as the Gallican
Psalter, and again, eight years later, directly from the Hebrew.

tions and the scholars' comments on them helped Purvey decide which reading he wanted to adopt. Gradually and very painstakingly, they compared their Bibles word for word and put together the one they would translate.

Purvey did not wish to translate word for word as Hereford had done. "At the beginning I purposed, with God's help," he wrote, "to make the meaning as true and clear in English as it is in Latin, or more true and more clear than it is in the Latin." They quickly discovered what all translators discover—the Latin vocabulary is restricted compared to the English vocabulary. One word in Latin has to serve for several in English. To be as accurate as possible, Purvey said they consulted "with old grammarians and old divines, of hard words and hard sentences, how they might best be understood and translated."

It is not known if these old grammarians and divines were living contemporaries or other commentators. The Biblical scholarship of the twelfth and thirteenth centuries, like that of Robert Grosseteste, did not continue into the fourteenth. Franciscans were still working in Biblical scholarship, as was Adam Easton, the Benedictine. It is unlikely that the friars were anxious to help anyone connected with John Wyclif, considering his attacks on them, nor would Adam Easton help.

John Purvey and his fellows did not finish the task for twenty years. And still, his translation differs from an accurate translation of the modern Latin text that has benefitted from the nearly six hundred years since Purvey. But no one has ever made a translation without errors, even in the many translations being made today. It was a tremendous accomplishment for John Purvey to make the translation at all. And it was important that he did it when he did. For the people who read English now had a complete Bible of their own. The stories of Adam and Eve, of Abraham and Isaac, of David and Absalom, the rhythms of the Psalms and of the prophets, the sermons of Christ, the visions of St. John all became part of the English idiom. And Wyclif hoped the ordinary priest and the ordinary person could discover for himself the true simplicity and purity of the Bible.

As soon as the church establishment discovered that Wyclif had inspired the new translation of the Bible, they fiercely opposed it. One of the chroniclers wrote:

> This master John Wyclif translated from Latin into English —the tongue of the Angles, not the Angels—the scriptures that Christ gave to the priests and wise men of the church so they could minister to ignorant and weaker souls. By this translation the scriptures have become vulgar, and they are more available to lay, and even to women who can read, than they were to learned scholars, who have a high intelligence. So the pearl of the gospel is scattered and trodden underfoot by swine.[6]

The Franciscans, tracing their own tradition of Biblical scholarship back to Robert Grosseteste, still regarded their order as the chief guardian of textual criticism. They recognized the errors that Purvey and his helpers discovered. They claimed that these errors would appear in the translation with more errors added, for English, they said, was not as exact a language as Latin. The errors upon errors would lead the uneducated English readers to heresy.

Wyclif had no trouble replying:

> The friars with their supporters say it is heresy to write God's law in English and make it known to uneducated people. Englishmen learn Christ's law best in English. Moses heard God's law in his own tongue, so did Christ's apostles. Latin is the mother tongue of Italy as Hebrew is for the Jews.[7]

---

[6]Knighton, *Chronica*, II, 152.

[7]"*de Officio Pastorali*," pp. 429–30.

He had heard a rumor that Anne of Bohemia, Richard's queen, had brought with her from Prague a Bible in two vernacular languages plus Latin. Wyclif wrote:

> It is lawful for the noble Queen of England to have the gospel written in three languages, that is in Czech, and in German, and in Latin; and it would savour of the pride of Lucifer to call her a heretic for such a reason as this. And since the Germans wish in this matter reasonably to defend their own language, so ought the English to defend theirs.[8]

As an additional part of his defense, Wyclif observed that the friars performed Biblical plays in York in which they recited the Lord's Prayer in English.

The sermons of Wyclif that were translated and copied as well as these Bible translations required not only an organization, but money, and lots of it. Who paid for the vellum? And who paid for the ink and the quills? Who paid the professional scribes and rubricators who wrote and decorated the sermons and digests?

The Latin Bibles and commentaries were more expensive than the sermons. One Bible cost as much as two hogs, and two hogs fed a family for a year. A complete Bible and a set of the "Common Gloss" would be equal to the price of a farm.

Wyclif had a pittance from St. Mary's, Lutterworth, but that church also supported John Purvey and another curate, John Horn. The position as regent-master paid Wyclif and Hereford only a little. None of Wyclif's followers at Oxford, Philip Repingdon, or John Aston had any more than Wyclif and Hereford, probably less.

Someone very wealthy must have supported John Wyclif's work at Oxford. Perhaps it was John of Gaunt. The

---

[8]Wyclif, *Polemic Works*, I, 168.

register of some of his disbursements has survived, showing that he was generous to religious institutions. They even show disbursements to his mistress, Katherine Swynford, whom he later married. But the register does not show disbursements to the Reverend Doctor John Wyclif. Of course people in the fourteenth century as well as in the twentieth have been known to spend money without entering it publicly in their books.

Other rich lords, who have come down in history as the Lollard knights, supported Wyclif and his followers. Sir Lewis Clifford, Joan of Kent's messenger to Lambeth Palace, was always sympathetic to Wyclif and his followers. He was not as rich as John of Gaunt, but he was wealthy enough to support the copying and translating at Oxford.

Sir John Montague, eventually earl of Salisbury, was a personal friend of Richard II and later of Nicholas Hereford. Sir John could have supported the work at Oxford. There were others, too. Unquestionably John Wyclif received a great deal of financial help, but there is no way of knowing who gave it to him.

It was not the attack on the Bible that would defeat Wyclif. He was still working on the problem of the Eucharist. His question, "How does the bread change?" and his eventual answer antagonized powerful men whom even John of Gaunt could not fight. Wyclif would have to stand against them alone.

CHAPTER SIXTEEN

Galileo's Ancestor

W HILE Nicholas Hereford was working on his translation and John Purvey was correlating the various
Latin Bibles, Wyclif was investigating the change of
the bread and the wine. He could still find no explanation in
the structure of the macrocosm to explain the mystery.

He was too good a teacher to teach something he could
neither explain nor defend to his students. So he took a
dangerous step: he would have to tell them that the bread and
wine changed at consecration, but that one could not perceive
the change.

Because he was so small, Wyclif probably gave his lectures
from a high, spidery stool so all the students who were crowded into the Austin refectory could see him. They listened
carefully as Wyclif divided perception into physical and mental parts. He told them that they could not physically see
Christ in the consecrated bread because of the nature of the
lens of the eye, an explanation he brought from his study of
optics from Grosseteste and his student, Roger Bacon. The
lens of the eye forms a triangle or cone within the eye itself,
he learned. This cone enables people to see in perspective to a
vanishing point.

Wyclif taught that the bread is broken so many times that
the body of Christ is fractured to a point smaller than the
vanishing point, and it could no longer be physically seen.
This does not mean it was not there, he was careful to explain. It was perceived mentally, by faith.

The bread and wine fed the soul, he said, and the change
that occurred at the consecration had to be understood by the
mind through various analogies. The light of the sun changed

when a person saw it through a prism, yet it was still there and not diminished in force. The flame of a candle, he explained in a second analogy, lights other candles, yet its own flame is not diminished.

His students wanted to hear the authorities who supported these analogies. Wyclif had assembled an impressive list: the Bible, first of all, then St. Augustine, St. Thomas Aquinas, John Duns Scotus, a philosopher of the fourteenth century who carried more weight than Thomas Aquinas, William of Ockham, the brilliant and revolutionary English scientist and thinker of the early fourteenth century, and Richard Fitzralph, whom Wyclif may have met at Merton.

But while investigating the problem historically, Wyclif discovered Berengar, the bishop of Tours in the eleventh century who believed in logic with the same dedication as Wyclif himself. Like Wyclif, Berengar believed that a word was a symbol and that the word corresponded closely to what it symbolized. When Berengar logically analyzed words, he believed he was simultaneously analyzing what the word symbolized. So to Berengar the words of the consecration were as important as the bread and the wine.

Wyclif maintained that in its first thousand years, the church believed as Berengar did, but it changed its beliefs during the reign of Innocent III at the end of the twelfth century, only two hundred years before Wyclif's time. So for his explanation of the mystery of the Eucharist, Wyclif looked to an earlier, simpler age as he had for his vision of Christian poverty.

Wyclif gathered his ideas together later in a work, *On the Eucharist*, but even before he published this explanation, what he had been teaching was known throughout the university. His students—the future priests, bishops, and archbishops—were hearing a doctrine completely different from what the church taught.

In the spring of 1381, Wyclif was lecturing, perched on his stool as usual, but his lecture was interrupted by a pounding on the door of the Austin refectory. His students opened the door and found nailed to it an order from William Berton, now chancellor of Oxford. John Wyclif had known Berton as a friend for twenty-three years. They had been together at Merton and had taken their master's degree the same year. Wyclif was astounded by what he read nailed to the door:

> William de Berton, Chancellor of the University of Oxford, to all our sons to whom this order may come, greetings and absolute obedience to our commands. Some people filled with the advice of an evil spirit ... teach a doctrine that the substance of the material bread and wine that exists before the consecration of the mass, remains after the consecration ... that the body of Christ and His blood are not in substance or in material but only symbolically present.... We have called together many doctors of sacred theology and professors of canon law ... who declare these statements are erroneous and repugnant to the church ... contradictory to universal truth.... No one may hold, teach, defend the before-stated erroneous statements in the schools or outside the university under punishment of imprisonment and suspension of every scholarly action and also under the punishment for a greater excommunication ... that if anyone hear the statements ... that he immediately flee and shun one so teaching as a serpent, spitting venomous poison ... the name of the doctors who especially gave their attention——[1]

Wyclif read the names of the doctors. John Wells, the famous Hammer of Heretics, a name he might expect. Henry Crump, an Irish Cistercian from Baltinglass in County Wicklow. Wyclif had debated with him and knew he had a savage Irish tongue and that he always could be found on the side of power. Then Wyclif saw the name of Robert Rigg. Rigg had been a student of his and Wyclif

---

[1]*Fasciculi Zizaniorum*, pp. 110–13.

thought of him as a special friend, a member of his surrogate family. Wyclif was shocked and confused.

The order did not mention him by name, and it misrepresented what he believed and taught. But there was no doubt
that the order was directed at him—it was nailed to the
door of his lecture hall where he could not miss it.

He felt his friends, William Berton and Robert Rigg, had
betrayed him. No one at the university had told him that
his ideas were being examined. The examination had been
in secret. He had received no word of what was happening
until he heard the nails going into the refectory door.

Of the twelve who signed the order, six friars and two
monks were not friendly toward Wyclif. But the others
were, like Robert Rigg, his friends. He should have heard
something from them.

Wyclif's confusion quickly changed to anger. Friendly or
unfriendly, his examiners had condemned him without a
hearing. As a regent-master he should have been given the
right to a hearing. They were calling him a heretic. He
knew he was no heretic. He was giving an explanation of a
phenomenon in nature based on his observations and years
of study. He was trying to bring knowledge to a mystery
that had not been explained satisfactorily though Thomas
Bradwardine, Robert Grosseteste, and Roger Bacon had
long ago given insights into mathematics and physics by
which the mystery might be explained.

He found out that the twelve examiners had at first split
seven to five for condemnation. The vote had been unani-
mous only after further discussion. "Some friars condemn
what they do not understand," he wrote later, "like the
seven doctors of Oxford who have condemned my doctrine
of the Eucharist. Though they clearly know nothing whatever of what it is, they have proceeded to determine how
Christ is present therein."[2]

---

[2]Wyclif, de Blasphemia, p. 89.

Until 1381 Wyclif's attacks on the church had been political. He had attacked the wealth of the abbeys and monasteries, the wealth of the hierarchy, and the failure of any of them to show responsibility for the poverty around them. He had attacked authority without virtue and wanted to take the church back to its roots, which he considered to be pure. Now Wyclif was probing doctrine, asking new questions. The man who asks new questions is always in danger. New questions give new answers, and new answers challenge the old ones. The establishment always has an interest in maintaining the old answers. It does not want new questions and it will not tolerate new answers. So at this point in the fourteenth century, the establishment decided to silence John Wyclif.

According to Berton's order, any student who heard Wyclif and did not report him would be as guilty as Wyclif was. Adam Stocton had heard Wyclif condemn the two popes and in his notebook had identified Wyclif as "this venerable doctor." Now he scraped off those words and substituted "damnable seducer."[3]

Thomas Netter had been a student "dumb-founded by Wyclif's powerful arguments." Now he wrote:

> When after some time I advanced my studies to the sacred books, it was not long before I discovered him even openly falsifying scriptures. He twisted scriptures with meanings opposed to that of all the commentators. He complicated passages that were self evident, hiding simple truths. Here he changed the sacred words with useless glossing; there he tore them up by the roots.[4]

Later Netter collected all the evidence of heresy that he could find in Wyclif's statements and published the case

---

[3]Aubrey Gwynn, *The English Austin Friars in the Time of Wyclif* (London, 1940), pp. 238–39.

[4]J.A. Robson, *Wyclif and the Oxford Schools* (Cambridge, 1961), p. 224.

against him in *Bundles of the Weeds of Master John Wyclif Together with the Wheat.*

When William Berton issued the decree against him, Wyclif had to make a choice. He could continue to speak out, but as soon as he did, he knew that he would be put in prison; then he could speak no longer. Or, he could remain silent on the mystery of the Eucharist—then he could stay at Oxford and continue to lecture and dispute, but only if he compromised what he believed to be the truth.

A prophet does not shadow his vision with compromise. Wyclif had another avenue open to him. He could appeal the chancellor's order in four ways. As a regent-master he could appeal to the Congregation of regent-masters, but the friars and monks among the regent-masters would surely sustain the condemnation. He could appeal to the Great Congregation of the university. The decision would probably be no different there. The chancellor of the university held power from the pope. He could appeal directly to Urban VI, but Wyclif had published his ideas on Urban VI in a book, *On the Power of the Popes.* He knew copies of everything he said and wrote were sent to Rome. Urban would not be sympathetic to a petitioner who had called him a dog snarling over a bone or had said that the pope's first concern was to glut his appetite and fill his coffers.

He still had one more possibility. The chancellor also held power from the king, and Oxford owed its independence to the king. Wyclif decided his only chance was to appeal to the king, so he sent a petition to Westminster Palace and waited for a reply.

He received an extraordinary one. John of Gaunt would come to Oxford to see him. When Wyclif was being tried at Lambeth Palace, a knight of the garter had been sufficient to bring a message. Now when Wyclif was condemned for his ideas on doctrine, the king of Castile and Leon, the duke of Lancaster, the earl of Lincoln and Leicester himself would answer the petition.

The trip could not have been made in secret. A man's position was advertised by the number of people who accompanied him, and a parade always accompanied John of Gaunt. He could not leave the Savoy Palace without being seen. The duke rode on horseback, the horse decorated with lions passant. Knights and wagons hauling equipment followed him. Messengers carrying his pennant galloped ahead to announce his coming. The parade entered Oxford through the Eastgate. Those who saw it as it passed the Trinitarian Friars, White Hall, and St. Hugh's would expect John of Gaunt to continue up High, through Carfax, then north to the royal retreat at Woodstock, a trip he had made many times before.

Instead they saw the parade turn right on Queen's Street just after it passed St. High's. Soon all of Oxford knew that John of Gaunt had stopped at Queen's College to visit Master John Wyclif.

Modern historians have wondered about this visit—that the king's brother would visit someone who was condemned for heresy is incredible. But the chronicle written at St. Mary de Pré, Leicester, is more accurate than the guess of the best modern historian, and this chronicle said John of Gaunt made the trip. In the chronicle, the attitude of the author—either Henry Knighton or his continuator—toward the duke now changes. Before the visit, he had called John of Gaunt a traitor and adulterer, the latter in reference to his unchanging love for Katherine Swynford. After the visit, the author called him "a brave soldier, wise counsellor, and faithful son of the church." This change of attitude is typical of the medieval belief that what a man did demonstrated his character. John of Gaunt condemned the heretical view of John Wyclif, and this act would be enough to show a change in the duke's character and effect a change in the author of the chronicle.

John of Gaunt knew that the learned doctor who had served him well had questioned a central belief of

Christianity, a belief to which the duke subscribed without question. But John of Gaunt was no scholar. He could not follow John Wyclif's careful reasoning nor his scientific analogies, and he had never heard of Berengar of Tours.

But he had been told about the chancellor of Oxford's decree. As a medieval lord, John of Gaunt felt he was responsible for the spiritual and physical well-being of those who served him, an old-fashioned idea in the fourteenth century, one that had been observed only in the mythical court of King Arthur.

But John of Gaunt was an old-fashioned man. He had already protected the physical well-being of John Wyclif at St. Paul's Cathedral and indirectly at Lambeth Palace. But he was the kind of man who felt it more important to protect Wyclif's spiritual well-being.

Their difference in age or learning was no longer important, so he ordered John Wyclif to abide by the chancellor's orders and be silent about the mystery of the Eucharist—to allow it to remain a mystery. Wyclif apparently told the duke that he could not remain silent altogether, but he promised he would not employ the terms "the substance of the bread and wine" if he wrote in English. By making this promise Wyclif inferred he would communicate only with those who shared his theological training and could understand the careful Latin vocabulary of religious disputation. John of Gaunt accepted the promise and returned to London.

John Wyclif was now under a "suspension of every scholarly activity." He could no longer lecture at the university nor enter a classroom. He left his room at Queen's College, his lecture hall in the Augustinian priory and his life in Oxford.

Departures are the most melancholy of remembrances, and John Wyclif's life had been relatively free of them. But leaving Oxford was probably the most traumatic experience of his life. He suffered the trauma of a teacher whose teaching, the focus of his life, was taken away from him. Only once in all his writings does Wyclif express his feelings about a place he had been. Remembering Oxford he wrote:

> For many reasons Oxford University is called the vineyard of the Lord, and deservedly. It was founded by holy fathers, situated in an agreeable place, watered by rivers and springs, surrounded by meadows and lawns, and stretching beyond it are valleys and dales. On every side the hills and uplands protect it from stormy winds, and nearby are lush farms and pastures. I can describe it with one name, the Elysian Fields, luxuriant and unsurpassed, most fittingly a dwelling place for gods, and rightly called the House of God and the Gateway to Heaven.[5]

Wyclif walked passed St. Michael's and through the Northgate for the last time and became the spiritual ancestor of Galileo. He had hoped to use his science to support his theology, but he could not unless he changed his theology. That change was impossible for him. Without wishing to, John Wyclif had split science and religion. That split widened with Copernicus and Galileo and has widened even further in the six hundred years since Wyclif started his forty-six-mile walk to Lutterworth.

Wyclif left behind him Philip Repingdon, John Aston, Lawrence Steven, Robert Rigg, and Nicholas Hereford, all of whom were still sympathetic. They and other masters would make sure his ideas would be heard and understood in the lectures and disputations at Oxford. His followers hoped that in ten years a new generation of Oxfordians could revolutionize England when they took the places of William Courtenay as bishop of London and of Simon Sudbury as archbishop and chancellor of England.

---

[5]Wyclif, *Opera Minora*, p. 18.

Wyclif probably took about two and one-half days to walk to Lutterworth. He walked through the town of Rugby and turned on to the Lutterworth Road where both roads cross Watling Street. The meeting of the roads was marked by a gibbet for local hangings.

This was an agricultural area and Wyclif saw spring crops well out of the ground—beans and peas, rye, wheat, and barley—all in open fields typical of Midland farming. Now in the distance he could see the tower of his parish church, St. Mary's, its spire forty-seven feet into the sky and all the more visible because Lutterworth was on a rise.

The road was uphill from here. South of the Spital Bridge over the River Swift, Wyclif saw the Lodge Mill where the townspeople brought their grain for grinding each day. Then at the base of High Street he passed the Hospital of St. John, which had achieved a reputation from Holywell Spring. The water of the spring was so full of minerals that travelers thought it was practically undrinkable, but most people stopped anyway. Water that strong would undoubtedly cure anything, they thought.

St. Mary's Church was not far from the river. And looking up High Street, Wyclif saw thatched houses, mostly single story, the better ones of brick and plaster framed in timber beams. High and the streets crossing it were lined with yews.

Most of the properties paid rent to Theodore de Verdun, Lord Ferrers of Groby. Lord Ferrers also held about a thousand acres worked by thirty-six tenant farmers who lived in the town. In addition, the prior of St. John's Hospital held 75 acres in his own right and 105 acres which maintained the hospital.

The people of the town already knew Wyclif, of course. He was their parish priest, at least in name, and undoubtedly had been there to give the sermon on important feast days. John Purvey and John Horn were the curates, but most of the parish duties fell to John Horn since both Wyclif and Purvey were busy at Oxford.

The men of Lutterworth—John Feilding, William Wilner, Walter Stephen, William Bonfaunts, Thomas Baker—all knew that something Wyclif had said or written had been condemned in some way. But they also knew he was a John of Gaunt man, and this was John of Gaunt country, as the duke had a castle a few miles north at Leicester.

The men of Leicester worked too hard raising rye and barley to know or care about theological arguments far away at Oxford, but they were proud to have a famous priest in Lutterworth.

Lord Ferrers was modernizing the church. He had brought a special glazer to Lutterworth from the west country who was making stained glass windows. A painter was doing a fresco of Richard II and the duke of Lancaster, leaving a place on the wall vacant. When the king married, his queen would be painted there. Negotiations for a queen were in progress, but his marriage to Anne of Bohemia was still a year away. The fresco of the Last Judgment seen today over the chancel arch was not painted until one hundred years later.

John Wyclif settled into the rectory. He had more parish duties now that he was living there, but John Horn still took care of as many of them as he could. Wyclif continued writing, especially defending himself against his condemnation in a work called *A Confession*, and he had been working on his own Biblical commentaries over the years. Nicholas Hereford, now a regent-master, was lecturing at Oxford, but he came up to Lutterworth every chance he had to continue with his translation. John Purvey transferred the work of editing a text of the Latin Bible to Lutterworth. In June 1381, they all were working too hard to pay much attention to stories of a rebellion in Essex and Kent in the east.

CHAPTER SEVENTEEN

Riot, Rebellion, and Retreat

*F*OBBING, ESSEX, IS A fishing village down river from London, where the Thames widens to form its mouth. Thomas, the baker of Fobbing, was an angry man on the first of June 1381. So was William Gildebourne and about one hundred of their fellow artisans in nearby Corringham and Stanford le Hope—fishermen, carpenters, boatsmen, and rope-makers. For the third time Parliament had authorized poll taxes. These men had paid it three times, and they weren't about to pay it again.

Not that they couldn't afford it, even now when the tax was raised to a shilling a person. William Gildebourne ran a band of seventy-two sheep and rented over one hundred acres of good land. The food he and his wife ate cost only two shillings a week.

The anger of the Essexmen had been growing for a long time. The taxes that they paid went toward the defeat at St. Malo of that arrogant John of Gaunt, who rode around calling himself a king. Now the French were invading England. They captured the Isle of Wight and raided the towns of Winchelsea and Lewes on the Sussex coast. They burned down the town of Hastings. In the west, the Spanish had attacked Cornwall and burned Fowey, a busy western seaport.

If it had not been for John Philipot, the wealthy London victualler, nothing would have prevented the French from coming up the Thames and raiding Fobbing, the Essexmen believed. With his own money, they knew, Philipot had outfitted ships and recaptured the English vessels the French took at Wight and then captured French and Castilian ships just for good measure. And he ran John the Mercer, a Scottish pirate, back to Scotland where he belonged.

What good was accomplished by paying all of these taxes if John Philipot had to handle the king's business at his own expense? Of course it was not the king's fault. His advisors were stealing all of his money. Everyone knew that, the Essexmen agreed.

John Bamptoun was also angry. He was one of the king's commissioners who had come from Westminster to the town of Brentwood, Essex, northwest of Fobbing. This latest poll tax had collected only three-quarters as much as Parliament had originally estimated, and the commissioners were authorized to go from shire to shire. If they found people whom they thought had not paid, the commissioners could put them in jail until they did pay.

Thomas Baker, William Gildebourne, and their angry friends marched determinedly to Brentwood. They told John Bamptoun that they had paid all the taxes they were going to pay. Anger met anger, and John Bamptoun ordered his two sergeants-at-arms to arrest every one of the protestors.

The swollen anger of the Essexmen now had a focus. It was John Bamptoun and the sergeants. With fists, scythes, rakes, and shovels they drove the king's commissioner and the sergeants out of Brentwood. The word spread, and more angry men gathered at Brentwood. Support for Thomas Baker grew.

When Sir Robert Bealknap in Westminster learned what had happened in Brentwood, he rode from the king's palace as fast as he could spur his horse. In the seven years since he had led the mission to Bruges with John Wyclif, he had become chief justice of the Common Bench and now had the special authority to try and hang troublemakers who defied the king's tax commissioners. But when Sir Robert arrived at Brentwood, the anger of the large crowd smoldering there exploded at him. To save his own life, he rode back to Westminster as fast as he could.

Now Thomas Baker, William Gildebourne, and the Essexmen were excited with a new discovery—acting together, they could exercise immediate power and achieve immediate results. They had certainly realized immediate results against the king's commissioner, the sergeants, and now Sir Robert Bealknap.

When men act as a mob, each man makes the man next to him stronger. Their excitement balloons, but the personal responsibility for what they do shrivels. It is fractured, actually, among all of them, so a man is not only very strong, he is also anonymous. It is the mob, not the individual, that possesses the power.

The exercise of this kind of power was a novelty to the artisans. It was like a drug, and one that addicts very quickly. They had to experience it again, and they did. They found three of John Bamptoun's clerks and beheaded them. They carried the heads around the town as proof of their power.

In Brentwood the men discovered some villagers who had given Sir Robert Bealknap testimony against them. The men exercised their new strength again. They beheaded the witnesses and destroyed their houses.

What is known as the Peasants' Revolt of 1381 had begun. The chronicles of the time called it "The Rising," a more accurate name. Today it would be called a riot.

An established political institution is able to store power like gunpowder, waiting to be exploded. In the fourteenth century the institution was made up of the fourteen-year-old king, Richard II, his chief justice, his commissioners, and his sergeants-at-arms. These officers represented the stored power of the government, its residual power.

In Brentwood these officers were overcome by the exercise of immediate power, a power that exploded spontaneously, set off by the anger of Thomas Baker, William

Gildebourne, and the rest toward John Bamptoun and Sir Robert Bealknap.

In the twentieth century, the police or the military exercise the stored power of political institutions. In the fourteenth century, there was no police force. The sergeants-at-arms were protected by chained mail and were armed with small, round shields about two feet in diameter and swords. At Brentwood, three sergeants had fought against two or three hundred angry men. Shields and swords were useless.

A village like Brentwood or Fobbing had a policeman of sorts, a common sergeant. Usually he was also the town crier employed by the mayor. The common sergeants of these villages depended on volunteers to help them.

To the north of Brentwood was the relatively large city of Norwich with a population of about thirteen thousand. It had sixteen constables who were no more effective than the sergeants in Brentwood. In London with its sixty thousand people, each ward hired its own watch like common sergeants or constables. In London the watch was mostly Flemish. When the watch tried to enforce the curfew law and keep people off the streets at night, they had to be ready to protect themselves. A man on a London street at night, perhaps stealing water from the conduit at Cheap, would not hesitate to beat the watch with what the law called "a blunt instrument," or if he was truly desperate, he might stab the watch. To really enforce the law, the watch had to depend on volunteers. The "hue and cry," an informal posse of citizens, helped the watch capture a suspected criminal and then took him to one of London's five prisons. A man could be fined for refusing to join the hue and cry, but few refused.

But the hue and cry carried no weapons. If a man wore chain mail or a breastplate and carried a sword and shield, by law he had better be a knight or at least a squire. If there had been knights in Brentwood, Sir Robert Bealknap could have gotten help and would not have been run out of town.

But even in London, no body of knights was readily available to the chief justice. John of Gaunt and an army of his knights were in the north negotiating with the Scots. Sir Henry Percy, earl of Northumberland and marshall of England, was patrolling the border between England and Scotland with more knights. A group of knights were in the south of England waiting to embark for France. These groups accounted for those immediately available.

Sir Robert Bealknap had no idea he would be needing knights, anyway. But if he wanted them, he would have to go to the king, who would send messengers to lords in various castles around the country. They would in turn send messengers to individual knights who owed them allegiance. Thomas de la Mare, abbot of St. Albans, was pledged to supply fifteen knights to the king, for example, but it would have taken him several days to round them up.

So Thomas Baker and his friends won the first explosion of power with their scythe handles and fists, but an explosion is not a revolution. Until the men of Essex had an organization with power in reserve, stored and ready to use when and where they needed it, they had no revolution. They had a riot, uncoordinated and disorganized. To have a true revolution the men of Essex had to transfer power to themselves from somewhere in the establishment, hopefully from the king.

Across the Thames another sergeant-at-arms, John Legge, aroused the anger of the people of Gravesend. Robert Belling, a serf on the estate of Sir Simon Burley, tutor to Richard II, had run away from the Burley estate to the town of Gravesend. In Gravesend, as in any town, he was automatically free and could be paid for his work.

John Legge and another sergeant found him in Gravesend. But the townspeople supported Robert Belling and felt that once he had entered Gravesend, he was a freeman. Anyway, they thought, serfdom should be abolished.

John Legge told them that they could free Robert Belling, and it would cost them only three hundred pounds of silver (about seventy-two thousand dollars). It was a ridiculous price, as much as a man earned in a lifetime of work.

No silver, no freedom said John Legge. Legge bound Robert Belling with chains and took him to a cell in Rochester Castle on the road to Canterbury. Then Legge returned up the road to Gravesend to arrest those who had taken the part of the serf. He found the men of Gravesend had joined together and blocked the road. He had to turn back. Like their brothers in Essex, these men experienced the novelty of exercising power, and they, too, became drugged with the new feeling. They marched down the Canterbury Road to attack Rochester Castle and free Robert Belling.

The main fortification of Rochester Castle towered ninety-three feet above the ground, and its walls were twelve feet thick. In 1087 King William Rufus had been unable to successfully besiege this castle, though the defenders had to surrender when their food supply became contaminated. In the thirteenth century, King John had taken three months to mine the wall before the castle surrendered.

The craftsmen, artisans, and laborers of Gravesend stood shoulder to shoulder at the base of this great keep with others who had come from Rochester. Sir John Newton, the captain of the jail, defended his prisoner from ninety-three feet above them—but only for half a day. The vehemence and frenzy of the mob was apparently more fearsome to him than the armies of two kings had been to his predecessors. Robert Belling was released, and Sir John Newton was made a prisoner of the mob.

Twenty-five miles farther south at Canterbury, other angry men exploded in a third riot. Two pages of court indictments, drawn up afterward, listed what they did:

Felonously killed four persons and carried away goods and chattel. Carried away muniments to the value of a thousand pounds. Burnt books, records, and muniments of our Lord the King's Crown.[1]

Sacking and looting Canterbury and other towns of Kent, the rioters revenged themselves on whomever they disliked locally. They were a mob, easily led, rampaging from one place to another, fascinated by their own looting and violence. In these early days of the Rising, the rioters had no issues. They only asked of whomever they met, "Are you for us or against?" as the mob in London had asked four years earlier, the mob that William Courtenay had prevented from destroying Savoy Palace. Henry Twysden and other Canterbury men strode to Archbishop Sudbury's prison at Maidstone, and as their indictment read: "Felonously broke into same and released and felonously set at liberty all the prisoners there imprisoned." Among the prisoners felonously released was John Ball, a tall priest with a red, flowing beard.

John Ball changed the nature of the riots in Kent. In June 1381 he was already well known. He had been in the Benedictine monastery of St. Mary's in York, but in the 1360s he had left the monastery and had begun preaching informally throughout England. He preached that a parishioner should give tithes and offerings to a priest or bishop only if he were richer than the priest or bishop. Unworthy priests were not entitled to gifts and tithes, and unworthy lords were not entitled to rents.

John Ball and John Wyclif had arrived at the same conclusions independently—the traveling preacher intuitively, the Oxford master by scholarship and logic. Neither was popular with the lords of the church. Very soon John Ball was forbidden to preach in any church, so he used the

---

[1]Reville, pp. 185-86.

meadows, roads, and market squares. Archbishop Islip had sent him a summons, but Ball ignored it. He was automatically excommunicated. Archbishop Sudbury, after he was installed in Lambeth Palace, finally captured John Ball, and since April 1381 Ball had been in the Maidstone jail.

The news of the revolt in Essex reached him in jail. Even before he was released, John Ball had letters smuggled to the rioters. One read:

> John Ball, priest of St. Mary, greets well all the people and bids them, in the name of the Trinity: Father, Son, and Holy Ghost, to stand firmly together in truth. Give Truth help, and Truth will help you. Now Pride rules in honor, and Greed is thought to be wisdom, and lechery is shameless and gluttony is blameless. Envy rules with reason, and Sloth is in high season. May God save you. Now is the time![2]

As soon as Henry Twysden and his men released John Ball, the priest started preaching around Kent. The rioters became rebels and took the first step toward revolution, for John Ball gave them a cause beyond local destruction and revenge.

John Ball preached that in the beginning all people were created equal. If God had wanted to create serfs, He would have done so in the Garden of Eden. He would have shown who was to be a serf and who was to be a lord. Serfdom was brought into the world by the oppression of men, he said, and was against the will of God.

John Ball gave to the revolt what every revolt needs—a slogan, one that is short, easy to remember and repeat. This slogan they had heard before:

> When Adam delved and Eve span,
> Who was then the gentleman?

---

[2]Walsingham, *Historia Anglicana*, II, 33-34.

The slogan lasted and was repeated by rebels for sixty years, long after John Ball had been executed. Even illuminations of the couplet showed up in manuscripts, Adam turning the ground over with his shovel, Eve making thread by rotating a spindle between her thumb and forefinger.

The lords had separated the people from their king, John Ball explained. And when rebels challenged anyone now, they asked, "Are you for King Richard and the true commons?" A rumor spread through Kent that the king was on their side; certainly, from him they would receive justice.

John Ball had changed the direction of the Rising of 1381. The action of the rioters was no longer fixed on immediate goals—a local house to be looted, a witness to be killed, an insult to be avenged. John Ball gave them a cause—freedom from serfdom and an end to all lordship but that of the king.

Now they were rebels with long-term goals and righteous principles to motivate them. John Ball was their voice. And they marched toward their goal with a new leader, Wat Tyler. Not much is known about him. His full name was Walter, and the chronicles, whose authors opposed the rebellion, say that his last name indicated his craft. Like most of the rebels, he was an artisan, not a peasant. He was a skilled craftsman who cut slate into tile shingles and laid the shingles on a roof.

Jean Froissart in his chronicles of *England, France, and Spain* said that Wat Tyler had been a soldier in France. He may have been; a good many were. But no other chronicle confirms Froissart. The chronicle from St. Mary de Pré described Tyler as "a skilled fellow with good intelligence," but it added, "If only it had been applied to a rightful purpose."

Wat Tyler had a plan for the Rising. The rebels would rid themselves of those traitorous advisors who stood between the people, who were the true commons, and their king, whom he thought was on their side. Wat Tyler was not a political theorist, but if the king was on their side, the rebels had the stored power, the residual power which they needed. They had a true revolution.

Wat Tyler tried to coordinate what had been isolated riots. He sent messengers to the north to Essex and Suffolk and to the South, through Kent, Surrey, and Sussex. Rioters who had thought they were acting alone streamed into Canterbury to join him and thus became rebels. They burst into Canterbury Cathedral and warned the monks that their archbishop, Simon Sudbury, was one of those traitors who stood between the people and their king. He would die a traitor's death. The monks had better elect a new archbishop. The rebels made the mayor and the bailiffs of Canterbury swear to be loyal to King Richard and the true commons, the people.

King Richard, Simon Sudbury, the king's chancellor, Sir Robert Hales, the king's treasurer, William Courtenay, Sir Thomas Percy, and others were at Windsor Castle discussing ways to combat the rebellion. Although he was only fourteen years old in 1381, the king was expected to act as a mature young man. The chronicles indicate that he did.

However, no leader, experienced or inexperienced, can act without accurate information. The king could discover what was really happening in Kent only through messengers. No other technique of communication was available. So he sent messengers on horseback to Kent, all carrying his banner.

The rebels told these messengers that they were true to King Richard and would save him from the traitors to the kingdom. In an exchange of messages, the king told the rebels that he wished to hear their grievances in person and would confer with them at Blackheath, a meadow across the Thames from the Tower of London. The rebels agreed, and the king and his counsellors hurried from Windsor to the Tower.

The king had focused the attention of the rebels on London, but from across the countryside south of the Thames, serfs, tenant farmers, and craftsmen jammed the roads to the capital. London is sixty miles from Canterbury, and in two days Wat Tyler and the rebels covered the distance to the suburban town of Southwark at the southern end of London Bridge, the only bridge into the city. London Bridge was actually a street one thousand feet long. There was a drawbridge, but there were also 138 shops and houses built wall-to-wall, a tavern at each end, and a church dedicated to St. Thomas à Becket.

But when they arrived, the rebels could travel only about one-third of the way down the bridge, for the draw section was up after the seventh pier and a large stone gate at the London end was closed. They were forced to remain in Southwark, a community of chapels, churches, rich homes, and famous inns like the Tabard, where Chaucer had begun his fictional pilgrimage. (The Tabard stood until the eighteenth century, when it burned down.)

Close to Southwark was Stewside, where houses of prostitution furnished an income to William Wykeham and the diocese of Winchester and helped support the bishop's new college at Oxford. The women, known as "Winchester geese," were burned out of their houses, symbols of lechery in high places to the rioters.

Not far away was Marshalsea Prison; its warden, Sir Richard Imworth, was known for his cruelty even in an age when all life was cruel. Before the rebels arrived, he escaped and found sanctuary in Westminster Abbey across the river. The rebels broke into the jail and released all the prisoners. Some of the rebels then continued up river to Lambeth Palace, hoping to find Archbishop Sudbury. They missed him, but they burned much of what they found— records, books, vestments, cloths—and destroyed the kitchen and wine celler. What wine they did not drink they poured on the ground, according to one of the chronicles.

Most of the southern rebels assembled on Blackheath, an open area where Greenwich Park exists today. Across the river in the Tower, the king and his advisors depended on the messengers and rumor. They knew the roads north and south of the city were clogged with rebels. Froissart reports that when Joan of Kent and her lady-in-waiting were coming from the shrine of St. Thomas à Becket in Canterbury, they were allowed to pass through the rebel throngs because Joan was still popular, though no longer a striking beauty. But the congestion on the roads prevented the king from calling on anyone for help. The watches inside the city were too few in number to give any protection. The king alone would have to deal with the rebels, for he had no way to oppose them.

On the morning of June 13, Corpus Christi Day, the king was true to his word. He left the Tower with several of his lords and traveled down the river to Greenwich to confer with the rebels. As usual, the statistics in the chronicles were exaggerated by the writers' fears of the rebels. Froissart estimated that there were ten thousand rebels along the riverside, sixty thousand altogether at Blackheath. The St. Albans chronicler, either Thomas Walsingham or a continuator, was even more excited and gave the number at two hundred thousand. Looking back, the true number of rebels at Blackheath is difficult to estimate. Even five thousand along the shore would have been enough to inspire fear as the king and his lords rowed by.

The king was advised against landing so they rowed up and down off the Blackheath shore. The leaders of the rebels shouted demands across the water to the barge. They called for death to the lords who stood between them and the king. Leading their list was John of Gaunt, who was still on the Scottish border negotiating a peace. The rebels had already threatened the archbishop of Canterbury, who was in the barge with the king. Also on their list were Sir Robert Hales, the treasurer, John Bamptoun, and Sir Robert Bealknap. They also asked for the death of William Courtenay, their hero only three and one-half years earlier.

Neither side communicated satisfactorily, even with their voices carrying across the water, and soon the king was rowed back to the Tower. Wat Tyler sent his demands by messenger and waited through the day for a reply.

That night, John Ball preached a rousing sermon to the rebels camped at Blackheath. Froissart reported a typical Ball sermon which established the principles for the revolt, and it was possibly similar to the one heard at Blackheath:

> We all come from one father and one mother, Adam and Eve. How can they say or prove that they are greater lords than we are? How can they make us earn the money and work for what they spend on themselves? They wear silks and velvets edged with fur, and we wear poor clothes. They have wine, spices, and white bread. We eat what is left and drink water. We have the aches and pains, the rain and the wind while we work in the fields, and they are comfortable in their beautiful houses.[3]

Across the river in the Tower, the king and his council learned what John Ball was preaching. It reminded them of John Wyclif. One of those who heard it was Bishop William Courtenay, and he began to see a pattern to the Rising. It seemed to him that the heretical ideas of John Wyclif had been translated into action—the Rising was a conspiracy centered at Oxford where those heresies began. At that moment, Courtenay's life was safe only if he remained in the Tower. But the day would come when he could combat this heresy, and he resolved to do so.

The next day, London Bridge was still raised, and the stone gate into the city was still closed. The king's advisors had little advice to give the young man facing his first crisis, and only a week away from the fourth anniversary of

---

[3]Dobson, p. 371.

his coronation. All those in the Tower knew that enough Londoners were sympathizing with the rebels to make their own situation precarious. Finally, William Walworth, the lord mayor, suggested that they send three aldermen across the Thames to negotiate, for no other alternative seemed open.

After the aldermen conferred with the rebels, one of the rebellion sympathizers inside the city, probably Walter Sibyle, an alderman himself, ordered the drawbridge lowered and the stone gates opened. The Kentishmen rushed in and were joined by friendly Londoners. They found that they had a common enemy—John of Gaunt. They joined forces, roared through the city, and poured out the city wall through Ludgate and over the Fleet River bridge. As they passed the prison, they released the prisoners, then clamored down Fleet Street into the Strand to the Savoy Palace.

The duke was not there, of course. Costanza, his Spanish princess, had fled earlier to Leicester, and the staff of servants for the palace had deserted it for their own safety. The portcullis was down, but the mob easily broke through the small gates beside it. Roger Leeche, a sergant-at-arms who remained by his post at the gate, was killed immediately. The duke's physician, William Appulton, a Franciscan friar and one of the most famous doctors in London, had also remained behind and was killed. The keeper of the wardrobe grabbed a single bed-hanging, ran through the orchards and gardens to the river, and furiously rowed to safety.

The rebels charged into the Great Hall and the apartments connected to it—the chancery, the wardrobe, the library, and the treasure chamber. They ripped the tapestries from the walls and shredded the cloths and covers they found in the wardrobe chests. They chopped to pieces the headboards of the beds, which were decorated with the various family coats-of-arms—Plantaganet, Lancaster, Castile, and Leon. The gold and silver plate were almost pure metal, easily bent but not easily broken. They hammered what they could and tossed what was left out the windows. Outside, others were burning benches, tables, chests, stools, and the illuminated manuscripts of the duke's library.

"No looting, no robbery," the rebels shouted. They were no longer rioters. They were fighters for a cause—freeing the king from the evil John of Gaunt. They were exercising the king's justice. Their purpose disciplined them. The gold, silver, and jewels that were thrown down to the lawn were then tossed into the river or pushed into the sewer openings that led to the river.

One of the rebels hid some silver in his loose tunic and ran away with it. Those who saw him enforced the rebel discipline. They bound him and threw him on one of the fires. Soon the palace itself was ablaze. The rebels who were still ripping out the interior of the quadrangle had to flee. In the armory among the lances, swords, and armor, some of them found three barrels filled with a dark gray substance. They smelled and tasted it, but no one could identify it. They let the barrels roll into a blazing room and fled outside. The barrels were full of gunpowder; a wing of the house exploded.

Unknown to the rest, about thirty-two rebels had discovered the duke's wine cellar beneath the palace. The barrels of wine were too heavy to carry outside, so they stayed inside and drank all they could. They did not notice that the fire and explosions had blocked the entrance to their cellar. They were trapped.

The chronicle of St. Mary de Pré said that for seven days following, Londoners visited the smoldering ruins of the castle. They could still hear the rebels beneath the ruins crying for help, praying for forgiveness, begging to be let out. No one helped them. The cries gradually weakened, then finally died out altogether.

CHAPTER EIGHTEEN

Attacks on the Monasteries

S EVENTY MILES TO THE NORTH of Savoy Palace was the monastery of St. Edmund's located in Bury, Suffolk. John of Cambridge, a prior, was acting as abbot. He had heard rumors that a mob led by John Wrawe was approaching the monastery.

John Wrawe was a priest from Ringsfield, a village in Suffolk, and had taken over as leader of the rioters on the Essex-Suffolk border. He quickly earned a reputation for violence by aiming the rioters' vehemence from one local object of hate to another but gave his followers no long-term aspirations as John Ball had done in Kent and Blackheath.

In Essex, just south of the border of Suffolk, the mob sacked the manor house of Richard Lyons, whose wealth had been confiscated by the Good Parliament five years earlier. Now he owned a chain of combined taverns and brothels, a mixture that in the history of enterprise has never been known to fail. In addition, he had been appointed sheriff by the king and was in charge of properties that lapsed to the crown for any reason. As sheriff, he was immune from any kind of prosecution.

John of Cambridge was no friend to Richard Lyons, but he knew that any riots in East Anglia would eventually be directed at the Abbey of St. Edmund's in Bury. It had happened that way sixty years earlier.

The abbey owned forty-three farms which supported the monks. The buildings of St. Edmund's were maintained by the craftsmen of the town, who had to give their skills for free, bound by agreements that dated before William the

Conqueror. Compared to other landowners, the monastery used a high percent of serfs. Most landowners used tenant farmers, sharecroppers who were somewhat better off than serfs since they could leave the land when they wished. Few left, because they had no other way of making a living.

The anger of the rioters sixty years before had been bequeathed to their descendents, who wanted title to the land they worked and freedom from any service to the monastery. They had heard priests say that they ought to have these rights. One family had to work twice a week for the monastery and give the monastery two hens and ten eggs a year for rent. Another family had to bind and cart the monastery hay during harvest when their own hay should have been cut, and then give the monks a chicken and five eggs for the privilege. The monastery was much richer than they were. If the monks wanted people to work their crops, why didn't they pay wages? They heard a priest say that was how it should be.

John of Cambridge knew the anger of these families. He knew that the sixty monks of St. Edmund's, even with their ninety-three servants, could not defend the monastery if John Wrawe and the rioters attacked them. So John fled to a daughter house at Mildenhall, twelve miles to the northwest.

He had been right to worry about his safety. The morning of June 13, while the king and his advisors had been rowing from the Tower to Blackheath, John Wrawe and his followers had crossed from Essex into Suffolk on their way to St. Edmund's. They had stopped at the town of Cavendish and decided to take revenge on Sir John Cavendish, a chief justice of the King's Bench, whose family had given the town its name. It had been Sir John's duty to collect the multitudinous fees levied by the monastery on its tenants. For the privilege of giving his daughter in marriage, a tenant had to pay the monastery a pound (more than $200). Five shillings ($50) were added to the fee if it could be proven that the daughter had fornicated before her marriage.

If any farmer left his fields, which were leased from the monastery, and went into a town to work for wages, Sir John collected a fine from him. If the son of a farmer wanted to join the monastery as a monk, he paid Sir John a mark ($175) for the right. Of course, the son of a serf could not become a monk no matter what he paid.

Sir John Cavendish enforced the law which said that everyone must bring his grain to the abbey mill to be ground into meal, and when the meal was made into dough, it must be brought to the abbey oven to be baked into bread. If Sir John found a hand mill in someone's home, it was confiscated with any oxen or horses the owner might possess. John Cavendish also saw that all wool was fulled at the monastery fulling mill, which charged the tenants for fulling their own cloth.

Before the rioters had arrived at Cavendish, Sir John had deserted his house and emptied it of all valuables. But Ralph Somerton, a dyer, told the rioters he had seen the valuables being hidden in the belfry of the local church. The rioters found them there, and carefully divided the velvets, worth more than twenty-six pounds, a silver candlestick worth seven pounds, and other valuables, so that all received an equal share. Then they resumed their march toward Bury.

A group of seventeen led by Geoffrey Parfay, a vicar from Sudbury, broke from the group and went to Thetford, twelve miles north. They collected forty gold marks from the mayor on the threat that John Wrawe would burn Thetford to the ground if he did not pay. A third group at Lakenheath, twenty miles northwest of Bury, accidentally discovered Sir John Cavendish walking across a field. He saw the mob and ran to the bank of the River Ouse where a boat was tied up. He could escape if he could cross the river to Ely. But Katherine Gamen, standing nearby, saw him running for the boat with the crowd howling after him. She shoved the boat into the current with her foot. In the fourteenth century, few people knew how to swim and Sir John

Cavendish was not one of them. The mob caught him as he frantically ran up and down the river's edge. The rioters beheaded him there, carried his head to Bury, and fixed it on a pillory in the market square in front of the monastery gate.

That evening, John of Cambridge also tried to escape from Mildenhall across the river to Ely. He, too, ran into roving bands. A group chased him into the woods about three miles from Newmarket. They formed a cordon around the woods and drove him out with the same system they used to hunt deer. Then they bound him with rope and took him to Bury.

Thomas Halesworth, an alderman of Bury, Robert West-broun, a member of the mercers' guild, and Geoffrey Denham, a land-owner, all leading citizens of the town, decided to join forces with John Wrawe and the rioters. Thomas Halesworth saw the riot as a chance to free Bury of monastery control once and for all and to obtain for its citizens the same rights that other towns in England enjoyed. After all, Bury was the fifteenth most populous town in England and was a prosperous center of the wool trade, but no office in the town government could be filled without permission of the abbot, and the abbey could even coin its own money and force all those living in the town and surrounding area to use it.

The rioters brought John of Cambridge into Bury. Thomas Halesworth and the townsmen voted with the rioters to execute him, and John of Cambridge's head was added to that of John Cavendish on the pillory.

Then they went to the monastery, into the cloister, and demanded to see John of Lakenheath, the keeper of the monastery land titles. When he appeared, he had to identify himself, for none of the townsmen knew him. He asked them what they wanted.

"Your immediate death," one of the townsmen is reported to have answered.

"I am prepared to die and willingly, provided the monastery should not be harmed because of me," he replied. He was dragged to the marketplace, where his head was added to the others.

The townspeople of Bury negotiated with the monks in the market square near the pillory, while the three heads stared lifelessly down on them. The men of Bury demanded that the monastery surrender all the charters of deeds that prescribed the obligations they owed the monastery. They also wanted the jewels of the shrine of St. Edmund, one of the richest shrines in England, to be given them as a guarantee that they would have those charters within forty days.

They demanded the release of Edmund Bloumfield from the monastery jail. He had been elected abbot and was sympathetic to the townspeople, but was soon deposed and imprisoned. The townspeople wanted him freed in time to celebrate the feast of St. John the Baptist, June 14. The monks agreed to all these demands, and for a short time, the townsmen of Bury were as free as Londoners.

St. Albans was sixty miles to the southwest in Hertfordshire. Like Bury, the town of St. Albans was under the control of a stern and wealthy Benedictine monastery. William Grindcobbe, William Cadingdon, Richard of Wallingford, and one of the monks rode hard for the twenty miles from St. Albans to London. Grindcobbe heard that in London Wat Tyler was freeing the serfs and hoped he could do the same for the townspeople of St. Albans. After all, Grindcobbe came from a family of burgesses, he had received a good grammar-school education from the monks themselves, and he could read and write legal documents in French, Latin, and English. He owned four houses in St. Albans, and his brother was a cloth dyer and guildsman in London.

Grindcobbe thought that the men of St. Albans had as good a case for freedom as the serfs of Kent. They had to harvest the abbey grain, make its beer, repair its walls, and clean its ditches. A tenant farmer worked 280 days of the year for the abbey and still had to pay rent. If a farmer did not fulfill his duties, the subcellarer of the monastery confiscated his plow, his cart, and his horse, and thus made him a beggar.

St. Albans was on the banks of the River Ver, but the townspeople had no fishing rights there. Like the men of Bury, they were not allowed to full their own wool or grind their own grain. The portable stone mills operated by hand, which their parents had in their own homes, had been taken away and built into the floor of the abbey reception room.

Three miles outside London, Grindcobbe and his companions passed the manor house of Sir Robert Hales, now with Richard II in the Tower. The manor was already burning fiercely. They had heard that the rebels were enforcing their demands by burning the homes of the king's advisors, but this was the first time they had seen with their own eyes what was happening.

When they arrived in London, they were told to go to the church of St. Mary le Bow, located where Cheap became Mercery Street. Other rebels were already meeting there and using the church as a headquarters where they coordinated their demands. The men of St. Albans learned that the king, standing on the wall of the Tower, had promised all rebels he would meet them at Mile End, a field northeast of the city. Grindcobbe decided that they would go there to petition the king for fishing rights on the Ver, hunting rights in the monastery forests, rights to milling and fulling in their own homes, and release from all labor obligations to the monastery. They hurried out of the city to Mile End.

Later the young king left the Tower in a ceremonious parade of earls, knights, and squires, joined by Joan of Kent, traveling in a small carriage. But remaining at the Tower were Simon Sudbury, Sir Robert Hales, and a few others whom the rebels wanted to execute. They hoped they could escape through the Watergate and up the Thames to safety.

The king's procession filed out of the city through Aldgate, where Chaucer lived. Chaucer, now controller of the customs and subsidy for wools, hides, and woolfells, was not seen during the time the rebels occupied the city. A skilled civil servant, he was staying out of trouble.

When the king's procession arrived at Mile End, the rebels had already gathered there in two long lines. They knelt and called out, "Welcome to our Lord, King Richard, if it please you. We will have no other king but you."

The anonymous French chronicle that relates this meeting in great detail states that Wat Tyler spoke for the rebels, asking that the king grant them the right to capture and execute traitors against him and against the law. The king granted this right, provided the treason was proven by law.

Tyler then asked that no man should be a serf or perform involuntary service for a lord, but rather pay four pence an acre for the title to the land he worked. This was granted. When the serfs and farmers heard they were free of their forced labor and could buy their land, they began drifting away from Mile End and London, back to their homes.

Now Tyler and the rebels who remained in London had authority from the king—legal power, residual power. Now the government was really "King Richard and the true commons." There were no lords between the people and their king. Or so they thought. Tyler and the rebels from the south left Mile End for the city of London.

When the southerners were gone, the king offered to receive the petitions from those who had come from other parts of the kingdom. Now it was the turn of the men from St. Albans. Grindcobbe bowed six times before Richard. The petitions were granted, freeing the townspeople from the obligations to the monastery and all restrictions

formerly imposed. The king promised to send a letter to the
abbot of St. Albans confirming their liberties. Grindcobbe
and Cadington took off immediately for St. Albans. But
they left Richard of Wallingford behind to wait for the documents which the king had promised.

The two men brought the news of freedom to St. Albans
and the townspeople were overjoyed. As a symbolic gesture
celebrating the end of their forced labor, they knocked
down the house in St. Albans that belonged to the subcellarer of the abbey. Now that they could hunt in the monastery forests and fish in the river they immediately burned
the fences and gates around the forests previously forbidden
to them.

That Friday night the serfs and tenant farmers from abbey lands came into town to buy their land at four pence an
acre, filling the square and the streets leading to the square.
They pledged to support the townsmen and the townsmen
pledged to support them. They slept where they could, in
the streets or on the square, and on Saturday morning they
released the prisoners from the abbey jail.

Now Richard of Wallingford, after a hard ride, arrived
from London carrying a pennant with the arms of St.
George, a crowned lion rampant. He dramatically planted
this in the ground beside his tired horse and told those who
had crowded around him what had happened in London.

First, he had the king's charter of freedom with him.
Everyone cheered. Then he brought the news that the archbishop of Canterbury, Simon Sudbury, and the treasurer,
Sir Robert Hales, had been taken from the Tower and
beheaded under the new law of King Richard and the true
commons. Again everyone cheered. Then Richard of Wallingford told the townsmen to wait, and with William
Grindcobbe, William Cadington, and a few others, he went
into the abbey.

Thomas de la Mare, from the same family as Sir Peter de
la Mare, speaker of the Good Parliament, was seventy-two
years old and had been abbot since he was forty. Thomas

was the ranking abbot of England, and his building policies had made St. Albans the richest monastery in England. He had built the gateway through which Richard, Grindcobbe, and the rest had just entered. They stood in a church that he had modernized with lamps brought from Italy and with walls newly decorated with murals and hangings. From Europe Thomas had imported embroidered, silk vestments, and golden vessels for the altar. Grindcobbe and the other visitors could not miss the huge eagle, its wings spread, that crowned the shrine of St. Alban, patron saint of the abbey.

Though he was not a scholar himself, Thomas de la Mare had built a library, organized one of the finest collections of books in England, and encouraged scholarship, such as the St. Albans chronicle that Thomas Walsingham had worked on.

Thomas de la Mare was no longer as strong nor as energetic as he had once been. He had barely survived the plague in 1361, and now facing William Grindcobbe, William Cadingdon, Richard of Wallingford, and the others, he was even weaker physically than most men his age.

He had already received a personal copy of the letter from the king:

Very dear in God: At the petition of our beloved lieges of the town of St. Albans, we will and command that, as law and right demands, you cause to be delivered to the said burgesses and good men of the town certain charters in your custody which we made by our ancestor King Henry, to the said burgesses and good men concerning common pastures, fishing rights, and several other commodities mentioned in the said charters; so that they may have no reason to complain hereafter to us. Given under our signet at London June 15, the fourth year of our reign.[1]

---

[1]Walsingham, *Historia Anglicana*, I, 472-73; Walsingham, *Gesta Abbatum*, III, 305-06.

Thomas de la Mare had had much experience with litigation and negotiation. He remained calm and respectful, explaining the intricacies of the law, the judgments given in the monastery's favor that existed in the records of Westminster Palace. Richard of Wallingford replied that he could order twenty thousand men to come from London and raze the monastery if he did not receive a charter which, according to legend, had guaranteed the town its freedom five hundred years earlier.

Thomas ordered a search, but this charter could not be found. Then Richard of Wallingford demanded that a new one be drawn up. This would take three hours, Thomas explained. While the clerks of the monastery drafted a new charter, Thomas gave Richard the documents of indenture, which were burned in the square. Townsmen wandering through the monastery found the portable hand mills that had been taken from their parents. They broke these out of the floor and returned them to the people of St. Albans.

That Saturday afternoon, messengers arrived from London with startling news—during a second conference with the king, Wat Tyler had been killed by either William Walworth, the mayor, or someone with him. Few rebels remained in London, they said. On London Bridge, the head of Simon Sudbury had been removed, and that of Wat Tyler put in its place. In spite of the news, Thomas de la Mare let his clerks finish the new charter and gave it to the townsmen. For a time, the people of St. Albans were free like those of Bury.

While the men of Bury and St. Albans were negotiating their freedom, another messenger from London rode his horse in panic into the city of Leicester. He told the mayor that a band of rebels was on its way to the castle of John of Gaunt. The rebels were going to burn it down as they had the Savoy outside London.

The mayor believed that he had two choices, both bad—he could resist the rebels and be killed, or he could grant their demands and be a traitor to the duke, his lord. Rather than choose on his own authority he called the leading townsmen together, and they decided that the better choice would be to resist. The constables and town criers called on everyone—rich and poor, lord, merchant, artisan, and farm worker—to arm himself. Early Sunday morning, June 16, they gathered on Gater Hill outside the town, twelve hundred of them, a chronicle reports. There they waited with swords, daggers, clubs, and scythes.

After escaping from the Savoy with his bed curtain, the duke's keeper of the wardrobe eventually arrived at Leicester. That very Sunday he commandeered all the carts he could, loaded most of the duke's valuables from the Leicester castle, and took them across the city to the Austin priory of St. Mary de Pré.

The prior was William Clown, named after a village in Derbyshire, not after a personal characteristic. But William Clown was afraid to take the valuables into the priory, so the keeper of the wardrobe led his procession of carts back across the city to a churchyard near the castle. They lined up among the monuments and waited forlornly.

But no rebels arrived at Leicester. The rumor of their arrival was the closest that John Wyclif, twelve miles away at Lutterworth, came to experiencing the Rising of 1381.

On the same day that the men of Leicester assembled on Gater Hill and the duke of Leicester's keeper of the wardrobe moved his carts from one side of the city to another and back again, Lord Henry Despenser, bishop of Norwich, learned of the riots in Suffolk. With eight of his knights and archers, he charged out of his manor house in Burleigh-on-the-Hill, Rutlandshire. The bishop of Norwich was noted for neither piety nor learning. He and his brother had fought for Pope Adrian against Bernabo Visconti of Milan,

and in 1370 Lord Henry was rewarded with the diocese of
Norwich for his military prowess. On this June 16 he was in
armor again, and happy he was once more a leader of
knights, if only eight.

After racing their mounts for sixteen miles, the bishop
and his knights found the townsmen of Peterborough,
Northamptonshire, at the gate of the Benedictine abby,
hoping to free themselves from the monks' control as the
townsmen of Bury and St. Albans had done. The bishop and
his knights charged into the crowd of protestors and hacked
all of them to death.

Continuing east, the bishop and his company met
another group of knights who were taking two captive
rioters to trial at Norwich. The bishop beheaded the rebels
on the spot. This second group of knights joined the
bishop's, and he led both groups north.

At North Walsham, Norfolk, a group of rebels were
warned of the bishop's approach. In the middle of the town
square, they piled up boards, shutters, and gates on one
side, carts and wagons on the other, in a circular barricade.
Around the barricade they dug a ditch and drove sharpened
stakes into the ground, and they believed themselves safe
inside their improvised redoubt.

Riding into North Walsham Bishop Despenser saw the
barricade. He did not slow his mount, but instead cradled
his lance and led a charge at a lope. The horses easily lept
the ditch and stakes, and the force of their charge knocked
down the boards, shutters, and gates. The carts and wagons
in the rear blocked the rebels so they could not retreat.
They were all slaughtered within their redoubt.

Wat Tyler's power, being immediate and not residual, had
died with him. He had set up no organization. The tenant
farmers and serfs who had joined the artisans and craftsmen
had left London thinking they had won their freedom. The
men of London, Kent, and Sussex had become satiated with
looting and beheading. Their immediate goals had been

realized. The Londoners had revenged themselves on John of Gaunt, Archbishop Sudbury, and Sir Robert Hales. They had eliminated the lords between them and the king. They had no further goals, so they drifted back to their homes.

Now the roads in and out of London were free. The king sent messengers in every direction, calling for volunteers to gather at Blackheath, but these volunteers were to be mounted, dressed in armor, and carrying weapons. Mounts, armor, and weapons meant knights only. In a few days the king had the army he needed. He could translate his own residual power into immediate action.

Petitioners from distant parts of the country who had not heard that the rebellion had collapsed arrived in London seeking their freedom like those before them. The king gave them a different message than he had given to the earlier delegates:

> Peasants you were and peasants you are still. You will stay as serfs and in bondage harsher than before. As long as we live and reign over his kingdom, by the grace of God, we will endeavor to suppress you with our mind, our strength, and our weapons so that your bondage will be an example to posterity.[2]

Within two weeks, King Richard had revoked all the charters he had issued at Mile End. John Wrawe was captured and taken to London, and though he turned state's evidence, he was hanged, then drawn and quartered.

When the men of Bury learned of these events, they realized that they had been defeated once again in their search for freedom. No new ideology, no new organization had taken the place of the medieval hierarchy and the power it brought from above. The men of Bury had always

---

[2]Walsingham, *Chronicon Angliae*, 315-17.

been true to the king and continued to be. Without royal support or a local leader, they had no choice but to return the treasures and surviving documents to the monastery. The town of Bury was fined two thousand marks for its acts against St. Edmund's.

At St. Albans, fifty knights arrived in the king's name and arrested William Grindcobbe, William Cadingdon, and fifteen others. They forced the men of St. Albans to return the charter that Thomas de la Mare had written for the town and the hand mills that had been pried up from the monastery floor.

A few days later, King Richard himself arrived at St. Albans with Sir Robert Tresilian, the new chief justice. John Ball had been captured, and they brought him along as prisoner. The king announced to the townspeople that they were still villeins of the monastery and had to perform all their hereditary work. William Grindcobbe, William Cadingdon, and the fifteen others were tried in the town of Hertford and condemned.

Before he died, William Grindcobbe spoke to his fellow townspeople:

> Fellow citizens, for whom a little liberty has relieved the long years of oppression, stand firm while you are able. And do not be afraid because of my persecution. For if it should happen that I die in the cause of seeking liberty, I will count myself happy to end my life as such a martyr. Therefore act now as you would have acted if I had been beheaded at Hertford yesterday. For nothing could have saved my life. They accused me of many things and had a judge who was partial to them and who was eager to shed my blood.[3]

Grindcobbe was right. His blood was shed. He and the others were hanged, then drawn and quartered as John

---

[3]Walsingham, *Gesta Abbatum*, III, 341–42.

Wrawe had been. And Grindcobbe had not been the worst of rebels. From London, William Courtenay, still the bishop, delayed John Ball's execution over the weekend, hoping Ball might recant and receive the last rites of the church. John Ball did not recant and on Monday died as the others had died.

This was one of the last acts of Courtenay as bishop of London. He was soon appointed the new archbishop of Canterbury. He remembered hearing the heretical ideas of John Wyclif in the sermons of John Ball, and he had seen those same ideas translated into action as the rebels attacked the monasteries. And the chronicles, written in the monasteries, joined the new archbishop of Canterbury in fixing the blame for the Rising on Wyclif:

> John Wyclif and his lackeys spread their preaching abroad by dogmatizing ther perverse and damnable doctrines of Berenger about the sacrament of the body and blood of Christ, and far and wide throughout the country defiling the people so that almost the greatest persons of the counties followed their errors. They knew that the ordinary people are easily turned with the leader.[4]

William Courtenay saw it as his first duty to cleanse the province of Canterbury of this heresy. He would start at Oxford, where the beliefs of a new generation of priests and bishops, he was convinced, were being formed in the mold of John Wyclif.

---

[4]Walsingham, *Historia Anglicana*, II, 11.

CHAPTER NINETEEN

Courtenay Begins His Attack

*T*HE STORY THAT HAS survived throughout history is that John Wyclif was already ill when he left Oxford in 1381 and while he was in residence at Lutterworth. This story originally appeared in the second edition of John Foxe's *Actes and Monuments of These Latter and Perillous Days,* familiarly known as his "Book of Martyrs." Foxe does not have the reputation of an accurate historian, and he repeats this story only as a rumor he heard:

> When Wyclif was lying very sick at London certain friars came unto him to counsel him; and when they had babbled much unto him, Wyclif, being moved with the foolishness and absurdity of their talk, with a stout stomach, setting himself upright in his bed, repeated this saying out of the Psalms: I shall not die, but I shall live and declare the works of the Lord.[1]

The facts of such a legend repeated over the centuries are usually false. But the spirit of the legend may be true. Wyclif may have been ill when he left Oxford. He was fifty-two, somewhat old for a fourteenth-century man. He may have already suffered a stroke, perhaps milder than the one he would experience in November 1382.

But as the spirit of Foxe's story implies, Wyclif was not subdued. He continued to write vigorously and continuously. Unlike Archbishop Courtenay, he did not attribute

---

[1]John Foxe, *Actes and Monuments,* III, 20.

the cause of the Rising to his own ideas. Wyclif recognized the economic causes.

He denounced the fines and taxes that the monasteries like St. Edmund's at Bury and St. Albans levied against its "villeins." He saw the system of fines and taxes as another example of the rich taking from the poor, and he knew the ways in which officers enforced the law. "If a poor man does not pay his rent," Wyclif wrote, "the lords seize their animals and harrass them without mercy, even when a person is in dire need, aged, and infirm."[2]

Wyclif knew it was the poll taxes that sparked the Rising and suggested that the church itself pay the poll tax:

> The clergy who possess the riches that belong to the poor should have paid the tax to the King. Oh, how glorious would have been this exchange of the goods of the common people! The clergy could have kept enough for their own food and shelter, and what was left would have satisfied the needs of the poor.[3]

He recognized that free tenants who were paid in wages did better work than serfs and sharecroppers who were paid nothing. Wyclif's solution to serfdom was evolutionary, not revolutionary: he wrote that the status of the serf should not be inherited. Everyone recognized that a serf often had gifted sons. If serfdom was not inherited, he reasoned, then the institution would die without bloodshed.

The violence of the Rising appalled him. He believed that the people had no right to take lives, that the Rising was not justice but an outburst of popular anger. He believed that the people did not punish according to the crime, that God

---

[2]"Servants and Lords," in F.D. Matthew, ed., *The English Works of John Wyclif*, pp. 233–34.

[3]Wyclif, *de Blasphemia*, p. 190.

would punish them as they deserved. And he regretted the death of Simon Sudbury.

"Although the clergy possesses superfluous wealth, still they should not be put to death for this reason," he wrote.[4] He observed, however, that if there had been a separation of church and state, if Sudbury had not been both archbishop of Canterbury and chancellor of England, he would not have been killed.

Like most political theorists of the fourteenth century, Wyclif accepted the basic division between the ruler and the ruled. It was a necessary division, he thought, because man had fallen from the innocence that existed in the Garden of Eden. Those who are ruled, he advocated, should serve their ruler loyally and gladly, and not be false, idle, grouchy, or slothful. They are actually being rewarded for being ruled. It is for their own good that God put them in the position of subjects. God did it to keep them humble and not proud and to keep them from idleness.

But Wyclif found a curious paradox in his own reasoning. A good man who obeyed the law of God would also have to obey an evil ruler who disobeyed the law of God. A good man, following God, actually obeys a bad man, following the devil. It was as if "God obeys the devil," he wrote.[5] To resolve the paradox, he repeated his basic concept that power must be united with virtue.

Wyclif's organization of scribes and copyists was now as active at Lutterworth as it had been at Oxford. His defense against his expulsion from Oxford, *The Confession*, and his ideas on the Rising, *Servants and Lords*, were translated, copied, and distributed, as were his sermons. Nicholas Hereford continued the first translation of the Bible, and John Purvey correlated the Latin texts.

---

[4]Wyclif, *de Blasphemia*, p. 191.

[5]Wyclif, *de Civili Dominio*, III, 40; *Sermones*, II, 311.

Courtenay was right in one of his surmises—Wyclif still had friends at Oxford. Robert Rigg, as one of William Berton's examiners, had originally voted against expulsion, and Rigg was now chancellor of the university. Friendly masters—Nicholas Hereford, John Aston, and Philip Repingdon—lectured on Wyclif's ideas to a new generation of clerks who eagerly participated in the disputations.

A year had passed since the rebels of Kent had assembled at Blackheath and John Wrawe had sacked the manor house of Richard Lyons in north Essex. On May 21, 1382, an earthquake, its epicenter in Kent, shook all of southern England. The bell tower of Canterbury Cathedral crumbled to the ground, and the nave itself was cracked, weakened, and now unsafe. Smaller churches in the county were destroyed "right down to their foundations," a chronicle reported.

In London, steeples and pinnacles rocked back and forth, then toppled into the streets. Smaller earthquakes followed and caused huge waves in the Thames, so powerful that in London harbor the ships were thrown around as if they were in a channel storm.

The huge Dominican monastery known as Blackfriars along London's west wall near the Ludgate was severely shaken. Here was one of the largest and most solid collections of buildings in the city, including a cloister, a chapter house, priory buildings, a huge church for the friars, and a smaller parish church, St. Anne's.

The people of England saw the earthquake as the third of three great calamities of the fourteenth century—first the Pestilence, then the Rising, now the Earthquake—all warnings from God that England was a sinful nation, one that was too patient with sinners.

In the chapter house of the Blackfriars, eight bishops, sixteen masters of theology, fourteen doctors of canon and civil law, six bachelors of theology, and the warden of Merton College had been called together by the new archbishop of Canterbury to examine for heresy twenty-four ideas taken from the writings of the Most Reverend Doctor John Wyclif, priest of Lutterworth. Among these prelates were William Wykeham, bishop of Winchester; Robert Braybrooke, the new bishop of London; and John Wells, Hammer of Heretics. The writings of the Reverend Doctor had not been examined for five years, since the Holy Inquisition had selected eighteen propositions for condemnation in 1377 and Gregory had sent his bulls to England just before his death.

But when the earthquake rocked the chapter house of the Blackfriars, the prelates were more worried about the motion of the earth than the ideas of John Wyclif. They too interpreted the quake as a sign from God. They believed He disapproved of what they were doing and that the conference should adjourn immediately.

In the past, William Courtenay had not been inhibited by the personal abuse of John of Gaunt nor by the mutterings of angry mobs. He strode into the chapter house and calmed the fears of the forty-four church leaders meeting there, though he was younger than all of them. He explained the cause of earthquakes to them: foul air and winds are bottled up in the bowels of the earth, he said, and these winds are expelled with great violence. Most scientists of the fourteenth century would have agreed with his explanation, but William Courtenay's interpretation of the earthquake was different from those of the other churchmen at Blackfriars. For him, the earthquake was a sign that the kingdom should be purged of its heresies that, like the foul winds in the earth, were bottled in the bowels of the wicked, waiting to explode.

The archbishop explained to those gathered that the attacks on the monasteries all over England were a direct result of Wyclif's belief that church wealth should be redistributed. Not only had St. Albans and St. Edmunds been attacked, but also the monasteries at Grace,

Dunstable, Redbourne, Worcester, and Peterborough. The priests and bishops of the future were being trained at Oxford, Courtenay reminded the prelates. If these young clerks were further exposed to the ideas of John Wyclif and then spread these heresies throughout England, only the chaos of more pestilences, more risings, and more earthquakes would result, and the true understanding of God and the world would be lost. On the other hand, when heresy is cleaned out of Oxford, order would be restored, and there would be no more pestilences, no more risings, and no more earthquakes.

The theologians were convinced by the force of the young archbishop's rhetoric and reasoning. That evening at Blackfriars, they declared that ten of the twenty-four ideas submitted by Courtenay were heretical and that the remaining fourteen were erroneous.

Condemned was Wyclif's explanation of the mystery of the Eucharist. This was the same concept that William Berton and his council had condemned the year before. Also condemned was Wyclif's principle that no power was rightly exercised without virtue, especially as Wyclif applied that principle to priests, bishops, and the pope. And the prelates at Blackfriars failed to see the humor in "God must obey the devil." They severely condemned this proposition.

Archbishop Courtenay announced that Wyclif's ideas threatened "to subvert the state of the whole church and of our province of Canterbury and the tranquility of the Kingdom as well." That last important phrase, "the tranquility of the Kingdom," was carefully chosen. Four years earlier Simon Sudbury had condemned Wyclif's ideas, too, but the visit of Sir Lewis Clifford had made it clear that the state would not support the church, and Wyclif had ignored the condemnation. William Courtenay was going to make sure that this time, the church and the state worked together.

He need not have worried. The king and his counselors had been as frightened of the Rising as the clergy. Like Courtenay they were convinced that the Rising had been God's voice crying out against heresy. The earthquake further convinced them of God's anger.

Then, within a week of the quake, in the slum area of Cornhill in London, the pestilence again began to kill in great numbers. The quake had shaken up the rats as it had shaken up the church and state. The king and the court did not doubt that God was still speaking to them through the pestilence, and speaking boldly and severely.

On May 30, 1382, the new bishop of London, Robert Braybrooke, led a procession through the streets of his diocese. He carried a consecrated host in a golden, jeweled casket called an ostensarium and was followed by chanting priests, monks, friars, and laymen. As their elders had done thirty-four years earlier, some Londoners beat their own backs with whips studded with horseshoe nails.

The march started at St. Paul's and wound through the streets from wall to wall, east to west, north to south, and returned to the yard of St. Paul's. Here John Kenningham, Wyclif's old adversary, read the condemnation of Wyclif's ideas. He announced that Archbishop Courtenay ordered each bishop in England to be his diocesan inquisitor and personally direct the work of stamping out heresy in order to rid England of the cause of the three calamities.

Parliament cooperated by passing a statute to enforce the condemnation. The statute required that if any priest reported that the condemned doctrines were being preached, the chancellor of England would order the sheriff to imprison the offending preacher.

By Corpus Christi Day, June 5, William Courtenay's efforts had some effect. The pestilence in London had receded. The earthquake had rattled Canterbury and southern England a few times after the initial shock, but these quakes did no further damage, and now the earth was still. Peasant and workers were rioting in Paris and Rouen, but the peasants of England were docile.

All over the country people celebrated their deliverance with plays that dramatized the history of man from the Creation to the Last Judgment. Great decorated wagons, like modern circus wagons but larger, were hauled by men from place to place, through many of the larger cities— Chester, York, Hereford, Leicester, Canterbury, Norwich, and probably London. The wagons were stages for the plays, the settings for Heaven, Hell, Jerusalem, and Bethlehem. The townspeople hooted and hollered at the devils who were thrown out of Heaven. The devils had huge, flapping wings and long tails and poured into the street out of dragon mouths that flamed and smoked and stank with smoldering sulphur.

The plays were as realistic as possible. A man playing God magically produced a bloody ox rib out of a naked, sleeping Adam and changed it into a naked Eve. A puff of smoke helped produce the illusion. The people laughed at Noah's wife, very drunk, refusing to go on board the ark. They were silent as Abraham moved steadily toward the sacrifice of his son Isaac, and they called out excitedly when, at the last minute, an angel in Heaven leaned out from a roof of one of the wagons and stopped Abraham's descending knife.

The Blessed Virgin carried a real baby in a specially constructed womb, and the birth was as true to life as the actors could make it. In another play, the horror of the massacre of the innocent children by Herod's soldiers was intensified by knights who went right out on the street, looking for babies in the crowd. The fright was softened by the ranting and strutting of Herod and by Watkins, a cowardly soldier. The women of Nazareth chased Watkins, beating on his head with their distaffs.

Nothing relieved the terror of the Crucifixion, for Christ lay on the cross in front of them, and they could hear the sound of the mallet hitting the nails and piercing his hands and feet. Christ's wounds bled from small bags of blood hidden between his fingers. People actually cried for joy when Christ first appeared to Mary Magdeline and she mistook him for a gardener. And everyone knew which side he had better be on when he saw God, from atop the last huge wagon, separating the saints from the sinners at the Last Judgment. Then devils went into the crowd and tried to capture prominent townsmen and take them off to Hell. A merchant or a blacksmith was not afraid to physically defend himself, and a devil had to be quick on his feet to avoid being beaten.

Not all towns were lucky enough to have rich guilds to support these elaborate cycles of plays. Smaller towns celebrated with simpler plays, dances, pageants, or singing carols, the name they used for circle dances.

Oxford may have had pageants or plays. There are references to them, but records and scripts have been lost. The scholarly clerks enjoyed a more intellectual celebration. The university celebrated Corpus Christi Day with a special sermon at St. Frideswyde and continual disputations that lasted through the weekend.

By April, Robert Rigg had chosen Philip Repingdon to give this special sermon. The choice honored Repingdon, for when Rigg chose him, he had not yet received his doctor of theology degree. The choice confirmed Repingdon's reputation as one of the most brilliant of Wyclif's students. Rigg expected that Repingdon would defend Wyclif's new thesis on the mystery of the bread and wine, for, after all, Corpus Christi Day had been set aside to celebrate the body of Christ.

When William Courtenay in London learned about Rigg's choice, it confirmed his worst fears about Wyclif's

influence in the university, so he sent Peter Stokes to Oxford. Stokes was a ruddy-faced Carmelite friar and a doctor
of theology who had already disputed on the Eucharist with
Nicholas Hereford at Oxford. Because of his white Carmelite habit, Wyclif had referred to him as "the white dog."

Peter Stokes arrived at Oxford on a Wednesday night, the
eve of Corpus Christi, and presented letters from Courtenay to Rigg. The letters ordered that before Philip Repingdon delivered his sermon, Stokes was to read the condemnation of Wyclif's ideas at the cross in the yard of St. Frideswyde. The orders also granted Stokes the power to prevent
the teaching of those condemned theses within the university. Stokes's efforts would be supported by the king and
the rulers of the kingdom, Courtenay explained, and he requested that Chancellor Rigg "assist our beloved son, Friar
Peter Stokes, diligently, in the publication of these
letters."

Rigg kept the letters and went on with the celebrations as
he had planned. He also made certain that all of Oxford—
clerks, masters, and townsmen—knew about this attack
on the university's integrity. "Neither bishop nor archbishop have any power over the university in matters of
heresy," Rigg maintained.[6] He promised that Oxford
would not be controlled by friars and monks like the University of Paris.

Rigg and the mayor of Oxford were part of the crowd that
went to St. Frideswyde churchyard to hear Philip Repingdon. Peter Stokes was there, but he could not read the condemnation of John Wyclif without Rigg's permission, and
Rigg had not given it.

The earlier riots had given Oxford a reputation for violence. Most in the crowd at St. Frideswyde were obviously
friendly to Repingdon and Wyclif, and Stokes was too
frightened to act alone. In the report he sent back to Courte-

---

[6]*Fasciculi Zizaniorum*, p. 299.

nay, Stokes said that he saw twenty men at the church with swords hidden under their clothes. The swords were probably figments of Stokes's panicked imagination, for there was no violence in Oxford during that Corpus Christi weekend.

In his sermon, Repingdon said little about Wyclif's stand on the Eucharist. He made a single statement that Wyclif was outstandingly orthodox and had "never advanced or taught any doctrine concerning the Eucharist which the Church of God had not held,"[7] a reference to Berengar, whose ideas on the Eucharist agreed with those that Wyclif was advocating.

Stokes reported to Courtenay that Repingdon incited the people of Oxford to insurrection and to plundering the churches. He added that Repingdon had assured the congregation gathered in the priory yard that the duke of Lancaster was impressed and would be willing to defend "holy priests," though Stokes used the term now becoming popular—"lollards." When the sermon was over, Stokes said that he saw Repingdon and Rigg laughing together. His report seemed to place Oxford on the verge of a second rising.

Wyclif's friends—Nicholas Hereford, Repingdon, John Aston, and others—celebrated the rest of Corpus Christi weekend in disputations in the halls of Oxford. Peter Stokes finally found the courage to enter one of these contests. When he arrived at the hall where the disputation was to be held, he said he again saw twelve men with weapons under their robes, and he left immediately for the Carmelite house. There he found a message from Courtenay ordering him to return to Lambeth Palace.

Robert Rigg did not join in the series of debates. Perhaps he learned of Stokes's excited report for on Saturday he and two university proctors left London to see Courtenay themselves and to tell him their side of the story. They

---

[7]Ibid., p. 307.

arrived in London on Monday but the archbishop refused to see them until Thursday and then only at a formal meeting of the same council that had already condemned Wyclif. As chancellor of Oxford, Rigg was entitled to sit as a member of this council. When he entered the hall on the second floor of the great monastery, however, he had to face the bishops and doctors and experience the full force of the archbishop's disapproval. Among his examiners Rigg saw some new faces. Henry Crump, the Irish Cistercian who had been among the leaders who expelled Wyclif from Oxford, was among them.

Courtenay had read Stokes's report carefully. He knew that Rigg had ignored his order to publish Wyclif's condemnation and that he had not rebuked Repingdon for defending Wyclif but instead had congratulated him "with a smiling face." Earlier Rigg had appointed Nicholas Hereford to give an important sermon on Ascension Sunday. To the archbishop of Canterbury it did not seem that the chancellor of Oxford was "well-disposed toward the enemies of heresy."[8]

William Courtenay did not use threats, but his understated manner was quiet and forceful. Courtenay never doubted himself. He knew he was right and had the power to enforce that right; he had no need to threaten. As for Repingdon's report that John of Gaunt would defend the heretics, he had confronted the duke at St. Paul's when he was bishop of London. He would confront him now as archbishop of Canterbury.

Courtenay handed Rigg the twenty-four condemned propositions and ordered him to publish them at Oxford in both Latin and English. Then Courtenay handed him a second document, in which Rigg agreed not to interfere with any agent of the archbishop.

---

[8]Ibid., p. 304.

As chancellor of Oxford, it was Rigg's duty to bar the following persons from preaching or teaching at the university until they purged themselves of heresy in the presence of the archbishop: John Wyclif, Nicholas Hereford, Philip Repingdon, John Aston, and Lawrence Steven. Further, if any clerk or master of the university favored the condemned propositions, the chancellor would take measures to force them to recant or leave.

King Richard had not yet signed the statute that allowed the sheriff to arrest heretics, but if Rigg had a lingering doubt that the state would not support the church in attacking heresies, William Courtenay ordered him to appear before the king's council to discover the truth for himself. Robert Rigg signed the orders and in doing so, he must have realized that he was being forced to become the inquisitor of the university.

On the next day, Rigg appeared at Westminster Palace and stood before Robert Braybrooke, bishop of London and now chancellor of England. William Courtenay sat beside the chancellor and next to him was the treasurer of England, the keeper of the privy seal, and other officers of the king's government. It was an impressive group. Only the king's uncle, the duke of Lancaster, who was returning from the Scottish border, was missing.

The chancellor of England ordered the chancellor of Oxford to follow to the letter every command of the archbishop of Canterbury. The king's chief officer did not have to threaten. Even without the statute he could imprison Rigg if he disobeyed. Rigg understood. In ridding England of heresy, the power of the state and of the church now stood side by side.

CHAPTER TWENTY

Hereford, Repingdon, and Aston

A S A MEMBER OF BERTON'S council just the year before, Robert Rigg had been forced to put aside his personal feelings and condemn his friend, John Wyclif. Now he faced the same painful duty once again. When he returned to Oxford, he told Nicholas Hereford, Philip Repingdon, and John Aston that they must stop teaching Wyclif's ideas and appear before the archbishop as heretics to recant.

Hereford had been working on his Bible translation at Lutterworth when he was not lecturing at Oxford. Typically, he attacked his new problem with immediate action. He instantly dropped the translation at the third chapter of Baruch, twentieth verse. With Repingdon he left for London to see John of Gaunt. Both believed what Repingdon had said in his sermon on Corpus Christi Day, that the duke supported their efforts, and they would need all the support they could muster when they faced William Courtenay.

John of Gaunt had returned from the Scottish border where he had negotiated a truce between the two countries. While he was in the North, he had learned that his beloved Savoy had been destroyed, so he moved out of the city to Tottenhall on the Oxford Road. Here Hereford and Repingdon visited him.

John of Gaunt considered himself a religious man. He had attacked the bishop of London as a politician, not as a churchman. He made large contributions to monasteries and supported the Carmelite friars, and at the same time defended John Wyclif, who attacked the monasteries and the friars. But there was no paradox here. He and John Wyclif were looking at the monasteries from different points of view. John Wyclif saw them economically, as existing only because they were supported by the sweat of tenant farmers and serfs. The duke of Lancaster saw them spiritually, as holders and preservers of God's truth.

Nicholas Hereford and Philip Repingdon understood the duke's attitudes. Like all Oxford masters, they were expert debaters. They tried to prove to the duke that Courtenay's new attack on Wyclif was an attack on the power of the young king, that the theological differences between the archbishop and Wyclif were misunderstandings in semantics.

Apparently their arguments were successful. The next day they planned to walk to the city and, supported by the duke of Lancaster, face Archbishop Courtenay.

Before they had a chance to leave Tottenhall, a second group of theologians arrived. They represented William Courtenay. They may have arrived by coincidence, but it is more likely that Courtenay had been told that Hereford and Repingdon had left Oxford to visit John of Gaunt. Oxford was a small community, everyone knew the business of everyone else, and Nicholas Hereford was never secret about his plans.

The newly arrived doctors brought the list of condemned ideas with them to show the duke. They, too, knew that the duke was a religious man. This list, they explained, contained the same propositions that Wyclif held when the duke visited him in Oxford before the Rising, especially the idea that the substance of the bread and wine remained the same before and after the consecration. Like all good fourteenth-century Christians, John of Gaunt had always believed otherwise. He did not understand how anyone could question that the bread and wine changed into the body and blood of Christ. The church had always said so; he had always believed so. And John Wyclif had promised him never to discuss this question again, at least in English.

The doctors showed the duke Wyclif's statement that "God must obey the devil." Of course, the doctors did not explain how the paradox had arisen, and, out of context, the statement was ridiculous.

For all their skill at debating, Nicholas Hereford and Philip Repingdon could no longer hold their ground. The duke was now convinced that William Courtenay was not attacking the king but that as archbishop of Canterbury, he was defending orthodoxy. The duke lectured the two Oxford masters on the meaning of the mass and with no uncertainty told them to obey the archbishop's summons and recant.

Hereford and Repingdon were disappointed that they had lost the duke's support, but by the time they had walked the two miles to Blackfriar's Abbey, they had decided on another defense. It was probably Hereford's idea, for he was never afraid to jump in a new direction.

While they were waiting at the monastery to appear before the council, they were joined by John Aston in his russet gown and bare feet. When the three Oxfordians appeared before the council, they noticed Peter Stokes had joined John Wells, Henry Crump, Courtenay, and the other inquisitors.

Courtenay handed Hereford and Repingdon a copy of the twenty-four propositions and told them to agree that these were heretical. Following their plan, Hereford and Repingdon asked to be allowed to reply in writing. Courtenay granted their request, provided they did not write their reply like a university disputation to confuse and obscure the real issues. The two masters agreed and left the council to prepare their answers.

Then the archbishop questioned John Aston. Aston immediately agreed not to discuss the propositions in public. Courtenay was suspicious of Aston's quick agreement because he had imitated Wyclif in his dress. He asked the astronomer-turned-preacher if he knew that both the archbishop and the Parliament had forbidden unauthorized preaching. Aston admitted he had, but added defiantly that he had ignored the prohibition. William Courtenay then directly ordered him to stop preaching and commanded him to appear two days later to explain why he should not be condemned as a heretic.

Hereford and Repingdon spent the two days before their next hearing in a frenzy of activity. They wrote their defense first in Latin, then in English. They arranged to have copies made, English copies to be distributed around London and Latin copies to be distributed around Oxford. The fastest system of copying available was to dictate to a room full of clerks. They probably used this method to accomplish their remarkable feat.

The English copies were posted or read aloud where people gathered—at the water conduit in the morning, along the river at Eastwatergate near Castle Bayard, at Paul Wharf, or down river at the London Bridge. They could also reach a lot of people at the markets, Cheap, Stocks, and Leaden Hall where the butchers, bakers, poulterers, cheese-mongers, and their customers gathered.

And the people listened. Heresy was a new phenomenon in England. These men might be heretics, and in other countries heretics were publicly burned. These men might soon be fighting for their lives, and such men often aroused a sympathetic audience.

Hereford's and Repingdon's defense moved the Londoners to their side. By the time of the second hearing, the Londoners crowded into the upstairs refectory, the dining room of Blackfriars where the hearings were being held. The visitors shouted their disapproval and tried to force Courtenay to stop the inquisition. William Courtenay was never intimidated. He quickly quieted the Londoners and then conducted his hearing in Latin so that they could not follow the proceedings.

Hereford and Repingdon admitted that Wyclif's propositions were undoubtedly heretical, but while admitting this, they made their answers as ambiguous as possible. For example, Hereford said, "God owes the devil the obedience of love," and he invited any member of the council to debate this point with him. The council ignored the challenge, and Courtenay polled each member on Hereford's and Repingdon's answers. The council found them insufficient, deceitful, erroneous, perverse, and heretical. Courtenay ordered the two of them to appear at his manor in Otford, Kent, the following week for sentencing.

After he sent away Hereford and Repingdon, Courtenay questioned John Aston in Latin. But Aston replied in English so that the Londoners who had remained could understand him. When Courtenay questioned him about theology, Aston, a Merton astronomer and mathematician, pleaded ignorance. "The speculation passes men's understanding," he told Courtenay. When the archbishop asked him what he believed about the mystery of the bread and wine at mass, Aston replied, "It is enough for me to believe as Holy Church believes." The phrase sounded innocent enough, but both he and Courtenay knew it was the same phrase that Wyclif had used at Oxford and that Repingdon had used in his sermon on Corpus Christi Day.

Courtenay then made his question more specific. He asked what happened to the material of the bread and the wine during mass. Courtenay used the Latin word *materialis*. Aston could not resist appealing to the crowd.

"*Materialis*," Aston repeated. "You may put the word in your purse, if you have one." The word *purse* was London slang for "scrotum," and while the Londoners in the refectory laughed at the crude joke, the archbishop of Canterbury did not. He declared John Aston a heretic on the spot and ordered the sheriff to take him immediately to the archbishop's prison at Saltwood Castle. The third meeting of the Blackfriar's council had ended.

Neither side was satisfied with the results of the hearing. William Courtenay decided that future meetings of the council would be held outside of London to avoid the possibility of a crowd interfering with the proceedings. But the defendants now had the sympathy of the Londoners, Hereford and Repingdon with their handbills and Aston with his dress, his plea of ignorance, and his joke.

Hereford and Repingdon obeyed the archbishop's order and appeared at his manor in Kent. Courtenay was not there but left a message that the two should present themselves at Canterbury Cathedral. But Hereford had decided on still another plan. He would now appeal personally to Pope Urban VI in Rome, the pope that Wyclif had called a "dog snarling over a bone." Hereford was always enthusiastic but naive. He thought he could convince the pope of the soundness of Wyclif's stands on the mystery of the Eucharist and on church wealth.

Hereford posted a declaration of his appeal on the door of St. Paul's and of St. Mary le Bow, the archbishop of Canterbury's church. Then he left for Rome. Repingdon went into hiding either in London or Oxford.

There was still plenty of sympathy in Oxford for Repingdon and all of Wyclif's followers. But the sympathy of the Oxford clerks or the Londoners did not stop the momentum of the church bureaucracy. Courtenay ordered Bishop Robert Braybrooke to excommunicate Hereford and Repingdon by "cross, bell, and candle," as the ceremony stipulated.

The ceremony took place at St. Paul's Cross on July 13. The bishop of London read the order from the archbishop to the crowd that had gathered around the Cross. They did not press too close, for they were familiar with the ceremony:

> In as much as Master Nicholas Hereford and Philip Repingdon, canons regular of the monastery of St. Mary's, Leicester, doctors of divine theology, are strongly suspected of heretical depravity, we charge and order you, firmly enjoining that you denounce publically and solemnly the said Nicholas and Philip on the same Sunday when a very large

multitude of people will have gathered at St. Paul's Cross to hear your sermon, holding the cross, lighting the candles, and then casting them to the ground, that they have thus been excommunicated by us and that they still are.[1]

Then Bishop Braybrooke carried out the impressive order. Standing on the platform of the Cross, he rang a hand-bell. He handed it to an acolyte who handed him the crucifix in his right hand, and a candelabrum, its candles lit, in his left. The bishop threw them both to the ground in front of him. The crowd had prepared for this, leaving him space in front of the platform.

When the candelabrum and the crucifix hit the ground, Nicholas Hereford and Philip Repingdon were no longer part of the church. They were still priests, but they could no longer say mass. They were masters, but they could no longer teach. They could make no contracts, for their oaths were no longer binding.

Henry Crump, the Irish Cistercian, was still a regent-master of Oxford. He returned to Oxford from Blackfriars and called Robert Rigg and Wyclif's other friends on the faculty "a bunch of lollards." Robert Rigg, as chancellor of the university, was glad to summon him for discipline. Having once faced him across the table at Blackfriars, the chancellor had been disciplined by a member of his own faculty.

But Crump did not appear, and Rigg suspended him from the faculty in the same way that Courtenay had ordered Wyclif, Hereford, Repingdon, and Aston suspended. It was a weak attempt at revenge, but at least it was some type of counteraction to what had happened to his friends.

In this fight for freedom of speech at the university, power had now shifted from the chancellor of Oxford to the archbishop of Canterbury. As soon as Courtenay learned of

---

[1]Dahmus, *Prosecution*, pp. 120–21, citing the Register of William Courtenay.

Crump's suspension, he asked Robert Braybrooke, in his capacity as chancellor of the king, to call a meeting of the king's council. Then the chancellor of the king ordered the chancellor of the university to appear before him. Rigg was handed two letters by the king's council. The first ordered him to restore all privileges of the university "to Brother Henry," and forbade any member of the university to annoy Brother Henry, Brother Peter Stokes, or any other scholar who might be concerned with this correction of the heresies and errors of John Wyclif, Nicholas Hereford, and Philip Repingdon. John Aston, still in prison, was not mentioned.

The second letter ordered Robert Rigg to establish a thorough inquisition at the university. Any friend of John Wyclif or anyone who communicated with him was to be driven at least twelve miles from Carfax, the center of Oxford. In addition, Robert Rigg was to search all college halls and houses for the writings of John Wyclif, which were to be confiscated and sent to the archbishop without any corrections. William Courtenay also ordered Rigg to perform the excommunication of Hereford and Repingdon in the courtyard of St. Mary's Oxford.

At the same time Courtenay asked the sheriff of Oxfordshire and the mayor of Oxford to assist the chancellor of the university in the purge of Wyclif's books. If Robert Rigg and the proctors of the university failed to obey the orders, "each and all privileges of the university would be suspended."[2]

Robert Rigg's attempt at revenge failed. Again the victory belonged to William Courtenay.

---

[2]Ibid., p. 124.

CHAPTER TWENTY-ONE

Courtenay Victorious—Almost

W HEN THE CANDLES AND THE crucifix hit the pavement in St. Paul's churchyard, Nicholas Hereford was already on his way to Italy. A sea trip in the fourteenth century was an uncomfortable experience. As soon as a traveler crossed the channel, he was usually glad to walk or ride horseback to his destination. It was not only more pleasant but also less expensive. Monasteries were situated a day's journey apart, and guidebooks told a traveler where he could find good water.

Hereford would have no language problem, of course, for Latin was the international language. But each country had its own Latin accent, and everywhere he went, Hereford would be recognized as an Englishman. Europe was still strictly divided between the two popes, Urban and Clement, and as an Urbanite, Hereford was safe only in the English-conrolled areas of France, Calais, and Bordeaux. Even the monasteries were divided. If he stopped at a monastery that supported Clement, he would be regarded as a heretic and an enemy and would be arrested and imprisoned. In Italy, feelings were especially high. In Clement territory, Hereford would have been executed. Actually, Hereford was a heretic even from the church that Urban ruled, but due to the slow and uncertain communications of the Middle Ages, the word of his excommunication would not yet have reached the Continent.

Hereford arrived in Rome safely, but the danger was not over. He could not have known how Urban's fortunes stood or how Urban regarded someone closely associated with John Wyclif. Fortunately, Urban showed his temperate side. He listened to Hereford's defense of Wyclif's theses. Then the pope called a special consistory of his cardinals and theologians. After long and frequent discussions on the subject, the consistory finally condemned Wyclif's theories and sentenced Hereford to death for advocating them. Urban clemently commuted the sentence to life imprisonment and forgot about Nicholas Hereford.

At Oxford, Robert Rigg's attack on Henry Crump had been a disaster for the university. The confiscation of Wyclif's books was completed. Those whom Wyclif had left behind to continue teaching his ideas slowly surrendered to orthodoxy. Lawrence Steven left Cornwall where he had been preaching and visited Bishop William Wykeham in Southwark. After the interview, Bishop Wykeham declared Steven clear of heresy. He returned to the university to further his studies.

The day after Lawrence Steven appeared before Wykeham, Philip Repingdon came out of hiding. He appeared before William Courtenay and some of the members of the Blackfriar's council. Now he accepted the twenty-four propositions culled from Wyclif's ideas as heresies and errors. He was restored as a regent-master of the university and started a climb up the church hierarchy.

William Courtenay decided to complete his victory over the university by bringing the Blackfriar's council to Oxford. He would avoid another London demonstration and inquire on the spot about the teaching of Wyclif's heresies. His visit would be a triumphant spectacle from Canterbury to London, with receptions at Uxbridge and Wycombe, and once at Oxford, a parade up the High. The university community, clerks and masters both, would see his power demonstrated, and seeing it, would understand and respect it. Courtenay would be joined by the bishops and abbots of England, including old Thomas de la Mare, who eighteen months earlier had won his victory over William Grindcobbe and the townsmen of St. Albans. Each church prelate would be preceded by knights, and all the bishops and ab-bots would be followed by a retinue of servants and clerks.

It was November. For the parade the lords of the church wore surcoats and capes decorated with their coats of arms, brilliant in blue, red, green, gold, and silver. The horses were covered with long clothes from the neck across the back to the tail. The caparisons were decorated with an animal or bird from the crest or shield of the arms—a crowned leopard on a blue field or a silver pelican on a red field. Some of the older members, such as Thomas de la Mare, rode in a cart with curtains similarly decorated. The parade was led by armed knights, their armor shining, their helmets plumed and ribboned. More knights followed, and the procession extended more than a half-mile on the road.

As they marched toward Oxford, the parade grew. Clergy from all over England wanted to join in the triumph and show their solidarity with the victorious archbishop, ready to humble his enemies and receive their surrender. The convocation at Oxford began with a solemn high mass at St. Mary's. As chancellor, Robert Rigg gave the sermon on the text: "They were gathered in the valley of Blessing," II Chronicles 20:26. The text referred to Jehoshaphat and the Jews gathering to give thanks for their victory over Am-mon, Moab, and the Edomites.

Jehoshaphat and the Jews at the valley symbolized Cour-tenay and the prelates at Oxford, Ammon, Moab, and the Edomites referred to Wyclif and his associates. Rigg had been humbled enough, so he did not mention that Jehoshaphat's victory came only as a result of Ammon, Moab, and the Edomites slaughtering one another.

After the mass, the visiting dignitaries paraded across the town, down Shipyard Street to St. Frideswyde. All who could crowded into the chapter house while lesser dignitaries, masters, and clerks crowded the cloister and halls of the monastery, hoping to catch a glimpse of the lords of the church.

William Courtenay announced that they had met "to root out certain heretics who have recently sprouted here."[1] The university chancellor would be a member of the committee to carry out the plan. This appointment was all part of the archbishop's spectacular show. The Blackfriar's council had accomplished everything Courtenay had asked of it.

Courtenay planned a second act for his show. Philip Repingdon was the symbol of defiance five months earlier when he gave that rebellious sermon on Corpus Christi Day. Courtenay would dramatize in Oxford, where the rebellion had started, that the weeds of dissension that Wyclif had planted had really been pulled up by the roots, and without destroying the wheat at the same time.

He ordered Philip Repingdon to appear before him and the lords of the church to repeat the order to "anathematize and abjure all heresy, and in particular the heresies and errors of John Wyclif, which were condemned and rejected by the council."[2] Repingdon had already "abjured all heresy" in London, but appearing at Oxford, he would make a public declaration that all could witness.

When Repingdon finished his performance, two monks helped John Aston through the crowd. Alone, infirm, and weak, he stood in his first appearance since his imprisonment in Saltwood Castle. Its dank, underground cells had obviously affected his health.

Archbishop Courtenay asked Aston his opinion on the mystery of the bread and the wine, repeating the question he had asked at Blackfriar's. Aston had been subdued by his stay in the Saltwood dungeon, but he still had some strength left. As he had first done in London, he pleaded that he was ignorant about the problem.

---

[1]Dahmus, *Prosecution*, p. 126

[2]Ibid., p. 127.

Courtenay was patient with him. He suggested that Aston eat something and invited him to join Chancellor Rigg, Abbot Thomas, and others at dinner, where he could confer with them about the subject. During dinner Thomas de la Mare, as diplomatic as he had been at the Rising, persuaded Aston to admit to heresy and join his old friend Philip Repingdon.

Aston, Rigg, and the abbot had eaten their dinner away from St. Frideswyde, and returning to the monastery, they had to force a path through the curious Oxfordians pressed into the building. Archbishop Courtenay and the rest had eaten their dinners in the monastery refectory. The crowds were so great they could not leave the refectory and return to the chapter house. Aston pushed on to the refectory and read his admission to Wyclif's heresies over the scraps of the archbishop's feast still on the tables. Then he apologized for his insult to the archbishop, referring to the joke about the purse. Three days later, Courtenay forgave him and restored him as a regent-master of the university.

After the archbishop and the lords of the church had left Oxford, Robert Rigg once again tried to counterattack. He charged Henry Crump and Peter Stokes with heresy. The ideas they taught in their lectures were questionable, he claimed. The two friars went immediately to Archbishop Courtenay and protested. The only ideas they advanced that may have been questionable, they said, were brought up in order to discuss and refute them. The archbishop accepted their explanation and dismissed the charges and he reminded Rigg that he had promised not to annoy the archbishop's representatives.

Courtenay ordered the Oxford committee which he had appointed to combat heresy to burn all Wyclif's manuscripts that could be discovered in the college halls. He was now certain that no future priests would graduate contaminated by Wyclif's ideas. The university would graduate only skilled, well-trained, submissive bureaucrats who were ready to take their place in the church hierarchy.

The danger of spreading heresy had been averted, he believed, and the chances of another rising, pestilence, or earthquake had been lessened.

During the lifetime of Archbishop Courtenay, there would be no more risings and no more earthquakes, but the pestilence remained. He might have been less confident about the spread of heresy had he known that in spite of his pomp and repression, Wyclif's ideas at Oxford were still discussed and the manuscripts still circulated.

On the surface, however, Oxford was subdued. Philip Repingdon and Lawrence Steven would remain orthodox members of the hierarchy. They were not cowards, but neither were they prophets. Their training at Oxford had been an exhibition of memory, rhetoric, and logic. For them disputations had been difficult challenges, but primarily intellectual games. It was the process that mattered, not the doctrines of the church, because the doctrines had been decided and were taken for granted.

But Wyclif had questioned the doctrines. He had continued his questioning as a doctor and a regent-master. He wanted to explain a mystery. For John Wyclif the logic and the disputations had been more than a process, more than a game. They had led him to his vision.

Repingdon and Steven had been excited by John Wyclif, himself, but they had not seen his vision at firsthand. They did not have the prophet's fire, anger, or stubbornness. Now they were willing to play the game within the boundaries which Courtenay had laid down.

John Aston was different. He, too, had seen the vision at firsthand. He had experienced the inside of the archbishop's prison. He may have been tortured, an accepted practice in the fourteenth century. Perhaps by this prison experience, perhaps by the old abbot of St. Albans, he had been persuaded to take part in Courtenay's spectacular at St. Frideswyde. But Aston would not stay within boundaries for long.

John Horn, a young curate at Lutterworth, has left a record that in November 1382, Wyclif suffered a stroke and was paralyzed. He described Wyclif at that time as being emaciated, spare, destitute of strength, and kept alive only by his indominable will. It is difficult to know exactly how much Wyclif was physically disabled. The term "stroke" is inexact even today. It is used to describe an interruption in the flow of blood to the brain, caused either by a stoppage or a rupture in one of the carotid arteries and resulting in a cerebral hemorrhage. The first is the more common cause.

Wyclif described himself as feeble and lame, at least one leg was permanently affected. In addition he may not have been able to use an arm or the muscles on one side of his face. Of course in the fourteenth century, with no knowledge of circulation, the cause of the paralysis was completely mysterious. Stroke was originally called "a stroke of God," and the usual treatment was to rub the affected arm or leg with a poultice of swine lard and wood-sorrel and to give the victim a decoction of cinnamon. At least these treatments would do no harm. But bleeding, the universal remedy, would more than likely kill the patient, or minimally spread the paralysis.

Wyclif survived this first stroke. But he suffered emotionally from the loss of those of his Oxford surrogate family who recanted—Philip Repingdon and Lawrence Steven.

In his writings there is more anger than affection. This is the prophet's way. His anger is public, his affection private. The affection is more striking because it is sudden and rare. He expressed his affection for Oxford, for William Woodford, and for John Uhtred of Boldon, although the friar and the monk both opposed his views. Wyclif addressed his followers at Oxford as "my sons." This is the usual way a religious superior addressed those for whom he was responsible, though technically Wyclif was no longer the religious superior of Philip Repingdon, Lawrence Steven, or John Aston, if he ever was more than a lecturer to them. But he voluntarily accepted responsibility for these associates. He had been forcefully separated from them, but they made up the most important group to which he belonged and were his only connections with Oxford.

Only Nicholas Hereford and John Purvey were closer to Wyclif than Repingdon, Steven, and Aston. Then he learned that this family at Oxford had publicly renounced the only inheritance he could leave them—his vision. Hereford's imprisonment disturbed Wyclif greatly, as is evident from his observations on "some men" suffering in Roman prisons and other remarks.

He never commented on the pain he underwent as a result of Courtenay's triumph, but a new attitude, an anti-intellectualism, began to seep into Wyclif's writings. For the first time he criticized the university. Courtenay had made it seem that Wyclif had lost all those who were to carry on with his beliefs, and that from now on, the university would allow only orthodoxy. Wyclif seemed to have accepted this triumph just as Courtenay had intended it.

Wyclif's first argument against the university was economic in nature. He wrote that the university took money from parishes that could use it to better advantage supporting their parishioners. He criticized the university because it was far from primitive, far removed from his age of simplicity:

> The apostles took no degrees and Christ forbad them to be called "master." The learned manner that studies brings out, is at variance with the gospel. As the preaching of the apostles was better than the preaching of these masters, so a priest without a school degree, may be more profitable to a Christian than these masters.[3]

---

[3]Wyclif, "*Officio Pastoralis*," in F.D. Matthew, ed., *The English Works*, pp. 427–28.

What Wyclif said is typical of the prophet—that his vision is sounder than learning, that the word of God is stronger than the word of the sage. This anti-intellectualism is also typical of the adult who is looking back and re-evaluating everything he has lived for. Wyclif had lived for his vision. It was the mountain peak of his life. Looking down from the peak, he could barely see the valleys, the twenty-three years of education that had led him to his vision.

After Wyclif suffered his first stroke he knew he was dying. The attitude toward death in the Middle Ages was different from modern beliefs. Throughout the Middle Ages and during Wyclif's own life, death had been an everyday occurrence, as common as eating and sleeping. No one tried to hide from himself or his friends. Dying was ceremonious. Friends visited the dying and talked openly about his soon departure. They wished the dying man well and gave him the respect they hoped for themselves when they would be dying, a respect given to someone of a slightly higher—but only slightly higher—rank.

Although Wyclif realized his death was coming soon, he did not surrender or despair. Throughout his life he had developed self-discipline into a habit; self-discipline freed him when he was a child watching over the birth of a lamb, later when he was studying at the manor church or at Oxford, and still later, working in his first parish at Fillingham.

The losses he suffered, physical and emotional, did not lessen his output. If he could not write, he could still dictate, and he continued his work. An organization at Lutterworth had escaped Courtenay's notice, and at least one other was functioning in Braybrooke, Northamptonshire, not far away, a village that was the center of the holdings of Sir Thomas Latimer, a wealthy midland landowner, friendly to Wyclif (but no relation to Lord Latimer, the baron condemned by the Good Parliament, 1376). Wyclif's assistants were quietly translating, copying, and surreptitiously passing on his manuscripts, which were replacing those destroyed, even at Oxford.

John Purvey continued revising the translation of the Bible that Nicholas Hereford had left behind. When he finished that task, his "many good fellows and cunning," as he described his learned helpers, prepared the new Latin text and from it Purvey made his own translation.

Thomas Netter wrote in *The Bundles of Weeds* that Purvey was the "valiant executor in all things and Wyclif's inseparable companion." No wonder Netter added that Purvey "toiled unweariedly."[4] While the work on the Bibles was going on, Wyclif churned out a mass of pamphlets that attacked the popes, the friars, and church wealth, his favorite targets. And he continued with his own commentary on the Bible.

He also applied in a new way a theory of predestination that he found in the writings of Augustine, a theory that God determined beforehand who was going to Heaven and who to Hell. Wyclif combined this theory with his principle of no virtue, no power. Living a life of immorality and vice was evidence that a person was predestined to Hell. Of course, Urban VI had displayed this kind of evidence. If he was on his way to Hell, Wyclif argued, it was obvious that the pope did not have to be obeyed.

Wyclif gathered together all his ideas, old and new, into a single, longer work, which he called the *Trialogue*.[5] The names of the three persons in the conversation were Greek,

---

[4]*Fasciculi Zizaniorum*, pp. 383–85.

[5]Wyclif understood the Greek word *dialogue* to mean a conversation between two people, not knowing the word meant simply a conversation. On the basis of his misunderstanding he called his work *Trialogue*, a conversation among three persons.

but were well-known to any person educated during the fourteenth century. They were taken from a text that had been used in schools as a model for Latin poetry; the eclogues of Theodulus, a ninth-century pastoral poet. From the poems Wyclif borrowed Alithia, Greek for "truth," whom he called "a reliable philosopher." Pseustis, or falsehood, "an insidious unbeliever," challenged Alithia, using the techniques of the university disputation. Their arguments were settled by Pronesis, or wisdom, "a subtle and mature theologian" and spokesman for Wyclif's ideas. These three debated the nature of God, the world of man, the virtues and vices, the sacraments, and the Last Judgment.

Wyclif knew what he was doing in borrowing these familiar Greek names, for the *Trialogue* became his most popular work. It continued to be read at Oxford twenty years after Courtenay thought he had rid the university of Wyclif's ideas and works. The popularity of the *Trialogue* showed that he had not succeeded in preventing the questions that Wyclif asked from being investigated by the Oxford scholars. It was copied in Austria, Czechoslovakia, and Germany. Ironically, it was the first of Wyclif's works to be publicly burned as well as the first to be printed.

Wyclif's ideas were also alive and spreading outside of the university. At Leicester, William Smith, Richard Waytestathe, and William Swinderby still occupied the Chapel of St. John the Baptist which served as a travelers' rest and school. William Smith was the blacksmith who taught himself to read and write. Little is known about Richard Waytestathe. The same chronicle that called William Smith "ugly" called Richard Waytestathe a "chaplain," but apparently only because he was associated with this Chapel of St. John the Baptist.

Wyclif's principles brought a new faith to these men. They responded to them not intellectually, like university scholars, but emotionally, like converts, and it was their emotions that moved them into the action. Without the discipline of university training they were more radical, more volatile than Philip Repingdon, Lawrence Steven, and even John Aston. William Smith, for example, gave up all meat, even fish, and drank only water, no ale or wine.

The last of the three, William Swinderby, was the most successful preacher of the group. He believed with passion, ardor, and vehemence. First he believed in the inherent wickedness of women. He denounced the women of Leicester so effectively that the women banded together and threatened to stone him and run him out of Leicester if he did not stop. He stopped.

He also believed in the evil of trade and wealth. He preached heatedly and frequently on Matthew 19:24: "It is easier for a camel to pass through the eye of a needle than for a rich man to enter the kingdom of Heaven." Again his preaching was very effective. Leicester had a thriving wool trade, and some of the weavers, fullers, and drapers took his words to heart and despaired of salvation. But others were annoyed, and eventually drove him out of the city.

Swinderby became a hermit in the woods near Leicester and quickly achieved a new reputation, this time for holiness. The people of Leicester made pilgrimages to him and brought him gifts, all of which he refused. He told his visitors that little was sufficient for anyone who had the help of God.

Eventually, he left the woods and was welcomed into the abbey of St. Mary de Pré, where Philip Repingdon and possibly Nicholas Hereford had been, and where Henry Knighton and his continuators later wrote the chronicle of these times. Using the abbey as headquarters, he became one of the most popular preachers in Leicestershire, visiting the magnificent churches in Melton Mowbry, Market Harborough, and Loughborough. Now he was welcomed back into the churches of Leicester, St. Mary de Castro, St. Nicholas, St. Martin's, and others.

After his successes as preacher, hermit, then preacher again, he left the Austin friars of St. Mary de Pré and joined William Smith and Richard Waytestathe at St. John the Baptist. On Good Friday, April 4, 1382, William Swinderby preached a sermon in one of the churches of Leicester—it is not known which one—before the mayor of the city, visiting priests, friars, and monks, and notables of the county.

In his preaching he stressed many of Wyclif's ideas and some of his own: that the friars lived off the poor rather than helping them; that parishioners should refuse tithes to sinful priests; that a call from God, not ordination, made a priest; and that men should not be imprisoned for their debts.

The Franciscans and Dominicans of Leicester who heard his sermons did not like what they heard. They resented his attacks on their calling, but they also saw him as a rival in popular preaching. And they recognized heresy when they heard it. They presented a case for heresy against him to John Buckingham, the bishop of Lincoln, old, venerable, and with a reputation for being honest. Under Edward III he had been controller of the wardrobe and keeper of the privy seal. His positions had enabled him to pay out money in the name of the king. He had been scrupulous and careful, and Edward had rewarded him with this bishopric.

Bishop Buckingham had jurisdiction over Oxford, and the friars of the university had always been annoyed that he had not acted against Wyclif in 1377 when Wyclif was attacking them. When Gregory sent the papal bulls to England condemning Wyclif, Buckingham never moved against him at all. Now in 1382 the friars of Leicester hoped he was finally going to act against William Swinderby. They listed sixteen heretical statements that they attributed to Swinderby. John Belvoir, a lowly but ambitious subdeacon, summoned Swinderby for preaching without a license. Swinderby did not appear and was automatically excommunicated. All the churches of the diocese of Lincoln were closed to him.

That did not stop Swinderby. He improvised a pulpit out of two large millstones, and standing on them, he attracted larger crowds than ever. While he was preaching from his millstones, John Belvoir sent a summoner with a beadle, and the two of them brought Swinderby to a church in Liddington, Rutlandshire, for trial.

Belvoir examined the list of sixteen heresies point by point. Swinderby denied preaching them, but Belvoir did not believe him. Belvoir ordered him to appear a month later with twelve orthodox priests to witness to his own orthodoxy, and he made him swear to stop preaching.

The friars were overjoyed with Belvoir's actions. They knew no priests would ever witness for Swinderby. When the month was up, they had already set a stake in place and surrounded it with dry brush. They had a blazing torch to set the fire that would burn the heretic, William Swinderby.

The trial for heresy was prepared, but such a trial needed more rank than that of a subdeacon, even an ambitious one. John Buckingham was present, and by his side was John of Gaunt's eldest son, Henry, earl of Derby, called Bolingbroke, for he was born at that castle east of Lincoln fifteen years earlier. The boy was already wealthy, powerful, and mature. Two years before he had married Mary Bohun, daughter and coheiress of the earl of Hereford, and through marriage was distantly related to William Courtenay. In 1399, seventeen years away, he would be crowned Henry IV, king of England.

The friars had been right. William Swinderby had not been able to bring twelve priestly witnesses. He did bring a letter with twelve seals of the mayor and burgesses of Leicester supporting him. But the friars produced twelve more witnesses against him, and the court believed the friars' witnesses.

Still, the old bishop and the young earl felt England was not ready to burn heretics. Swinderby had to recant his heresies at Lincoln Cathedral during mass on Sundays and on successive Sundays in the churches of Leicester where he had preached. He was also forbidden to preach within the diocese of Lincoln.

Swinderby agreed. After he had visited the churches as he was ordered, he left Leicester for Coventry. Here again he was accused of heresy and of preaching without a license, so he crossed the Severn River into Wales and preached in the valleys of the border country where he could easily escape into the hills if any churchmen came after him.

John Buckingham did not wish to continue his fight against heresy. He had always believed that as long as a threat to the organization was a quiet one, it could be ignored, for the organization could survive the quiet threats to its existence. He allowed William Smith and Richard Waytestathe to continue with their school and hostel at the Chapel of St. John the Baptist.

Another word was being heard throughout England, and in a much louder tone. It was the word *crusade!* In the fourteenth century, this was a magic word. For a while, the church in England turned its attention from frail John Wyclif, his followers, and his heresies to the fighting bishop of Norwich.

CHAPTER TWENTY-TWO

Wyclif's Last Debate

O N December 6, 1382, Henry Despenser, bishop of
Norwich, who had subdued the Rising in East Anglia
eighteen months earlier, called this magic word *crusade* from the pulpit of St. Paul's in London. In the name of
Urban VI, he called for a crusade against Clement VII and
all those who followed him.

England had not been called to a crusade for two hundred
years. What the people who heard the bishop knew about
crusades they had learned from minstrels who sang and
recited rhymed adventure stories, the popular entertainment of the fourteenth century. These adventures
fascinated ale drinkers in taverns, wine drinkers in castles,
bargain-hunters at the markets, and revelers at the fairs.

The minstrels sang about Richard the Lion-Hearted conquering Acre and Jerusalem, and how he would not give up
his faith for all of Saladin's gold. They sang about Charlemagne bringing back the nails of Christ's cross and the
thorns of His crown from the emperor of Constantinople.
They sang about Roland converting the giant Vernagu
before he chopped off the giant's head, King Horn killing
Saracens to save Queen Rymengild, and Floris rescuing
Blanchefleur from the sultan of Babylon.

The crusade of Henry Despenser would be closer than
Jerusalem, Constantinople, or Babylon. It would be a short
journey to France. The French had allied themselves with
the antichrist, Clement, and the dream of fighting in
France had almost as much allure as the dream of fighting
in Jerusalem, Constantinople, or Babylon. The battles of
Crécy and Poitiers were only a generation passed, in 1346

and 1356. Plenty of soldiers who had gone with the Black Prince to Bordeaux and Limoges were still alive. In the twelve years since Limoges, the days of the Black Prince were filled with images of glory. Bishop Despenser had brought together two dreams bound to be popular all over the country—fighting in France and going on a crusade.

The crusade had been Urban's idea. He had given England two choices for a crusade: this one, announced by the bishop of Norwich, or a second one to Castile to be led by John of Gaunt, who hoped to be king of Castile and Leon.

Henry Despenser was not going to give up this chance to lead an army. He got a jump on the duke of Lancaster and made the announcement of his own crusade without the authorization of Parliament on the authority of the pope alone. His life had been too peaceful since he and his knights had slaughtered rioters in East Anglia.

All England received the bishop's announcement of the crusade with hysterical enthusiasm. But it was not only this enthusiasm that convinced Parliament to support the bishop's crusade to France rather than the duke's crusade against Castile. Parliament had a good economic reason as well.

The French had conquered Ghent and seized Bruges and its warehouses of English cloth. The seizure had stopped the trade between Flanders and England as well as the money from tariffs that the wool trade yielded, the king's chief source of income. In Parliament, the knights of the shire, the burgesses, and the lords of the realm believed that Despenser's crusade would not only be good for Christianity, but also good for the treasury of England.

The church bureaucracy functioned well for Bishop Despenser. The authority for his crusade came from three papal bulls that he had received even before the Rising. The first of these bulls gave an indulgence to all those who would serve in the bishop's army for a year or who would contribute substantially to its success. The second order gave

Bishop Despenser the power to use church clerks to organize his army. The third gave the bishop the power to arrest the followers of Clement in England and to confiscate their property.

The Franciscan and Dominican friars cooperated with the bishop to carry out these papal orders. At each monastery, Despenser appointed a friar commissioner and a clerk. They would arrive at a parish and immediately go to the parish priest and impress him with their authority.

The friar then circulated through the parish, whipping up enthusiasm for the crusade. He led a parade up High Street, passing shops, taverns, inns, and houses to the market square. Here the friar eloquently proclaimed the holy war against the pagan. The knight, the archer, and the lancer would wear white tunics, not with their lord's coat of arms, but with the simple red cross of the crusader for Christ. They were soldiers of the Lord. There would be no buying a replacement, no looting, no women followers, at least not without the permission of Bishop Despenser of Norwich.

The friar explained that the indulgences were issued not only for those who went on the crusade, but also for their loved ones in Purgatory. The indulgence worked like this: Christ, the Virgin Mary, and the saints had built up a great storehouse of grace in Heaven, like grain stored in a barn after a good harvest. Everyone understood this comparison. A crusader, or one who contributed substantially to the crusade, could partake of this great storehouse of grace so his own sins would be forgiven, and if he died he would go straight to Heaven, bypassing Purgatory. Or his loved ones could be forgiven. An angel from above would descend to Purgatory and carry his loved one's soul immediately to Heaven. Of course, an indulgence was not bought and sold like grain. It would be effective only if the crusader or the contributor performed his duty and was in a state of grace.

This appeal spread throughout England. There was a Dominican or Franciscan house in every major city—Carlisle, Lincoln, Cambridge, Winchester, Guildford—and in every shire. Knights offered their services to the crusade and the services of any followers who owed them allegiance. The appointed friar took the knight's name, and the knight signed an indenture for a year, to begin when the crusade began.

The friars also kept an account of the gifts received: gold and silver, jewels, necklaces, spoons, brooches, tankards, goblets, and dishes. Each person, rich or poor, had to give according to his ability or the indulgence was refused. No one wanted the indulgence refused, so each person thought of his loved one in Purgatory and gave according to his ability.

The country was swept up in the magic of the new crusade. William Courtenay joined with the people and gave the crusade his enthusiastic support. Thieves, always following a sure success, impersonated friars, took gifts in the name of the crusade, and pocketed them. Some of these impersonators were discovered with the help of local constables and had to volunteer for the crusade or be hanged.

One man strongly and violently opposed the crusade. It was the crippled John Wyclif at Lutterworth. His body was weakened, but his energy was not diminished. The crusade confirmed everything he had said about the pope and the papacy since the schism and everything he had felt about the friars. He wrote forcefully and prolifically against the crusade, the pope, and the friars.

He wrote that every war is evil in itself, but a war initiated by a pope is equivalent to the work of Satan. Therefore all association with the pope should be terminated. Wyclif reasoned that the pope was guilty of apostasy by inciting to war instead of humbly following Christ, the Prince of Peace. Urban, prince of liars, was unquestionably Satanic and diabolic, according to Wyclif.

In one attack, Wyclif wrote as ironically about the crusade as he had about the schism. He quoted St. Paul's letter to the Romans (8:28): "All things work together for good of those who love God," explaining that the crusade exposed the pope's hypocrisy and worldliness. In this way the crusade was not evil in every respect—at least it illustrated Urban's perversity.

Wyclif also attacked the friars for so effectively preaching the crusade. He was particularly critical of one of the stories the friars liked to tell. It was about a woman who dreamed that all those who were killed on the crusade were taken directly into Heaven. Wyclif observed, "They do not preach from the gospel as Christ bids, but they urge the people to fight from dreams and fictitious stories."[1]

Wyclif's criticism of the crusade and the friars' support of it was copied at Lutterworth and distributed as his other manuscripts had been. These new attacks reached his followers at St. John the Baptist in Leicester, in the West and Midlands, where there were sympathetic priests, and in Cornhill, London, where William Langland and his wife, Kit, lived. John of Northampton was lord mayor of London again; he remembered Wyclif when, only six years earlier, he was scurrying from church to church at the request of John of Gaunt.

John Aston was aroused again. There is a record of a sermon he gave in Gloucester criticizing the crusade. There may have been others, but Wyclif complained that priests who opposed the crusade had trouble finding a way to be heard.

In January 1383, eighteen-year-old Richard II was temporarily distracted from the crusade by marrying Anne of Bohemia. From Prague she brought with her her own chaplains, ladies-in-waiting, and a learned staff. Wyclif and others heard the rumor that she had also brought a Bible in

---

[1] Wyclif, *Sermones*, II, 166.

three languages, Latin, German, and Czech. And there is a
record that John Purvey presented her with his translation
of the four gospels in English.

John Hus, a schoolboy in Husinek, was still three years
away from beginning his theological studies at the University of Prague. At Prague, members of the university faculty
and churchmen had been crying out for church reforms for
twenty years in this country where the church and monasteries owned half the land.

The new royal channel made communication between
Bohemia and England easier, and reform-minded Czechs
read Wyclif's criticism of the church sympathetically.
Copies of Wyclif's manuscripts began to move from Oxford, Lutterworth, and even Braybrooke, to Prague. They
would be waiting there for John Hus when his own ideas on
change were forming.

In the month after the royal wedding, Bishop Henry
Despenser sent the word from London for his recruits to
assemble at Sandwich, a port on the seacoast. The recruits
drifted to Kent in small numbers. Some were convicted
felons or thieves who had impersonated friars and who had
chosen the crusade in place of hanging. Others were debtors
who chose the crusade in place of payment. Others were
friars, monks, and priests who had taken advantage of a
papal bull releasing them from their more peaceful duties if
they would fight the antichrist. The monastery of St.
Albans, for example, sent a lively group of young monks.
The sheriffs were to deliver bows and arrows, but few arrived at Sandwich.

On April 8 the bishop ordered messengers to gather up
the gifts and money collected in his name. He expected a
normal delay, for the messengers had to leave London for
the various Franciscan and Dominican houses, make their
collections, and return.

Henry Despenser waited for their return. He waited and
he waited. Finally some messengers returned. Most had
fewer jewels and valuables than had been promised. For

some of the commissioners who had collected the jewels and money, the temptation of this wealth had been too great. When the messengers came to John Karlel for the treasures he had collected, they discovered that he had left for Ireland. He lived the rest of his life there, a much richer Irishman.

Wyclif had always maintained that the church system failed because those who were supposed to make it function lacked virtue. Now the bishop of Norwich learned the same lesson. He had collected only half the money he needed and about half the number of men. He commandeered all ships from the mouth of the Thames around the coast of East Anglia to King's Lynn, where the River Ouse empties into the Wash. These were for transportation to Calais. The ships' captains were ordered to gather at Sandwich on April 8. However, the equipment, men, and ships did not join together in numbers enough to transport the crusade to the Continent until May 16. That evening, the invasion fleet left Sandwich on the tide and with a good wind arrived at Calais the next day.

In spite of the limited size of his army, the bishop had some initial success. He marched twenty miles from Calais to Gravelines. Here he ordered the garrison manning the town walls to surrender. They refused. The crusaders built ladders and after a two-hour attack they took the town, took all they could grab, including the contents of a monastery, and slaughtered all the townsmen.

Then the army marched sixteen miles to Dunkirk. This city surrendered without a fight. There the crusaders learned that a French force was only one and one-half miles away. Louis the Bastard, the French ruler of Flanders, had hastily organized garrison troops and peasants of nearby towns into an army of sorts. The English quickly beat them back on St. Urban's Day, May 24, a sure sign to them that God was on the side of Urban VI. Bishop Despenser ordered some of the priests who had joined him to sing *Te Deum* to celebrate the victory.

The crusaders now believed that, though fewer in number, they were equal in valor to the armies of Edward III and the Black Prince. Their victories would be remembered like Crecy, Poitiers, and Nájera. The bishop thought that the crusaders' third victory would be against Ypres. It did not worry him that West Flanders and Ypres, its capital, supported Urban VI. Flemish allies who had joined the bishop wanted to attack the city, and the bishop rationalized that since Ypres was actually under the control of the French, and the French supported Clement, he could attack Ypres in good conscience.

Ypres was a walled city, and the crusaders needed siege weapons to enter it. The bishop carried several kinds of catapults called Canterbury guns. One was a giant spoon under tension which was drawn back with a windlass, then released with a trigger. A second was a giant sling set on an arm with a counterbalance. Medieval catapults could throw heavy stones from two hundred to four hundred yards, depending on the size and tension of the catapult in relation to the weight of the stone. They could also throw fire bombs, flaming pitch, or even decomposed horses, dogs, pigs, and sheep to contaminate the city and start a plague. It was germ warfare before it was known that germs existed.

At Ypres the bishop tried catapulting giant rocks, but the walls of the city and the inhabitants withstood them. If he tried fire or pestilence, these did not weaken the defense. Then he realized that the only way to bring down the walls of Ypres would be to undermine them; that meant filling the ditch surrounding the city, digging out the foundations under the walls, bracing them with wood, then burning out the wood.

As the crusaders began this tedious operation, the bishop received word that Philip, duke of Burgundy, was approaching with a large French army. John of Gaunt tried to persuade the newly wed king to send reinforcements. But young Richard, enamored of his new wife, delayed, and when he did send help, it was too late. Bishop Despenser wisely decided not to try to duplicate Crecy, Poitiers, or Nájera. He left Ypres, and retreated down the channel coast, finally abandoning all the territory he had occupied except Bourbough, a walled town south of Gravelines. He left a small garrison there, which surrendered to an army that the king of France himself brought up to the walls.

The crusaders did not return to England in triumph. They drifted across the channel a few at a time.

The stories that the king's army told about their crusade were subject to the medieval law of rumor. The soldiers themselves exaggerated the odds they had faced, then these stories ballooned as they spread. And the new versions started a panic in the land. People heard stories of a huge French army, the combined forces of the duke of Burgundy and the king of France, poised on the shore of the channel ready to invade England. They heard that town criers were circulating through the cities of Flanders and France, calling for a general muster to help the Scots fight the English, a story that was based on fact.

Sir Michael de la Pole, now chancellor of England, with the king and the duke of Lancaster, conducted a special impeachment trial of the bishop. For his sentence, they deprived him of his income-producing lands for two years.

When the crusade had failed so completely, Wyclif extended his attack on the crusade to an attack on all wars. Earlier, in *On the Duties of a King*, he had condemned wars in which Christian fought Christian. This was against the law of nature, he had argued. After all, a wolf respected another wolf, a snake another snake. A man loved a bird, a horse, or a dog, but still treated his fellow man cruelly. Now Wyclif attacked wars of all kinds. His sermons emphasized the cruelty and evil of war and its denial of the basic law of God's love.

From Lutterworth Wyclif had a chance to defend John of Gaunt. It was at a time in Wyclif's life when old friendships were important to him, especially since he had lost the friendships of Philip Repingdon and Lawrence Steven during Courtenay's purge.

John of Gaunt was being accused of plotting to kill his nephew, the accusation a product of the complicated politics of Richard's court. A Carmelite friar had said mass for the king, and when mass was over, the friar suddenly announced to the king that his uncle had organized a conspiracy against him in London, Coventry, and some of the other larger cities. The king abruptly ordered that John of Gaunt be seized and executed, but his advisors calmed him. When John of Gaunt heard the charge, he denied it, of course. Every witness called by the friar to substantiate his story also denied knowing anything about a conspiracy.

Without the knowledge of either the king or the duke, two court officers tortured the friar to discover who and what was behind the accusation. The friar never talked before life left his mutilated body.

Stories of the friar and his death spread from London throughout the country. And as usual the stories quickly became exaggerated, and distorted. The friar had become that medieval hero, the saint. The wood of his coffin had sprouted leaves, people said, and when a blind man touched the coffin his sight had been restored. After the friar had been buried, it was said that a light shimmered over the grave.

The old hatred of the duke was revived. The conspiracy was soon discredited, and even the king no longer believed it. Still the rumors spread that what the friar had said was true. The leaves on the coffin and the miracles proved that. People believed that the duke himself had had the friar killed to keep him from talking.

It is impossible to know what kind of information John Wyclif received about the conspiracy and the friar's death. Rumor spreads falsehood more quickly than truth spreads fact. Certainly the rumor of the duke's guilt reached Lutterworth before the truth of his innocence.

John Wyclif wrote that the friar's accusation against John of Gaunt was a plot of the Carmelites to have the duke killed because he "did not wish to punish faithful priests who demonstrated by their life and their work they are champions of God's law."[2] Of course, Wyclif was wrong about the Carmelites. John of Gaunt had always been a friend of the Carmelites, and the friars knew it. The order announced that they had no part in the accusation against him. Two years later, in 1386, John Kenningham, a Carmelite and eventually their provincial, would be John of Gaunt's personal confessor. At Oxford, a Carmelite preached a sermon against the duke, and the order promptly muzzled him.

What John Wyclif said was interesting, however. The statement is evidence that he knew, or believed, that the duke was still friendly not only to him personally but also to his followers, such as John Aston, who preached in western England, and William Smith and Richard Waytestathe, at the Chapel of St. John the Baptist in Leicester. And someone, perhaps the duke, still financially supported the copying of manuscripts and the translating of the Bible.

But soon the copying ended at Lutterworth. On the day of Holy Innocents, December 28, 1384, John Wyclif suffered his second stroke while hearing mass. John Horn, the curate, said it was at the very moment of the elevation of the host, but this is the story a good curate would tell of his rector. Wyclif was not serving mass himself; apparently he was not strong enough for that. The stroke caused "a severe paralysis of the tongue," Horn wrote. The indications are that the hemorrhage affected the cerebral cortex. John Wyclif died three days later.

---

[2]Wyclif, *Polemic Works*, I, 95.

CHAPTER TWENTY-THREE

The Vision Lives On

*T*HE MESSAGE OF A PROPHET usually ends with his death. His vision is personal. His anger is directed at events of his time. And after his time, these events are no longer relevant. But John Purvey and other followers of Wyclif were determined that his vision would not be forgotten. When Wyclif died, Purvey left Lutterworth but continued to translate the Bible and disseminate Wyclif's ideas. He had finished the first English version of the Bible, the one abandoned by Nicholas Hereford, and he had started on the second translation. He took time off to preach, probably at Bristol in the West. When he preached, he did not wear the long russet gown as Wyclif and Aston had done, but he always dressed in everyday working clothes—a simple tunic of some dull color, tied and bloused around the waist and extending below his knees, with a high circular neck, no collar, and long sleeves. He wore heavy, wool stockings, also a dull color, and light, leather slippers.

He spread Wyclif's ideas both in oral sermons and in manuscripts which he distributed throughout the Midlands and the west. When he finished the second translation of the Bible, he had to defend his work from the same attacks that Wyclif had experienced. The attackers said that those who could read English—and the numbers were growing rapidly now—did not know enough theology to understand the Bible. Purvey reminded his critics that some of those who wrote the Bible were shepherds and fishermen. But his arguments did not stop the church establishment from burning the English Bible wherever they found it.

John Aston was already at Bristol, also preaching Wyclif's message. He knew authorities would pounce on him at any time. The church bureaucracy was especially interested in relapsed heretics, those who had renounced their preachings but later took up the same ideas. In case of danger, Aston hoped he could escape over the Severn River into Herefordshire where the towns were farther apart and where he could vanish into the rolling hills. John Swinderby was preaching in Herefordshire, too, and he was just as successful there as he had been in Leicester and Coventry.

In June 1385, six months after Wyclif died, Urban VI was in Nocera, a town south of Naples and besieged by Charles, the very man whom he had made king of Naples. Now the two were scuffling over the spoils. Urban had been away from Rome for two years, torturing cardinals and massacring laymen. In his absence, the Romans had rioted against him. They had invaded the Vatican palace and released all of Urban's prisoners from his jail.

Among these prisoners was Nicholas Hereford, who had been there three years. The imprisonment had been especially hard on him. He was an active man, always wanting to do something, to devote himself eagerly to a cause.

As soon as he was freed he hurried back to England. Courtenay heard that he was in the country and ordered a warrant for his arrest. But Hereford joined Purvey, Aston, and Swinderby in western England. Hereford stayed in Shenley, Herefordshire, at a manor belonging to Sir John Montague, who became the earl of Salisbury in 1397. Sir John was steward of the king's household and a personal friend of Richard's, one of few friends, for Richard had become more and more unpredictable. Sir John Montague was a powerful protection for Nicholas Hereford. Hereford was able to write pamphlets and distribute them from the manor and use it as a home base when he went to the west country to preach.

When John Wyclif died, the connection with John of Gaunt was broken, but Purvey, Hereford, Swinderby and the others had aroused the sympathy of important lords. Sir Lewis Clifford, who, on behalf of John of Gaunt, had interceded when the archbishop was trying Wyclif at Lambeth Palace, was still sympathetic to Wyclif's followers. Even while Wyclif was alive, Sir Thomas Latimer had allowed a group of Wyclif's copyists to use Braybrooke for their work, and now he extended his hospitality to them in the rest of his vast estates throughout the diocese of Worchester.

William Courtenay thought that he had stopped the spread of heresy with his spectacular triumph at Oxford and his seizure of Wyclif's writings. Now he realized that he had to attack again. He sent a letter from Lambeth Palace reminding Henry Wakefield, the bishop of Worcester, that unlicensed preachers were "sowing weeds instead of wheat in the Lord's fields."

Upon receiving the message, Bishop Wakefield ordered warrants for the arrest of Nicholas Hereford, John Aston, and William Swinderby. At the same time, Parliament ordered the works of John Wyclif and his followers confiscated.

Not long after the sheriff issued Wakefield's warrants, Nicholas Hereford's natural enthusiasm got him into trouble. He preached too far away from Sir John Montague's protection. He was arrested and locked up in the gloomy Nottingham castle, high above the town. It was a terrifying place filled with secret passages and cells that were actually holes carved in the rock.

Hereford had no chance to escape. From Nottingham he was transferred to Archbishop Courtenay's own dungeons in Saltwood castle. Three years after Courtenay had imprisoned Nicholas Hereford, Hereford publicly renounced Wyclif's beliefs and returned to orthodoxy. Wyclif's other followers were stunned and hoped the renunciation was the result of torture. But judging Hereford's personality from the meager records that remain, torture would have only made him more stubborn, and his torturers would probably have killed him. When he was convinced of a cause, he followed it with great dedication. Three years of William Courtenay's arguments and persuasion would have been more effective than torture on Nicholas Hereford. And he was the kind of man who would return to orthodoxy with the same resolution he had earlier given to the tenets of John Wyclif.

Hereford officiated at the trial of William Brut, a Welsh follower of Wyclif's. He preached against his former friends. He was made chancellor and treasurer of Hereford Cathedral by John Gilbert, who forty years earlier had led Wyclif and the other commissioners to Bruges. Hereford received a good income from properties belonging to the bishop of Worcester. John of Gaunt's son, Henry IV, made him an annual gift of a barrel of wine, worth about one thousand dollars today.

Just as suddenly, Nicholas Hereford changed again toward the end of his life. He gave up his positions and wealth to enter the Carthusian monastery of St. Anne in Coventry.

The ideas of Wyclif that Nicholas Hereford had earlier advocated grew out of learning, logic, and reason. The orthodoxy of the late fourteenth and early fifteenth centuries, too, was a careful synthesis of learning, logic, and reason. But Hereford had left behind logic and reason and looked to mysticism. There is no logic and reason in the silence, the ascetic exercises, and the solitary meditation of the Carthusians, the most stringent of Western religious orders.

For the third and last time, Hereford's conversion was dramatic, dedicated, and absolute. Always a man of talk and action, he spent the last years of his life in silence. The action of his life was restricted to prayer seven times a day, while kneeling on rock. He lived in a cell smaller than those in the dungeon at Saltwood or the papal prison in Rome. He drank only water. He ate one meal a day, usually vegetables, some of which he raised in a small garden outside his cell. At night he slept in a pine box just large enough for his body. In a few years that box would serve as his coffin.

Nicholas Hereford deserted the vision of John Wyclif and his friends. But in that Carthusian monastery, he lived in simplicity and purity, more strictly than even Wyclif had lived. In the discipline of the Carthusian life he did his penance. Perhaps in his cell he learned who Nicholas Hereford really was and who God is.

CHAPTER TWENTY-FOUR

Death and a Beginning

*B*ISHOP HENRY WAKEFIELD WAS NEVER ABLE to have a warrant served on John Aston. Aston had been in the archbishop's prison and knew just what would happen to him if he were caught a second time, so he escaped, probably into Wales. It was reported that he preached Wyclif's vision until he died in 1388.

While John Aston made his getaway, William Smith and Richard Waytestathe were still in their Chapel of St. John the Baptist. They had escaped the notice of John Buckingham. In the four years since Wyclif's death, six skilled artisans had joined them: a tailor, a goldsmith, a maker and seller of parchment for manuscripts, and others. Over the years, William Smith had collected an extensive library of writings on the New Testament and on church doctrine, all in English. Apparently his school was flourishing.

Followers who survive a reformer often distort his original ideas by concentrating on only a few of his conclusions and then exaggerating this selection. William Smith, Richard Waytestathe, and the six others at the Chapel of St. John demonstrated this tendency. Going beyond Wyclif's attitudes, they were vehemently contemptuous of pilgrimages to shrines popular in the fourteenth century: the shrine of the Virgin Mary at Lincoln, the well of the Virgin at Walsingham (a corner of Norfolk near the sea), and even the famous shrine of St. Thomas á Becket at Canterbury. Shocked witnesses heard them refer to the Virgins of

Lincoln and Walsingham as the "witches of Lincoln and Walsingham."[1]

They also disapproved of the veneration of the saints. Witnesses against William Smith told a story that one day those living at St. John's chapel were hungry. They had some cabbage but no fuel for a cooking fire. They noticed a wooden statue of St. Catherine in one of the niches of the chapel.

"Dear friends," William Smith is reported to have said, "I see God has provided us with fuel to cook our cabbage. This holy statue will make a holy fire for us. The saint will suffer martyrdom again, this time by fire and axe. And by these tortures possibly she will meet the Queen of Heaven."

One of them removed the statue from its place and another grabbed an axe. "Doubtless we will prove whether she is a true saint," Smith continued, "for when we chop off her head, any bleeding will prove she must be adored as a saint. If there is no bleeding, though, then we will be able to cook our cabbage." The record ends there, but apparently St. Catherine cooked their cabbage.

In the fall of 1389 Archbishop William Courtenay made an official visit to the abbey of St. Mary de Pré, and while he was there, those at the Chapel of St. John the Baptist were reported to him as heretics. He summoned them to appear before him at the abbey on All Saints' Day, November 1.

They did not appear. At vespers on All Saints Day, Courtenay organized another of his spectaculars. He called the friars and the priests into the chapter house and while each held up a lighted candle, Courtenay pronounced the sentence of excommunication. Then they extinguished all of the candles. The next day, Courtenay confirmed the sentence with the complete ceremony, candles, crucifix,

---

[1]Knighton, *Chronicon*, II, 182–83.

and bells. But the spectacular did not bring in William Smith.

The archbishop, continuing on his official visit into Northampton, left orders for the sheriff to arrest the eight excommunicants. After a ten-day search, bailiffs found William Smith and two others and brought them to the Church of Saints Peter and Paul in Dorchester, an imposing abbey church of the Augustinians. It provided an impressive setting with the forceful and dramatic presence of William Courtenay standing before the altar.

William Smith was overawed. He renounced his errors and heresies. For penance, Courtenay made him walk around the marketplace of Leicester dressed only in an undershirt carrying a crucifix in his right hand and a statue of St. Catherine in his left. The witnesses against Smith were satisfied, and the affront to St. Catherine was atoned. It was a cold November, and Courtenay thoughtfully revoked the need for Smith to strip to his undershirt. But the archbishop confiscated Smith's library, a sad loss to the man who had taught himself to read and write.

Nothing was heard again of the school at St. John the Baptist. Smith, Waytestathe, and the others probably vanished into the Welsh hills, as did so many of Wyclif's close followers.

The most successful member of the original group at St. John's had always been William Swinderby. Seven years earlier, he had escaped the fire that the friars had prepared for him when Bishop Buckingham and John of Gaunt's son, Henry, made him recant and swear never to preach again without a license.

But Swinderby was never silent for long. He left Leicestershire and started preaching on the western side of the Severn in Herefordshire and Monmouthshire along the Welsh border. The country there was isolated. The farms were dispersed, the villages tiny, and parish churches solitary, often hidden in the woods. These were not the

magnificent edifices of Leicester. The border people
responded to Swinderby as enthusiastically as the people of
Leicester had. He preached in the valleys, and if he learned
a summoner or a bailiff had been inquiring about him, he
climbed into the hills of the Black Mountain country.

John Trefnant was now bishop of Hereford. A Welshman,
his name came from a village in North Wales. He had been a
skilled church bureaucrat, and held a position as an auditor
at the papal court in Rome where he investigated specific
legal problems for the pope.

In Herefordshire, Trefnant tried to use his legal expertise
in the daily affairs of his diocese, arguing in depth over
trivial questions with other bishops, even with William
Courtenay. He did not seem particularly interested in ridding the diocese of William Swinderby or the Wyclif heresies. An order for Swinderby's arrest, which Trefnant's
predecessor, John Gilbert, had requested, was still in the
hands of the sheriff of Herefordshire.

Finally, Trefnant got around to officially denouncing
Swinderby, and Swinderby read the document at Mon-
mouth. When the bishop was visiting the parish church at
Pembridge, a small town fifty miles from Hereford,
Swinderby made a sudden and unannounced appearance,
talked with the bishop, and left again for the mountains.

In June 1391, Swinderby agreed to appear at Kington, and
Bishop Trefnant, as a good lawyer, gave him from June 14
to June 30 to prepare his defense. The bishop also promised
that if Swinderby appeared voluntarily, he would be free to
leave without being arrested, a perfectly legal procedure.

William Swinderby appeared at Bodenham Church on
June 30 as arranged. He had written out his defense in
English, although the hearing would be in Latin. He was
charged with still preaching the eleven heresies which
Bishop Buckingham of Lincoln had charged him with nine
years earlier. Fifteen new heresies were added from
evidence of those who had recently heard him preaching.

Swinderby did not try to argue law with Bishop Trefnant. He knew he could not do that. Instead he called the charges against him the work of friars and lecherous priests. He cited the authority of the Bible and St. Augustine for his preachings.

True to his word, Bishop Trefnant allowed Swinderby to leave, but he cited him to appear again during the summer. Swinderby finally agreed to appear a second time, and he again defended himself in English and by the authority of the Bible. Again the bishop let him go, but this time he condemned him as a heretic. When Swinderby did not return for sentencing, he was excommunicated.

Swinderby sent a letter of appeal "to the knights in Parliament," asking them to stand up against "spiritual cowardice and the devil."[2] Nothing came of the letter. In January 1392, Bishop Trefnant ordered a royal warrant and King Richard instructed the sheriff and bailiffs to bring in Swinderby. He was always able to avoid the sheriff and bailiffs and was never captured again. There is evidence he continued preaching in the green and golden lowlands of Herefordshire and on the wooded slopes of the Clun forests of Shropshire, escaping into the hills when pursuit came too close.

In 1395, John Purvey finished his second translation of the Bible and continued to defend an English Bible, not only against attacks but against burnings. The archbishop of Canterbury signed an official order that no one could translate the Bible nor use a translation without the approval of his bishop or some provincial official.

On a January morning in 1395, the archbishop of Canterbury and the residents of London and Westminster read a manifesto that had been nailed to the door of St. Paul's Cathedral in London and the abbey church in Westminster.

---

[2]Foxe, III, 128–30.

It was a demand to the lords of Parliament to disendow the church of its material possessions and its income-producing properties throughout England, and by confiscating its wealth to return the church to true Christian poverty, as Wyclif had advocated.

Bishops convened at Canterbury and petitioned the king to extend the death penalty to all heretics. They sent a copy of the manifesto to Pope Boniface IX. He replied with a letter to the king, the bishops, and the mayor and sheriffs of London, urging them to suppress such "pseudo-Christians" whose doctrines could lead only to the subversion and ruin of all authority, secular and religious.[3]

The following year England had a new archbishop of Canterbury, Thomas Arundel, formerly bishop of Ely, archbishop of York, and chancellor of England. He believed that the manifesto was the result of persons, both at the University of Oxford and outside it, who were still reading the works of John Wyclif. He decided to attack the most popular of these works, the *Trialogue*, and appointed a special examining commission whose members declared the *Trialogue* was heretical in eighteen places. The archbishop then ordered William Woodford, now an old man, to write a reply, as if he were still debating with his university antagonist, sixteen years after Wyclif had died. While Woodford was preparing his arguments, all copies of the *Trialogue* that could be located were burned in the middle of Carfax at Oxford.

It was now the fifteenth century. England had a new king, Henry IV, son of John of Gaunt. The earlier request of the bishops that heretics be burned was granted by Parliament, but with some restrictions. The fire was to be used only for those heretics who had renounced their false beliefs but later changed their minds and returned to them.

---

[3]*Register of Bishop Trefnant*, pp. 405-7.

Under the new statute, these heretics were to be handed over to the sheriff and burned to death "on some high place."

Under this law, England witnessed its first burning at the stake. William Chatris was the priest at two poor parishes—St. Margaret's in Kings Lynn, Norfolk, and Tilney in the back-country swamplands. He was the kind of priest who had seen Wyclif's vision and believed in it.

The fighting bishop of Norwich, Hugh Despenser, subdued since the crusade had failed sixteen years earlier, heard reports of William Chatris's preaching and convicted him of heresy. The priest spent nineteen days in the bishop's prison, nineteen days of "mature deliberation," as the chronicle put it,[4] not mentioning the glowing irons and stretching rack that encouraged mature deliberation. William Chatris finally "understood" his errors and renounced them.

He moved from the diocese of Norwich to that of London, and under the name of William Sawtrey became the priest of St. Osyth the Virgin, a tiny church in the ward of Walbrook. On Walbrook Street, in the many skinners' workshops, fine furs were scraped, soaked, and tanned into leather, all very smelly tasks. The area was dominated by the great church of St. John's Walbrooke. The priest of little St. Osyth's should have gone unnoticed.

Unfortunately he was not. Two years after his first conviction for heresy, he was convicted again, and Bishop Arundel declared him a relapsed heretic. He was burned at the stake at Smithfield where Wat Tyler had once met the fourteen-year-old King Richard and had also been killed.

John Purvey had also been captured and was imprisoned in Saltwood castle, where Aston and Hereford had been. Two days after William Sawtrey met his death, Purvey was

---

[4]Foxe, III, 222-29.

examined before a council of bishops at St. Paul's. He was convicted of seven heresies, but it was the first conviction, so he was returned to prison. A week later, he renounced those heresies from St. Paul's Cross in the cathedral yard, and five months after the renunciation, he was sent to a parish in West Hythe, Kent, not far from Saltwood, as its priest. Two years later he vanished from his parish and was never heard from again.

One of Wyclif's surrogate family at Oxford and his own pupil, William Thorpe, was now arrested and tried. For the twenty years since he had graduated, he had been successfully preaching the ideas of his master and once again had been arrested for his activity. But in both that trial and this one, he demonstrated that he had mastered the skills of disputation, and in neither trial was the archbishop able to trap him into a statement of belief that could be condemned as heretical. Thorpe was freed without recanting or punishment.

By 1414, Wyclif had been dead for twenty years. He had been buried in the consecrated ground of St. Mary's Church, Lutterworth. November 5, 1414, a papal council gathered in Switzerland on the rolling hills surrounding the green waters of Lake Constance. Relying on the council's promise of safe conduct, John Hus, already excommunicated for advocating the beliefs of John Wyclif, travelled from Prague to Lake Constance to defend them.

Queen Anne of Bohemia, Richard's queen, had died in 1394, but Czech students were still at Oxford and carried the manuscripts of Wyclif from both Oxford and Braybrooke. At Prague, Hus had read them, absorbed them, translated them into Czech, and as rector of the University of Prague had defended their ideas in his annual quodlibet disputation. He was a hero at Prague, for he had wrested the university from German control and had made it a Czech institution.

At Lake Constance, the members of council first condemned the beliefs of John Wyclif as heretical on 260 counts. Then, in spite of their promised safe conduct, they arrested Hus, tried him for holding the newly condemned ideas, and condemned him. He was burned at the stake, and a tradition has survived that he died singing "Kyrie eleison," the Greek chant in the mass meaning, "Lord have mercy on us." His ashes were shovelled with those of the pyre into a wheelbarrow and dumped into the Rhine River where, at Lake Constance, it begins its long journey to the sea.

Now in death, Wyclif became the heretic he had not been in life. The council ordered the bishop of Lincoln to remove the bones of John Wyclif from St. Mary's Church and destroy them. The bishop of Lincoln was now Philip Repingdon, and he did not obey the order.

Thirty-three years earlier, Repingdon had defended John Wyclif in the churchyard of St. Frideswyde on Corpus Christi Day. Something of that day must have stayed with him. Perhaps he recalled some memory of the vision he had once seen.

The order to exhume John Wyclif was carried out on December 16, 1427, by Repingdon's successor. The bones were burned and the heap of ashes thrown off the bridge just below St. Mary's where it crosses the River Swift.

These men had started a rebellion among the English, and among the Czechs; and it would soon spread to the Germans. In history books, the rebellion is called the Reformation.

Bibliography

General and Special Histories

Bloch, Marc. *Feudal Society*. Translated by L.A. Manyon. London, 1961.

Duby, Georges. *Rural Economy and Country Life in the Medieval West*. Translated by Cynthia Postan. London, 1918.

Gimpel, Jean. *The Medieval Machine: The Industrial Revolution of the Middle Ages*. New York, 1976.

Knowles, David. *The Evolution of Medieval Thought*. London, 1962.

Lyon, Bryce. *A Constitutional and Legal History of Medieval England*. New York, 1960.

McKisack, May. *The Fourteenth Century*. Oxford, 1959.

Pantin, William A. *The English Church in the Fourteenth Century*. Cambridge, 1955.

Trevelyan, G.M. *England in the Age of Wycliffe*. London, 1909.

Biographies of John Wyclif

Hague, Dyson. *The Life and Works of John Wycliffe*. London, 1935.

Lechler, Gotthard V. *John Wiclif and his English Precursors*. Edited and translated by P. Lorimer. London, 1884.

McFarlane, K.B. *John Wycliffe and the Beginnings of English Nonconformity*. London, 1952.

Stacey, John. *John Wyclif and Reform*. London, 1964.

Wilkins, Henry J. *Was John Wycliffe a Negligent Pluralist?* London, 1915.

Workman, Herbert B. *John Wyclif: A Study of the British Medieval Church*. 2 volumes. Oxford, 1926.

263

The Works of John Wyclif

Arnold, Thomas, ed. *Select English Works*. 3 volumes. Oxford, 1869–71.

Hudson, Anne, ed. *Selections from English Wycliffite Writings*. Cambridge, 1978.

Matthew, F.D., ed. *The English Works of John Wyclif Hitherto Unpublished. Oxford, 1880.*

S. Harrison Thomson, ed. *Summa de Ente*. Oxford, 1930.

Works Published by the Wyclif Society, London (unless noted)

de Apostasia. Edited by M.H. Dziewicki. 1889.

de Benedicta Incarnacione. Edited by H. Harris. 1886.

de Blasphemia. Edited by M.H. Dziewicki. 1893.

de Civili Dominio. 4 vols. Edited by R.L. Poole and J. Loserth. 1885, 1900–04.

de Dominio Divino. Edited by R.L. Poole. 1890.

de Ecclesia. Edited by J. Loserth. 1886.

de Eucharistica. Edited by J. Loserth. 1892.

de Logica. 3 vols. Edited by M.H. Dziewicki. 1899.

de Officio Pastorali. Edited by G. Lechler. Leipzig, 1863.

de Officio Regis. Edited by A.W. Pollard and C. Sayle. 1887.

de Potestate Papae. Edited by J. Loserth. 1907.

de Simonia. Edited by Herzberg-Frankel. 1898.

de Veritate Sacrae Scripturae. 3 vols. Edited by R. Buddensieg. 1905–07.

Opera Minora. Edited by J. Loserth. 1913.

Opus Evangelicum. 2 vols. Edited by J. Loserth. 1895.

Polemical Works in Latin. 2 vols. Edited by R. Buddensieg. 1883.

Sermones. 4 vols. Edited by J. Loserth. 1887–90.

Trialogus. Edited by G. Lechler. Oxford, 1869.

Medieval Chronicles

Anonimalle Chronicle. Edited by A.H. Galbraith. Manchester, 1927.

Fasciculi Zizaniorum Magistri Johannis Wyclif. Edited by W.W. Shirley. London 1858.

Froissart, Jean. *The Chronicle of Froissart.* Translated by Sir John Bourchier, Lord Berners. Edited by W.P. Ker. London, 1892–1909.

Knighton, Henry. *Chronicon Henrici Knighton.* Edited by J.R. Lumby. London, 1895.

Walsingham, Thomas. *Chronicon Angliae.* Edited by E.M. Thompson. London, 1874.

_____. *Gesta Abbatum Monasterii Sancti Albani.*

_____. *Historia Anglicana.* H.T. Riley, ed. London, 1863.

Chapter 1. Early Years at Wycliffe Manor

Chaucer, Geoffrey. *The Complete Poetry and Prose of Geoffrey Chaucer.* Edited by John H. Fisher. New York, 1977.

Clarkson, Christopher. *The History of Richmond in the County of York.* Richmond, Yorkshire, 1814.

deMause, Lloyd, ed. *The History of Childhood.* New York, 1974.

Erikson, Erik. *Childhood and Society.* 2d ed. New York, 1963.

Leadman, Alexander D.H. *Battles Fought in Yorkshire.* London, 1891.

Nicholson, Ranald. *Scotland in the Late Middle Ages.* Edinburgh, 1974.

Chapter 2. John's Future Is Chosen

Boccacio, Giovanni. *The Decameron.* Translated by G.H. McWilliam. New York, 1972.

Dugdale, Sir William. *Monasticon Anglicanum.* Edited by J. Coley, H. Ellis and B. Bandinel. London, 1846.

Knowles, Dom David. *The Monastic Order in England.* Cambridge, 1950.

_____. *The Religious Orders in England,* vol. 2. Cambridge, 1957.

The Towneley Plays. Edited by George England. London, 1897.

Chapter 3. A Farm Boy Masters Latin

Leach, A.F. *The Schools of Medieval England.* London, 1915.

Plimpton, George A. *The Education of Chaucer Illustrated from School Books in Use in His Time.* Oxford, 1935.

Rogers, E.T. *A History of Agriculture and Prices in England from 1259 to 1793.* Oxford, 1866.

Watson, Foster. *The English Grammar School to 1600.* Cambridge, 1908.

Werner, Jakob. *Lateinische Sprichwörter und Sinnsprüche des Mittelalters.* Heidelberg, 1911.

Chapter 4. Oxford

Crombie, A.C. *Robert Grosseteste and the Origins of Experimental Science 1100. 1700.* Oxford, 1953.

Chapter 5. The Black Death

Campbell, Anna M. *The Black Death and Men of Learning.* New York, 1931.

Levett, Ada E. *The Black Death on the Estates of the See of Winchester.* Oxford, 1909.

Ziegler, Philip. *The Black Death.* New York, 1969.

Chapter 9. The Prophet as Envoy

Power, Eileen. *The Wool Trade in English Medieval History.* Oxford, 1941.

Chapter 10. Preaching for John of Gaunt

Armitage-Smith, Sidney. *John of Gaunt.* London, 1904.

Baker, Timothy. *Medieval London.* New York, 1970.

Owst, Gerald Robert. *Literature and Pulpit in Medieval England.* Cambridge, 1933.

_____. *Preaching in Medieval England.* Cambridge, 1926.

Robertson, D.W. *Chaucer's London.* New York, 1968.

Salusbury, G.T. *Street Life in Medieval England.* London, 1939.
Thrupp, Sylvia L. *The Merchant Class of Medieval London.* Ann Arbor, Mich., 1962.

Chapter 11. Wyclif Faces Courtenay

Allen, Thomas. *The History and Antiquities of the Parish of Lambeth and the Archiepiscopal Palace.* London, 1826.
Chrimes, Stanley B. *An Introduction to the Administrative History of Medieval England,* 2nd rev. ed. Oxford, 1959.
Dahmus, Joseph. *The Prosecution of John Wyclif.* New Haven, Conn., 1952.

Chapter 13. A War, a Pope, and a Debate

Chandos, Herald. *The Life of the Black Prince.* Edited and translated by M.K. Pope and E.C. Lodge. Oxford, 1905.
Emerson, Barbara. *The Black Prince.* London, 1976.

Chapter 14. The Fame of Wyclif Spreads

Hudson, Anne. *Notes and Queries.* 20 (1972): 443–53.
_____. "A Lollard Compilation and the Dissemination of Wycliffite Thought." *Journal of Theological Studies,* 23 (1972): 65–81.
_____. "A Lollard Sermon-cycle and Its Implications." *Medium Aevum* 40 (1971): 142–56.

Chapter 15. The Bible Is Translated

Deanesly, Margaret. *The Lollard Bible and Other Medieval Bible Versions.* Cambridge, 1920.
Fristedt, Sven L. *The Wycliffe Bible.* Stockholm, 1953.
The Holy Bible made from the Latin Vulgate by John Wycliffe and his Followers. 4 vols. Edited by J. Forshall and F. Madden. Oxford, 1850.
John of Gaunt's Register. Edited by S. Armitage-Smith. London, 1937.

McLuhan, Marshall. *The Gutenberg Galaxy.* Toronto, 1962.
Smalley, Beryl. *The Study of the Bible in the Middle Ages,* 2d ed. New York, 1952.

Chapter 16. Galileo's Ancestor

Crombie, A.C. *Medieval and Early Modern Science.* 2 vols. New York, 1959.

Chapter 17. Riot, Rebellion,and Retreat

Dobson, Richard B. *The Peasants' Revolt of 1381.* London, 1970.
Hilton, Rodney and Hyman Fagan. *The English Rising of 1381.* London, 1950.
Loftie, William J. *Memorials of the Savoy.* London, 1878.
Reville, Andre. *Le Soulement des Travailleurs d'Angleterre.* Paris, 1898.

Chapter 18. Attacks on the Monasteries

Lobel, M.D. *The Borough of Bury St. Edmund's.* Oxford, 1935.
Oman, Sir Charles. *The Great Revolt of 1381.* Oxford, 1969.
Powell, Edgar. *The Rising in East Anglia, 1381.* Cambridge, 1896.

Chapter 19. Courtenay Begins His Attack

Dahmus, Joseph. *William Courtenay, Archbishop of Canterbury, 1381–1396.* University Park, Penn., 1966.
Daly, Lowrie J. *The Political Theory of John Wyclif.* Chicago, 1962.
Dyson, A.H. *Lutterworth, John Wycliffe's Town.* Edited by Hugh Goodacre. London, 1913.

Chapter 20. Hereford, Repingdon, and Aston

Dahmus, J.H. *The Prosecution of John Wyclif.* New Haven, 1952.

Chapter 21. Courtenay Victorious—Almost

McFarlane, Kenneth B. *Lancastrian Kings and Lollard Knights.* Oxford, 1972.

Perroy, Edouard. *L'Angleterre et le Grand Schisme d'Occident.* Paris, 1933.

Trefnant, John. *Registrum Johannis Trefnant.* London, 1916.

Chapter 24. Death and a Beginning

Lambert, M.D. *Medieval Heresy: Popular Movements from Bogomil to Hus.* London, 1977.

Leff, Gordon. *Heresy in the Later Middle Ages.* Vol. 2. New York, 1967.

Peter of Mladenovic. *John Hus at the Council of Constance.* Edited and translated by Matthew Spinka. New York, 1965.

Spinka, Matthew. *John Hus, a Biography.* Princeton, 1968.

INDEX

Abbeys, 11. *See also* Bury St. Edmund's; Saint Albans, abbey of
Abelard, Peter, 25
Accounts: keeping of, 5, 64
Aelfric (Old English translator), 140
Albert the Great, Saint, 21, 25
Alfonso de Robagorza (count of Denia). *See* Denia, count of
Alfonso (prince of Denia), 113, 122
Amos (prophet), 77, 81
Anglo-Norman language, 140
Anne of Bohemia (queen of England), 151, 163, 239–40
Apostasy. *See* Wyclif, John, works of
Aquinas, Saint Thomas, 21, 25, 148, 154
Arabic language, 38
Arabic numbers, 74–75
Aramaic language, 146 n.4
Aristotle, xi, 28, 35, 38, 39
Arundel, Thomas (archbishop of Canterbury), 258
Aschenden, John, 47, 52, 133
Aston, John: appearance before Courtenay of, 222–23; arrest escape of, 253; at Corpus Christi disputations, 207; and Courtenay, 215; declared heretic, 209, 211; imprisonment of, 224; opposition to Norwich Crusade of, 239; poverty of, 151; preaching of, 248; as regent-master at Oxford, 161, 200; and Wyclif, 132, 133
Astronomy, 38, 133
Augustine, Saint, xi, 28, 53, 64, 77, 148, 154, 228
Avarice, in churchmen, 81
Averroes, 35, 38
Avicenna, 38, 46

Avignon: papal palace at, 43, 67, 70, 78

Bacon, Roger, 21, 153, 156
Ball, John, 171–73, 177, 195
Balliol Castle, Durham, 33
Balliol College, Oxford, 32–37, 61–62, 76. *See also* Wyclif, John
Bealknap, Sir Robert, 84, 166, 176
Beaufort, Pierre Roger de. *See* Gregory XI
Becket, Saint Thomas à, 175, 253
Bedeman, Lawrence. *See* Steven, Lawrence
Belvoir, John, 231–32
Benedict, Saint, 55
Berengar (bishop of Tours), 154, 207
Berton, William, 51, 57, 155, 156, 158, 200
Bible: celibacy in, 61; commentary on, of Lombardin, 38; copying of, 145–46; cost of, 151; early English translations of, 140–41; first complete translation of, 2; Grosseteste's scholarship for, 52; in libraries, 143; handwritings in Wyclif's manuscript of, 143; new Latin translation of, 102; opposition to English translation of, 150; Oxford study in, 70, 72; parish church holdings of, 142–43; primitive church in, 77; and Purvey's achievement, 149; as verbal utterance, 74; Vulgate edition of, 52, 141; Vulgate editing of, 144–46. *See also* Wyclif, John
Black death. *See* Pestilence
Blackfriars Abbey, London, 200
Black Prince of Wales, 87, 115
Boccaccio, Giovanni, 22, 125–26
Boethius, 35

271